LIVE IT
LOVE IT
EARN IT

MARIANNA OLSZEWSKI

LIVE IT LOVE IT EARN IT

A Woman's Guide to Financial Freedom

PORTFOLIO

PORTFOLIO
Published by the Penguin Group
Penguin Group (USA) Inc., 375 Hudson Street,
New York, New York 10014, U.S.A.
Penguin Group (Canada), 90 Eglinton Avenue East, Suite 700,
Toronto, Ontario, Canada M4P 2Y3
(a division of Pearson Penguin Canada Inc.)
Penguin Books Ltd, 80 Strand, London WC2R 0RL, England
Penguin Ireland, 25 St. Stephen's Green, Dublin 2, Ireland
(a division of Penguin Books Ltd)
Penguin Books Australia Ltd, 250 Camberwell Road, Camberwell,
Victoria 3124, Australia
(a division of Pearson Australia Group Pty Ltd)
Penguin Books India Pvt Ltd, 11 Community Centre, Panchsheel Park,
New Delhi – 110 017, India
Penguin Group (NZ), 67 Apollo Drive, Rosedale, North Shore 0632,
New Zealand (a division of Pearson New Zealand Ltd)
Penguin Books (South Africa) (Pty) Ltd, 24 Sturdee Avenue,
Rosebank, Johannesburg 2196, South Africa

Penguin Books Ltd, Registered Offices:
80 Strand, London WC2R 0RL, England

First published in 2009 by Portfolio,
a member of Penguin Group (USA) Inc.

10 9 8 7 6 5 4 3 2

Publisher's Note
While the author has made every effort to provide accurate telephone numbers and Internet addresses at the time of publication, neither the publisher nor the author assumes any responsibility for errors, or for changes that occur after publication. Further, the publisher does not have any control over and does not assume any responsibility for author or third-party Web sites or their content.

A portion of author's royalties will be donated to nonprofit organizations dedicated to empowering, educating, and assisting women and girls.

Olszewski, Marianna.
     Live it, love it, earn it : a woman's guide to financial freedom / Marianna Olszewski.
        p. cm.
     Includes index.
     ISBN 978-1-59184-255-2
  1. Women—Finance, Personal. I. Title.
     HG179.O458 2010
     332.0240082—dc22
                              2009035782
Printed in the United States of America
Set in Whitman
Designed by Pauline Neuwirth, Neuwirth & Associates, Inc.

For my parents,
ALBERT AND SANDRA OLSZEWSKI
I love you both—thank you for everything.

■

Contents

Introduction

GROWING UP, I was just like so many other girls pining for a life that seemed out of reach. My journey to independence and financial freedom began when I was just twenty-three years old. There were no thunderbolts and blaring trumpets; it happened after crossing the George Washington Bridge in my old gray clunker.

It was close to midnight, and I was going home to my small apartment that I shared with two other girls. At the time, I had a management-track job at IBM and was working toward my MBA and waitressing at night. Building my career day and night, paying off college loans, and taking care of monthly bills and expenses were definitely taking a toll. I had no money to show for my efforts and I was exhausted.

As I made my way over the bridge, I suddenly noticed clouds of smoke billowing out from the edges of the hood and heard the engine making funny noises. I tried to shift gears, but all I managed to accomplish was spilling my coffee all over my white shirt. I stepped on the gas and nothing happened. Nearly to the end of the bridge, the car finally decided to die. As it sputtered to a grinding halt, I had just enough time to navigate safely to the side of the road. I got out to check the engine—completely ridiculous because I knew nothing about cars—and as I opened the hood puffs of thick steam engulfed me. Standing in the rain next to my wheezing rattletrap, I felt very alone.

No one stopped to help me for at least thirty minutes. And as I looked around I thought, Marianna, if this situation isn't a metaphor for your life I don't know what is—stuck on a bridge, broke, and broken down. This was not the life I wanted to be living. I made a vow in that moment to earn enough money not only to buy a decent car but also to have the financial freedom to create a life I could love. And I did.

Have you ever felt as if you were trying to cross a bridge, one step away from disaster? Are you living paycheck to paycheck? Overwhelmed by debt? Have you caught glimpses of your dream life on the horizon, but just can't find the path to get yourself there? Well, I'm happy to tell you that you can cross over to prosperity! Discovering the secret to living and loving the life you want and earning enough to create it for yourself is doable for everyone. I'm going to show you how. Even with a weak economy, discouraging employment statistics, and a topsy-turvy real estate market, you can change your current situation. Not only that, your life and your financial state can be even better than you imagined.

I know you're motivated (indifferent people don't often read personal finance and self-improvement books). That's a great start. The good news is that you already have the power to create happiness, control your destiny, and become financially free and independent. You, like the women I coach, just need information. A lack of financial knowledge prevents you from undoing bad money habits and creating wealth. With the right education you will realize that there's nothing wrong with, and everything right about, wanting, making, and having money.

If you feel trapped by your financial situation, my effective strategies will help you take control of your life so that you can make money work for you. I will talk you through debt reduction, raising your credit score, retirement planning, investing, and making sense of your taxes in language that you can relate to and understand. You won't find complicated algorithms or pie charts. So don't worry about getting bogged down with unnecessary theoretical gobbledygook. I'm not going to do that to you.

With the information in this book, you will be able to finally open a credit card bill without shaking, save enough for a 20 percent down payment on a home, and handle a health emergency or a broken-down car without worrying about where the money will come from. And once you've conquered the essentials, you can bring your dreams ("I want to open a shoe store," "become a yoga instructor," or "travel around the world") and ideas ("I found the secret to a stocking that will never run," or "a nail polish that never chips") to bountiful fruition.

As we travel up the road to independence through the pages of this book you'll meet remarkable women who have reached incredible heights. Award-winning designer Diane von Furstenberg; shoe mogul Tamara Mellon of Jimmy Choo fame; Elaine Crocker, president of Moore Capital and one of Crain's "100 Most Influential Women in NYC Business"; Nina DiSesa, chairman of McCann-Erickson North America and one of *Fortune* magazine's most powerful women; and Congresswoman Marsha Blackburn are just some of the women who share their wisdom. Their stories are both inspiring and instructive. Most came from ordinary beginnings, yet they have the courage, commitment, and curiosity that they used to help them succeed.

You'll also read the true stories of women just like you: those who are in the throws of overcoming financial challenges, looking for a first job, climbing the corporate ladder, changing careers in midstream, building (or dreaming of) a business, moving to a new town, getting married, starting a family, going solo after a divorce, or simply wanting to make a good life more fabulous. To protect their identities I have changed the names of many of the women whose stories I tell in the book.

There's Gabrielle, who overcame a mountain of debt; Greta, who finally got her act together by reclaiming her health and building a nest egg; Fruzsina, who followed her passion and created an amazing jewelry line; and Katherine, who recognized a need and turned it into a booming business. Dozens of other women were generous enough to divulge their aspirations and disappointments, accomplishments and challenges. Their stories have inspired me to continue to reach new and higher goals I set for myself, and I hope they'll do the same for you.

A few years ago I first started to think about the tools and techniques I used to help me succeed as a process. As I began to write them down I realized that they could be used by anyone to get ahead, to live their dreams. My tools have evolved and matured, as have I, but the fundamentals remain the same:

1. Act as master of your life by putting your health, well-being, happiness, and education first.
2. Become absorbed in and joyful about what you are doing.
3. Have confidence in your ability to design the life you want.
4. Love money by overcoming fear and anxiety about money, getting out of debt, cleaning up your credit, and learning to prosper within your means.

5. Respect money by learning the fundamental principles of spending, saving, and investing.
6. Create a better life on your own, without secretly hoping or waiting for someone else to do it for you.
7. Become exactly the person you want to be.
8. Take the right next actions, and never procrastinate again.
9. Appreciate what you have so you can have more.

There's more to being rich, happy, and fabulous than the items on this list, of course. You found your way to this book because you were intrigued. Don't stop here. Settle in, turn the page, and get going. Think of *Live It, Love It, Earn It* as your success GPS. You are on your way!

HOW TO USE THIS BOOK

Live It, Love It, Earn It can be read like any book, straight through from start to finish. I have tried to make it as interactive as possible, including numerous exercises and activities, to engage your mind, body, and spirit.

I suggest you start a *Live It, Love It, Earn It* group with two or three or even more individuals who like and respect one another, have different life and work experiences, and want to create wealth with the help of one another. Meet on your own, at regular times, over a four- to six-week period, or even longer. In my experience, women who practice my nine tools, exercises, and Success Secrets with other like-minded women experience something magical. The power of the tools is enhanced, and abundance comes to all of us much more quickly than if we are working on them by ourselves.

If you create a group like this you can use *Live It, Love It, Earn It* as a study guide. Read, review, and discuss a different chapter, or aspect of a chapter, each week. To get the ball rolling, open each meeting with a Desire Exercise. Set a timer for two minutes and write down a list of financial dreams and desires (e.g., "pay off credit card debt," "own my own home," "save for retirement," "travel around the world," "make more money at my job," or "go back to school"). Once the two minutes are up, read your list to the other women (or woman) in the group. They should respond with: "You can have all that and more." This sets the tone for the rest of the session and puts you in an abundant frame of mind. Enjoy!

My Story

IT'S IMPORTANT TO me that I share my background with you because I don't want you to think that I got to where I am today without a struggle. The story of my life is classic American Dream material, from its rough beginning straight through to the happy ending. I sincerely hope it becomes an example of what can be achieved with an open heart and mind.

My early life was a determining factor in my success, and really, I don't think this book (or my current life) would exist had my childhood been different. I grew up in a big family. My father, an assembly-line worker at Ford Motor Company, supported us while my mother stayed at home to look after us—raising five children was a full-time job. We all loved, cared for, and learned a lot from one another. My mom and dad were always there for us and gave us discipline, strong values, independence, educational opportunities, and confidence in our abilities to become whomever we wanted. My dad always used to say, "Marianna, the whole world is in front of you, just waiting. You can do anything you want." There was a wide and interesting world beyond our neighborhood, and my parents didn't want me to miss out on it.

Frankly, we didn't grow up in the ideal neighborhood with white picket fences and tidy sidewalks. Instead, we lived so close to the railroad tracks I could hear the trains rumbling by day and night. Our apartment was directly above a butcher shop, and every morning I was awakened by the noise of meat being processed directly below my bedroom. As I left to go to school each morning, I was greeted by cow sides hanging in the butcher's window, the sound of knives slamming against the massive cutting boards, the grinding screech of the sausage-making machine, and the butchers shouting at one another above the din. Around Christmas-time, one butcher's favorite "holiday tradition" would be to tell my sister and me that the stag hanging in the window was Rudolph the Red-Nosed Reindeer, which would, obviously, make both of us cry.

Because my parents taught me the true value of money, it dawned on me at a young age that most circumstances, including my own, could be changed with a bit of effort. There should be more of that kind of teaching by parents today. For instance, to demonstrate how work and money go hand in hand, my dad had me wash the windows and stairs in our apart-ment for ten cents a day when I was a young girl. The old adage "Buy low, sell high" was drummed into me before I was ten years old, as was the idea that a penny saved was a penny earned. If I "traded" one dollar of my hard-earned money for a piece of pizza, that money would be gone forever. Was the pleasure of the pizza worth it, or should I save the money for something else? I always asked myself that question before making a purchase, and I still do today.

By the time I was twelve years old, I was very aware of the ins and outs of our household finances. I knew what bills were, and why they must be paid on time. An emphasis on buying an item only if it could be done so with cash (not credit) was a constant and lasting lesson. In fact, the very first apartment I bought was paid for with cash, as was my second, my third, and pretty much everything else that I own. I understand that this is very unusual and I don't expect or even recommend that most people make large purchases this way. However, the "Use cash as much as pos-sible" philosophy contributed to my ability to create wealth, and I believe it can help others do the same.

Education was incredibly important to my parents, and they provided the best for my siblings and me, making many sacrifices to do so. Although neither of them had the opportunity to go to college, they are extremely well read, particularly about history and politics. They believed, rightly so, that education would give me more options. My mom and dad corrected every paper I wrote. They reviewed—again and again—my math and Eng-lish homework to make sure I understood it all. If I got a 97 on a test, they asked why I didn't get 100. I had to push myself too, and find the discipline to get better grades—even if it meant staying in and studying when other kids on my block were playing outside. I looked ahead because I under-stood that to do more you need to know more.

My drive to have more opportunities in life resulted in an intense work schedule that started when I was still a teenager. I took on many adult responsibilities at home, such as helping my mom take care of my younger siblings. In high school I worked multiple odd jobs simultaneously; the summer I was sixteen I had three jobs. I recall quite clearly waking up at five A.M. and walking two miles all by myself in the black morning hours to the next town to clean rooms at the Ramada Inn. After my shift, I walked to a monotonous data-entry job at a medical clinic until late in the day. In the evening, I was an off-the-books waitress at a local restaurant. You'll never hear a complaint from me—I have always known that honorable wealth comes from hard work, ingenuity, and enthusiasm.

When it was time to go to college, I was uncertain about what path to take. Other than my mom and dad, there were no role models in my neighborhood to inspire or guide me. Most of the girls in my town were pregnant dropouts by the time they were fifteen; many of the guys didn't finish high school either, and entered the local workforce, which didn't afford many opportunities beyond a paycheck. College degrees, white-collar jobs, and big houses didn't exist in my insular world. Midway through senior year, my high school guidance counselor asked me what school I planned to attend, to which I replied, "I haven't thought about it." I had a high GPA, so my counselor urged me to apply to Rutgers University. But because it was already so far into my final year at school, I rushed to take the SATs and submitted a "late" application quickly. When Rutgers accepted me, my world opened up.

On the first day of classes, I had fifty dollars in my bank account and a student loan to pay back. I worked day and night to pay the remaining tuition, sometimes skipping classes because I was so exhausted from the assortment of waitressing, lifeguarding, and tutoring gigs I juggled. I'm grateful that I worked my way through college. And I know that whatever sacrifices I made were worth it because I believe there is no better investment you can make than in education. After four years, I graduated cum laude from college. I was on my way.

It took several years, but I did make more money than I ever dreamed of in a very tough business, and at thirty years old I found myself in the top 1 percent of income earners of any age or gender. A few years later I was living mortgage-free and debt-free, and had I created a portfolio of assets, investments, and real estate that provides me with lifelong financial freedom and independence. I also am blessed with a great family and a wonderful baby and husband. I tell you all this with a great deal of humility and thanksgiving. I am grateful for the hard work, adversity, and triumphs that pushed me from one success to another.

IT'S YOUR TURN

Now I spend my days sharing everything I have learned about financial freedom and prosperity with women who feel stuck in small towns, crummy apartments, mind-numbing jobs, or bad relationships, their noses pressed up against the window of happiness and independence. Anyone who feels stuck about money can get unstuck. You can change the way you feel about yourself and the world, learn to focus on what you want, and get out of your comfort zone and take appropriate action to reach your goals. If I did it, so can you.

"I have found that if you love life,
life will love you back."

—ARTHUR RUBINSTEIN,
POLISH-BORN U.S. COMPOSER/PIANIST (1886–1982)

■

LIVE IT
LOVE IT
EARN IT

PART ONE

Prepare Your Potential

Each one of us holds the promise of greatness within our hearts, minds, and souls. Our potential and where it leads us are as unique as our fingerprints, yet the way to access what is possible is universal. Affirm your life; find joy every day, even in the mundane; and embrace your strengths and use them to better yourself and the world. Part 1 of this book will ready you to tap into your limitless ability to create financial independence and the life you want. If you follow this path I promise that the door to prosperity and good fortune will open wide.

1.

Say Yes to Yourself

"Believe in your dreams and they may come true; believe in
yourself, and they will come true."

—ANONYMOUS

LET'S START ON the right path to prosperity by learning how to take care
of ourselves, and affirming and developing our talents and interests. Doing
so gets us where we want to go more quickly than when we neglect these
areas of life: a healthy mind, body, and bank account are all connected.
I realize this is a surprising way to begin a book about wealth creation
and personal finance. However, I have met many successful, wildly creative people who have richly charmed lives. Those who take care of their
health—mind and body—stay on top of their game and have an edge when
it comes to their competition.

Begin your own journey to well-being by turning *toward* people, behavior,
and situations that enhance your life and well-being, and *away* from those
that don't. I call this saying yes to yourself. Until you start affirming your
self-worth and your future through both thought and action, your efforts to
improve your finances and create wealth will not be met with success.

The moment you say yes to yourself, life will improve.

■

We will come back to personal well-being and confidence again and again in *Live It, Love It, Earn It*. When we take care of ourselves we are better equipped to look after other people. Consider what happens on an airplane. The flight attendant reminds passengers to, in case of emergency, put on an oxygen mask *before* tending to the person sitting next to them. How could a traveler gasping for breath help another? Think of saying yes to yourself as your oxygen mask for life.

For those of you who may be stressing out at the thought of how much saying yes may cost, rest assured that most of what I suggest requires very little if any money at all. And I will show you throughout the book how to fund those small pleasures that do require a small investment.

YES TO BALANCE

Putting your life into harmony and balance is the first best way to get into the habit of saying yes. By balance I mean ordering your days so that they enable you to get both personal needs and outside obligations met without feeling pinched and frustrated at the end of the day. Have you ever noticed that when your life is in balance days pass with ease and are often filled with accomplishments big and small? We're productive and energetic. Stability and calm enable us to make sound judgments on just about everything—from who we date and marry to what kind of job we go after to how many pairs of shoes we buy to what kind of food we eat. We're able to perceive potentially stressful situations as benign, and handle them objectively. We can take a deep breath, step back, and see the big picture. When we are balanced, we can look inside ourselves without fear of what we might find. We are at peace and can flow with the inner guidance we are getting, and can tap into it successfully.

When we're out of balance, things never seem to go as well, do they? Annoyances and distractions seem to happen *to* us, as if some force of the universe were willing bad stuff to happen. Imbalance tends to focus us on abstract matters and we may push off more immediate concerns. For instance, I have a friend who when overwhelmed by a busy schedule has a tendency to dwell on events not scheduled for months, and forgets to pay bills that are sitting on her desk, staring at her. We've all been there, so there's no blame and shame. When I am out of balance I don't feel like myself, centered and confident. The risk of making bad decisions increases, as does the chance that I will repeat mistakes. I think of this as being in a split state, when I am thinking one thing and doing something else.

> *Achieve peace and emotional balance by paying attention to intuition and feelings, observing them, listening, and then acting.*

■

For instance, as I wrote this chapter, the stock market was tumbling to record lows. While I understand that such upheavals are partially cyclical, and that markets usually rebound, the day after a particularly steep drop I woke up feeling very negative. "What's going to happen today?" I thought with dread. Not helpful! So what do I do in these instances? Instead of calling my broker and crying, "Sell!" or pulling the covers back over my head, I consciously shift my thinking and remind myself to focus on what I can control, not on what I can't. I can't control what the markets are doing but I can take appropriate actions for my investments. I called my financial adviser and a few trusted friends, weighed the different courses of action, and made a clear decision aligned with my best interests. I'm not saying this was easy! I had to consciously and deliberately shift my thinking, and make sure my actions were in sync with my best interests.

This kind of realignment will help to keep you from making unintentional mistakes—the day goes well despite the fact that markets are down or business is slow or whatever trials and tribulations are happening. Everything is okay, the world keeps spinning, and I keep producing and moving forward toward my goals. The trick is to *respond*, not react, to events, particularly those you cannot control, like the weather, the stock market, or politics. There is absolutely no profit in that—after all, we can't choose our weather or manipulate the marketplace to our liking, and we don't have any say in global economic policy. Focus attention on the things that can be changed and accept the things that can't, as the old saying goes. We *can* control where we keep our money and how it is invested. We *can* ensure that we don't overspend or indulge in food or drink that will impact our health negatively. We *can* control our attitude and outlook on life situations.

That said, maintaining our emotional equilibrium is more doable when we are not flooded with a torrent of obligations, requests, and unreasonable expectations. Face it, it is easier to project our worries onto a failing stock market, tornadoes in the Midwest, or global famine relief than to face a coworker, spouse, or friend and tell her we can't add one more thing to our already full plate. Yes to balance is, in large part, achieved by learning to say no.

A Fine Balance

The physical ability to balance helps steady us emotionally, especially during times of stress and uncertainty. So says board certified master physical instructor Malcolm Milton, NASM, CES. "Having a strong sense of balance goes right to the core of your being. Applied to everyday life, physical balance actually helps you focus on things that give you stability—like satisfying work and loving relationships." If you have never tried a balance exercise, Malcolm recommends the following to improve stability. Do it each morning or evening—or both:

1. Stand up straight and close both eyes. Have a chair nearby, for safety's sake.
2. Without holding on to the chair, raise one leg a foot off the ground and to the side.
3. Extend both arms out to the side.
4. Maintain your balance in this position for a count of 10.
5. Repeat with the other leg.
6. Perform the sequence five times.

"NO" IS A COMPLETE SENTENCE

Have you ever noticed that when you ask a guy to do something he doesn't want to do, he just says no, without guilt or explanation? Discussion over. It usually sounds something like this:

You: "Will you go shopping with me this afternoon instead of watching the football game?"
Him: "No."

We make our own choices; *we* are responsible when we say yes to something we do not have to do. Yet "no" is out of our comfort zone. As a result we tend to give in when a request comes our way because we (unnecessarily) want to make everyone happy, be perceived as good or loyal, or we believe that the requester is going to be angry with us if we don't. There is a chance that people who are used to hearing "yes" will be annoyed when they hear "no" coming out of our mouths for the first time. They'll survive. And they may even respect us for not being a pushover.

Remember too that understanding the feelings of a person who receives our no is one thing—caving into them is quite another. Acknowledge his or her feelings simply without changing your stance: "I am so sorry you're disappointed, but I still have to say no." The idea is not to make the other person feel wrong for asking. A clean, honest, and friendly delivery is essential. For example, if a guy asks you for a date and you do not want to accept, tell him, "I'm so flattered, you made my day, but I can't." If a co-worker asks for help on a project, respond with a genuine smile and tell her, "My schedule is full, I cannot do that for you, but good luck getting it done."

Another part of the no scenario is ensuring that our physical reaction is neutral and our body language relaxed. A lot of women get noticeably tense when they say no. Their shoulders hunch, they stammer, mumble, or raise their voice, and they may back away or cross their arms tightly. Obvious discomfort makes the other person feel as if they've done something wrong. Stay loose and stay centered.

Just Say No

Practice makes perfect when it comes to no. One of the exercises I like to do in my abundance workshops with Elizabeth Webb, a relationship coach and CEO of La Vida Femme, is to go through a list of requests and questions and have the participants reply "no" until they are comfortable saying it. Below are some sample questions (you can access a longer list on liveitloveitearnit.com).

Have a buddy ask you each question. Reply "no" after each question. The first few times, saying "no" might make you feel very uncomfortable. You may have to do this exercise several times before saying no loses its hold on you. Then trade places.

1. Can you help me with my project?
2. Can you walk my dog?
3. Can you lend me one hundred dollars?
4. Can I borrow your new shoes?
5. Can you do some research for me?
6. Can I leave early today?
7. Can you cancel your workout and come out with us instead?
8. Can I leave my storage boxes in your basement?
9. Can you read this report for me? It's due tomorrow.
10. Can I use your Rolodex for contacts?

YES TO YOUR INSTINCTS

The same reason we find it difficult to say "no" (wanting to be liked and approved of, or perceived as loyal and open-minded) can lead us to ignore our instincts. Most often, our instincts are right. Unfortunately, we often work at cross-purposes to our own best interests, even when our minds and hearts are telling us loudly and clearly to avoid certain relationships or activities. When warning bells are ringing in your ears, listen, and stop caring so much about what your friends, colleagues, and others think.

Recent scientific research supports the accuracy of our gut instincts. People who deliberate are *less* likely to consistently make the right decisions, say psychology researchers Loran F. Nordgren and Ap Dijksterhuis. They found that those who make so-called "snap judgments" based on their gut instincts are more likely to make better decisions—especially complex ones. Northwestern University psychologists also concluded that many gut feelings are not impulsive judgments or baseless guesswork. Rather, our brains quickly access unconscious memories and use them to make fast, but considered, choices.

Intuition, if we pay attention to it, can play an important role in finding answers to all sorts of problems in everyday life, according to these scientists. Our instincts help us steer clear of dangerous or unproductive situations, as well as lead us to many "lightbulb moments" and solutions to difficult problems. It's not so much a matter of rediscovering our instincts; they are there and communicating with us all the time. We have to start paying attention to them, giving them credence, and following through. We often get so wrapped up in over-thinking or justifying choices that go against our feelings that decisions at odds with what we know to be true can blow up in our faces.

How many times have we talked ourselves into believing a person we think is our friend is not really lying to us or talking about us behind our backs even when there is evidence—and instinct—to the contrary? How many of us have tried sticking it out at a failing company even though we know we should be looking for another job? Have you ever been in a situation with work, friends, or a relationship where you stayed even though deep down inside you knew the situation would never improve? I have.

After I had opened my own marketing business, a colleague of mine referred me to a financial firm that was in need of my services. This person had told me it was a very well-run office. The catch? My friend said that while the fund was reputable, the person running it, Mike, wasn't. He had a history of never signing contracts or paying on deals he made with other marketers, despite the fact that they brought in business that helped him build large profits.

When we met, I was immediately struck by his shady vibe. I should have walked out of his office and never returned after our first meeting. Instead, I pushed the feeling down, attributing it to the influence my colleague's opinion of Mike was having on me. How could someone so well known in his industry be so dishonest? I didn't want to believe it and so Mike and I came to a verbal agreement. However, each time I asked him to sign a contract, he refused. Despite this, I kept working for him, telling myself it would all pay off in the end.

After months of getting nowhere with Mike, I told one of my mentors about my frustrations. He suggested writing an informal handwritten list of the work I had done for Mike and asking him to initial it. The next day I casually walked into Mike's office, put the list in front of him, and said, "If you are not going to sign my contract, at least sign this paper to acknowledge that you agree that I've done this work." Thinking it was meaningless and to get me off his back, Mike signed the paper.

Flash forward one year. I met with Mike and was insistent that he pay me for the work I had done. His response was devastatingly simple: "Thanks for all your work. I appreciate your help but I don't think you deserve what you want to be paid." Hearing him say those words was like going down in an elevator really fast and being punched in the stomach at the same time. This time, I did what I should have done from the beginning: I walked out and never came back.

Trying every possible way to get paid by Mike, I sent legal letters, called repeatedly, and did everything else in my professional power. I didn't want to give up and just walk away; that's what Mike expected. It took me another year of legal wrangling to receive the compensation that was due to me. The sheet of yellow legal paper that Mike had initialed held up as a binding agreement. Handshake deals and verbal agreements, I'm afraid, are not worth the air they use up. Was all the trouble I endured to get paid worth it? Yes and no. Yes because I stood on principle and was eventually paid. But on the other hand, I should have listened to my gut and never accepted the project in the first place; getting the money from him afterward was costly to me both emotionally and financially.

Not following our instincts can cause us to miss opportunities or disregard brilliant ideas. I should have followed my instincts and put my energies into an opportunity that felt positive from the beginning. In retrospect, I ignored a chance to be part of a very lucrative business opportunity because I was so wrapped up in the drama of worrying about whether or not Mike would pay me. Since that time I have learned to "go with my gut." If a potential business partner gives me a bad feeling, I seek a partnership elsewhere. If an acquaintance makes me feel uncomfortable when I am with her, I don't pursue the friendship. On the other hand, if I feel a tingle of excitement during a business meeting, I am likely to follow the feeling. My instincts protect and serve me well.

A friend of mine told me of a similar gut-wrenching episode that happened to her. She had hired a decorator to do some work on her new apartment. The two hit it off and Barbara loved the decorator's ideas. "We agreed that the designer would charge a flat fee for her services, plus ten percent commission on anything she bought. This seemed reasonable to me, so I signed the contract," Barbara told me. The design project commenced, and at the beginning, things went smoothly. The decorator filled Barbara's apartment with lovely furniture and accessories exactly to her taste and specifications. When she received the decorator's bills—which did not have the pieces itemized, but only stated the total amount owed—Barbara sensed something strange but paid the bills without asking for explanation or itemized receipts for the purchases. "The prices just seemed weird, but I put it out of my mind," she says. "I felt like I was imposing or asking too much to see the breakdown of the charges."

Through the process Barbara continued to ignore a strange feeling she had about the transactions. "One day a few weeks after the project was completed, I was just not feeling right about it. I liked what the decorator had done, but somehow I couldn't push the feeling away that something was a bit off." Finally and very hesitantly she asked the decorator for an itemized bill, to which he defensively objected, accusing her of not liking his work and mistrusting him. "It was hard to be firm and ask for what I wanted, the itemized receipts," says Barbara. But she firmly asked again for the details, and when she did finally receive them and went over each one, she realized that the decorator was indeed overcharging her. There it was in black and white. The prices the designer had charged were 20 percent, not 10 percent, above the sale price. So the designer *had* charged her more; her instincts were right all along.

Barbara realized she had to go through the designer's bills and every manufacturer and store to confirm prices. In every case, the prices were 15 to 20 percent above the retail price. This was devastating for Barbara because she had a written contract with the decorator that specified payment of a flat fee plus 10 percent. She wrote a letter to the designer detailing what she had learned. It took several letters and phone calls and many months of work to get everything straightened out. "I did get a refund from the designer," says Barbara, "but I wish I had followed my gut from the beginning and insisted on seeing the actual receipts for the items."

Barbara was right. In hindsight she should have been more vigilant about looking over receipts and trusting her gut. But so often belief and faith in a relationship is hard to discourage, especially for us women. We are trusting souls, but we have to get back in touch with our survival instincts. We have to confront the situation when our instincts tell us to do so, and then move on and cut our losses.

SUCCESS SECRET:

Red Flags Are Red for a Reason

When you have an immediate good or bad feeling, acknowledge it and act on it. Don't spend time explaining away red flags—heed them. For example, say you go on a job interview and meet several people in the company. Yet, you do not really click with the person who would be your boss or like the feeling you get from the office environment in general. Then they offer you the job. Should you take it? What's your initial reaction—*without* ruminating? If it's no, don't take the job. It it's yes, accept. If you are *still* confused and can't make a decision, *do nothing*. Wait and know that the right direction and answer will come, often when you are doing something else (that's your intuition tapping you on your shoulder). By using this method, on the whole, I have learned how to respond and make the decisions that are right for me.

YES TO SELF-RESPECT

Call it the digital age, the information era, or a time of change—we live in a fast-moving world that offers many ways for us to communicate, connect with new people half a world away (or down the block), express our individuality, and share our views. Couple this with a trend toward informality in all things, from dress to dining, and we may be left with the idea that it's safe to reveal our private lives in a public way.

According to experts at the American Psychological Association, many of us have become insensitive to our own privacy interests. Even though social networking sites (Facebook, MySpace, Twitter) are wonderful ways to keep up with friends, and blogging offers an accessible and exciting way to express opinions, write about our interests, and share prized images, these technological wonders can also be slippery slopes to personal and professional disaster. Making our personal indiscretions available on the Web, or casually offering our personal data electronically to others, can lead to regret and some scary scenarios.

The woman who posts revealing photos of her topless Caribbean vacation on the Internet may be in for a surprise when she returns to her office. Embarrassment is the least of it. Many employers have ethics and moral codes, which allow them to fire a worker for disregarding those standards. It may be hard to find another job, because once something is on the Internet, it's just a Google away from being discovered. Before you post a picture or an opinion or send an e-mail or a text message consider how it reflects on you and your values. Everything you "put out there" should reinforce your dignity and high standards. Likewise, always present yourself in a ladylike fashion. I am a modern woman living a contemporary life, yet I know that poise and composure will never go out of style.

SUCCESS SECRETS

Maintain Poise, Polish, and Professionalism

Not much has changed in terms of gender and office politics over the years, no matter what kind of industry you work in. Men set the social bar higher for women. This may seem unfair, and it probably is. But why not keep your dignity? It's easy enough and you can do what you like with discretion in your private life. Just don't let it spill over into the professional arena because you will be the one to take the hits. When you are at a conference, company party, after-hours meeting, or other work event that involves a social component, wear conservative business clothes and make sure not to drink too much. If it gets late, leave with another woman, because if you are seen leaving with a male colleague the rumor mill could move fast the next day. These are rules I live by and they have served me very well.

YES TO YOUR HEALTH

Good health puts us in a position to work better, stronger, harder, and smarter on our goals. When we eat nutritious, healthy whole food we are truly saying *yes to life*. Unfortunately, one out of four women ages twenty-five to forty-five have "disordered eating behaviors," according to a survey done by *Self* magazine and the University of North Carolina at Chapel Hill.

Another 10 percent of women report engaging in drastic behaviors such as bulimia and anorexia. According to The Renfrew Center, a nationwide clinic that specializes in eating disorders, many of these girls and women establish rigid rules around food as part of their disorder (e.g., no butter, no bread, no carbs, no sugar, or no eating after ten o'clock). Breaking the "rule" often leads to inward anger, depression, binging and purging, starving, and other serious health risks.

Eating disorders is a subject I know quite a bit about. I have suffered from food issues since I was thirteen years old; between my teen years and my twenties I had numerous bouts of anorexia and bulimia. I am tall and naturally thin to begin with, and never had the need to lose weight or diet. Yet I would either stuff myself with all sorts of junk, which I would throw up an hour later, or I would not eat at all. There was a point when, at five feet ten inches, I weighed about one hundred pounds. Size 0 was barely an option for me—I could fit into children's clothes. I weighed myself constantly, thought about food all the time, and isolated myself from others. I often felt dizzy and could not concentrate.

One part of my issue with food stemmed from an overwhelming school and work schedule, which often seemed chaotic and beyond my control. I could, however, control what I ate. Or so I thought. My sorority sisters taught me how to throw up my food after binge eating. There were days when I threw up more than fifteen or twenty times, ripping my knuckles apart in the process. I was hurting myself very badly, body and mind. I tried to fill this emotional hole with "comfort" treats such as cookies, potato chips, candy, or ice cream, and even so-called healthy foods. I once went on a binge with carrot sticks, and another time with bowl after bowl of oatmeal. What I thought would be a once-in-a-while thing became a hard-to-break habit.

After years of struggling with food, in my mid-twenties I sought professional help at a hospital outpatient program. I learned that when you overeat, as we all do from time to time, you have to forgive yourself for "making a mistake" with food and be gentle and loving toward yourself. Eating issues can be difficult to resolve on our own because they are tightly bound up with emotional issues. If we can identify our emotional binge or starve triggers—in my case it was anxiety over all the jobs and schoolwork I had to juggle—we can learn to stop and think before reacting by overindulging in or withholding food. One exercise that helped me stop binge eating was to write down all the people, events, and situations that made me feel angry, fearful, and anxious. Instead of heading directly to the fridge (or the bathroom), I learned how to take a moment and ask myself what it was that I was feeling angry about and why. It might have been a particularly difficult project at work. So I'd think, "Oh, I get it, I'm stressed about finishing the report on time. Right. That's no reason to force-feed sixteen doughnuts down my throat." Even if I did eat the doughnuts, I would still have to do the project. Or, "I see, I am upset that what's-his-name didn't call me back. That's no reason to purge my lunch."

Other suggestions that helped me when I wanted to overeat and purge was to distract myself immediately by getting out of the kitchen or restaurant, going for a walk, heading to the gym, taking a bath, or talking to a trusted friend until the craving passed. We women who have or are struggling with eating disorders know how hard this is to do—the physical craving seems overpowering—but I promise that if you start slowly with these few suggestions and others from eating specialists, it will get easier with time.

I no longer fixate on what and how much I eat, and I do not avoid any particular food. I am at a healthy weight for my frame and build. My philosophy about eating is practical: eat three balanced meals and two healthy snacks every day and live life in between. It's a simple and satisfying way to eat. I may have two serving-size containers of yogurt for breakfast because my body type needs more protein than carbohydrates. For lunch I often have eggs, a turkey sandwich, a chicken salad, or a slice of pizza and a salad. For dinner, I may have whole wheat pasta with meat sauce or poached salmon with a cucumber salad or vegetables. Nuts make great snacks, and I always have them available at home or tucked into my bag. A piece of fruit or a small bagel with cream cheese are other snack stand-bys. Twice a day I take vitamins, omega-3's, -6's, and -9's, and extra magnesium.

SALLY'S NEW OUTLOOK

My friend Sally was in the midst of a painful and unpleasant divorce. There were young children involved, and many years of accumulated belongings and property that she and her husband had to divide. She was so stressed and upset that she, in her own words, "ate and ate and ate, and then I ate some more." She gained fifty pounds in about six months. It was stress eating, yes, but she was also punishing herself. Sally felt guilty that she could not make her ten-year marriage work, especially for the sake of her three girls, who would no longer have both parents always available. The breakup was a heavy burden for Sally to bear, and she used food to help carry the load.

Eventually, with the help of a nutritionist and a therapist, Sally learned how to stop using food to combat the stress and disappointment she felt over the dissolution of her marriage. "Whenever I feel the pull of the fridge, I distract myself with a walk, a shower, or a phone call to a friend until the feeling passes." Sally also keeps cards in her purse and in her kitchen that remind her that overeating negatively affects her health and her girls. "My favorite, most effective, card is the one that says 'My girls are more important than more food.' It keeps me focused on my goal to lose the extra weight and provide my family with healthy food." So far Sally has taken off twenty-five of the fifty pounds she gained, and is providing her family and herself with fresh, wholesome food.

GRETA'S JOURNEY

Greta had been thin all her life. "I never needed to diet," she says. "I really had no issues surrounding food and I was fairly athletic." Then Greta took a job that sounded great on paper: a move to a new company and a new city, a promotion, an executive title, and an impressive raise. "After a few weeks I realized that taking the job was the worst mistake of my life. The company had a very different corporate style than I was used to, and it seemed very clubby to me in an unpleasant way." On top of that the new city made her feel very isolated, so she turned to her new best friend: food.

The result was that Greta would go across the street to the local shopping center and bring back enormous quantities of food to eat at her desk. "After downing a platter of sushi, a bowl of soup, bread sticks, and a salad, I'd be starving for more. It seemed as if I could never have enough. I'd go back out and get cookies, candy—anything to push down the dread and disappointment I felt."

After eighteen months on the job, Greta jumped at the chance to take a layoff package the company offered, which shocked her boss and coworkers. "The sad part is, I walked into the job a thin person, and I walked out a fat one. I gained sixty pounds in less than two years." It took Greta nearly ten years before she was able to lose it all. In that time she learned how to stop using food as an emotional crutch and start seeing it for what it is—fuel that keeps the body in peak condition and a source of energy that helps us face every circumstance that comes our way.

MINDFUL EATING

Lisa Talamini is no stranger to stories like Sally's and Greta's. As a nutritionist and vice president of research and program innovation for Jenny Craig, the diet and lifestyle firm, she has a firsthand understanding of the kind of food-related issues and challenges that face women every day. "It's not just what you eat, it's how you think about what you are eating. Take time to eat mindfully so that you are *present* for the experience. You will feel fuller on a lesser amount of food than you think, because you are truly enjoying it," she says.

When we observe that we aren't making the best food choices, we can quickly respond and make the needed adjustments by checking in with ourselves, says Lisa. "You may even find that it's not food you want at all. You may have fatigue, not hunger. Maybe you need a break. Sit outside in the park for a while, walk around the block; if you're home, lie down for ten minutes," she advises. Lisa says that self-awareness allows us to structure our environment around healthy choices.

I love that Lisa always keeps fresh flowers on her desk at work. What does that have to do with food and eating? "My schedule is really busy and when I see those flowers it brings me back to the moment. It's a little reminder of my humanity—I don't need to eat a bag of chips." Lisa also carries healthy foods—a bag of carrots, some almonds, or yogurt—with her when she knows she's got a jam-packed day in front of her. "If I know I am not going to have a chance to get lunch, then I want to have foods on hand that give me energy and satisfaction." That's easy for anyone to do—no cooking required.

I used to think I could eat junk food, pop a vitamin, and I'd be fine. Not so! We need plenty of whole, natural foods and few processed snacks and sweets. For women age eighteen to forty, or those in peak childbearing years, Lisa says it is crucial to make sure natural folate and calcium are part of our diet. Folate-rich foods include calf's liver, lentils, pinto beans, chickpeas, asparagus, peanuts, spinach, black beans, navy beans, kidney beans, and collard greens. As for calcium, you can find it in low-fat yogurt, sesame seeds, milk, spinach, collards, turnips, dark leafy greens, mozzarella cheese, and black-strap molasses. We also need iron for sustaining energy and focus throughout the day. Beans and greens offer a healthy dose of iron, as do pumpkin seeds, tofu, venison, lean beef, and spinach.

Women over forty-five need these nutrients as well, but must also make it a point to eat foods that contain vitamins B12 and B6 and omega-6 fatty acids. These have been shown to help reduce the risk of cardiovascular disease. Best of all, these foods fight the aging process. The fiber, carotenoids, vitamin C, and antioxidants found in fresh produce are vital for heart health. Animal proteins, such as those in lean lamb, salmon, scallops, snapper, and halibut, are great sources of B12 and B6. Vitamin C is found in oranges and orange juice, but there's more of this nutrient, per serving, in papaya, red bell peppers, broccoli, Brussels sprouts, strawberries, cantaloupe, kiwifruit, cauliflower, and kale. Bottom line: *most* of our food should come from the perimeter aisles of the grocery store—the fresh produce, meat, and dairy departments.

GET MOVING!

I am not a fanatic about fitness, although there was a time when my food drama was wrapped up with exercise drama. Some of you may recognize this routine: I would eat four cookies and "balance it out" immediately by going to the gym and running for forty-five minutes on the treadmill. Or I would indulge in too much dessert after a date, and then add two hours the next day to my already heavy workout schedule. Now I see exercise as part of my mental health. We have one body and one mind, and they need to be strong and in sync to accomplish our goals. Vigorous movement relaxes me and clears my head. I walk instead of jumping into the car, run in the park as often as I can, stretch when I wake up I the morning, and swim in the ocean every chance I get. In fact, whenever I am at the beach I soak up the sun (with sunscreen), relax, play volleyball, and swim. This approach seems to me to be a very natural way to incorporate movement into my life. There's no pressure to make it to the gym or stick to a rigid routine.

Incorporating movement into our daily routine pays huge dividends in terms of increased energy and focus, as well as elevating our mood and happiness. Physical activity can be a social event. "In days gone by we used to ride our bikes after school, or take a walk, or play a game outside," says Lisa Talamini. "Now we meet at the coffee shop or a fast-food place. So much of entertainment is centered on eating. Think of entertaining as a people event, not a food event."

Instead of meeting friends for dessert and latte, organize a trip to the local driving range and hit a few balls (what a way to work out all our stress!). Go to the park for a power walk, or meet at the local bowling alley or golf course. Take a Pilates class with a few friends, play doubles at the local tennis court, or take a horseback riding lesson. If you do go out for dinner with friends, can you walk to the restaurant and then back home? Try thinking about how you can make movement a part of your everyday life.

SWEET DREAMS

Getting enough sleep is *extremely* important and often forgotten as a heath issue. After all, it can be tough to get enough. With days jam-packed with work, social life, chores, and obligations, sleep seems like a sidebar we fit in when we've reached the exhaustion point of no return. At that point we can be so tired, falling asleep is difficult. Studies suggest that lack of sleep can lead to irritability, chronic fatigue, and weight gain. We should all get a minimum of seven hours a night. If doing so means going to bed an hour earlier, so be it.

Our beds should be comfortable—the right mattress; soft, smooth, sweet-smelling sheets; and comfortable pillows all add to our ability to drift off peacefully. If you have trouble sleeping, or staying asleep, ask a doctor or sleep professional for help. Before committing to taking a pill, keep in mind that researchers say that meditative sleep techniques are more effective and a whole lot safer than pharmaceutical solutions. Soak in a hot bubble bath for fifteen minutes, drink warm milk right before you go to bed, or give yourself a head message while lying in bed. Saying to myself, "I'm sleepy," over and over again works for me. Try to shut off all the noise (TV, radio, MP3). Mentally take all the events of the last twelve hours and put them in a big hatbox. Take the box and watch yourself use a stepladder to place it in a closet, on a high shelf, out of sight and reach. Then relax with an empty mind for several minutes and feel your body relax and drift.

Diane von Furstenberg

DESIGNER

Designer Diane von Furstenberg first arrived on the fashion scene in 1972, and by 1976 had sold millions of her signature wrap dress. In 1997, Diane reemerged on the New York style stage with the re-launch of the iconic silhouette for a whole new generation of women to enjoy. Through the years, one thing is certain—Diane said YES to herself. That has been the driving force behind her personal and professional success.

How do you approach life?

With everything I have. Two years before I was born my mother was in a concentration camp and survived. The fact that she was not even supposed to live makes my birth a miracle, and that certainly influenced me to live life fully every day. You are going to be living your life; no one else is, so therefore it has got to be good.

How did you start your career?

I started in fashion when I was twenty-two. I did not have a real vocation. No formal background or training. However, I did know what I wanted to be: an independent woman. I had a clear picture and I became it. I was interning in Italy with a friend of mine who had a printing and knitting factory. My college boyfriend came back to Italy from America and I was pregnant. I thought to myself, here I am, pregnant and about to get married. This is horrible! I explained the situation to my friend at the factory and asked if I could make a few samples of a dress I had designed. And then the fairy tale happened. I was lucky—I had the right product and a strong will, and ended up living the American Dream. It wasn't all roses, of course. I sold my company and then started it again eight years ago.

What about your "Second Time Around"?

I wanted to create my wrap dress again because I saw hip, young girls buying the vintage pieces. But I had no idea whether it was going

(continued)

to work. I also wrote a book as a way of making a line between the past and the present (*Diane, A Signature Life*). I would ask myself, why am I writing the book and what if it fails? Yet it turned out to be very good. But you never know for sure—no one does. How can you know how other people will react, what other people will do? As far as starting my dress business again—well, you always have resistance. But I had trust in the idea, and strength from knowing that I had all the solutions inside of me—it wasn't going to happen from anybody else. I went toward the dress line slowly, and then saw there was traction. It is always about taking little steps before reaching the final destination, and finding a place for yourself. So find your place. It's there.

What's your definition of success?

There is no success without humble pie. You have to use rejection and frustration as fuel—it happens all the time, it happens every day. It's inevitable, part of life. The earlier you become your best friend, the better off you will be. The only thing that will never go away from you is your character, so be honest with yourself. You can lose everything money, wealth, beauty, and youth—but not your good character. I never felt like I had to be anything for anyone—I always trusted myself.

The best advice I can give women is don't be afraid of your own strength—what a woman can endure and deal with is incredible. I have yet to meet a woman who is not strong—all women are strong. Some of them are afraid to show it and they hold it back because of lack of education, or a husband. But it's all there in all of them. Therefore my mission at this time is to empower women—I try to do it with my clothes, my company. The biggest barrier to success is not letting your strength out. Just let it out.

YES TO YOUR MIND

Self-improvement, higher education, keeping abreast of current events, and enjoying art, music, and literature are essential elements of saying yes to yourself. Enriching your mind builds self-confidence in an authentic way.

There are different points in our lives when we are consumed with building a business, closing a deal, or caring for a child, and our ability to stay in touch is sidelined. That's okay. In fact, when we are really busy with life, spending an hour a week on anything that expands our mind (like reading the arts section of the newspaper, or taking a class) is just fine. At least once a day see what is going on in the world—current events and the news, lifestyle, fashion. Scan the newspapers, watch the morning or evening news, or check in on Internet current events sites. There's no need to read every word of every major paper, or every book on the best-seller list. Read about what interests you—whether it's fiction, fashion, history, politics, sports, or food.

This effort offers two benefits. The first is that when we take the time to find out what is going on in the world, we very often come across a topic that holds serious interest for us. Delve into whatever sparks the imagination. Doing so can lead to brilliant ideas, deeper enjoyment of life, and true happiness. Psychologists who study happiness have found that pursuing interests and becoming deeply involved in an intellectually or physically demanding activity that we enjoy—*especially if it is difficult or challenging*—provides deep and lasting satisfaction.

Second, keeping abreast of cultural knowledge gives you an advantage in life and in your career. As a result of my own interests and pursuits I can chat about cricket, shooting, hunting, and fishing quite comfortably with a British lord, discuss private equity with a money manager, and trade insights on modern painting with an art collector. If you think this ability has not helped to enrich my life, think again! For example, I have an interest in modern art. While I do not have a degree in art history, I have read and learned about the periods I am interested in (modern and contemporary art, with a passion for abstract paintings).

Discovering art is much like learning about a really interesting new person or place. It broadens my perspective on the world. I love traveling to different cities, and taking in great architecture, and looking at the work of regional painters. Few Saturday afternoon outings are more enjoyable to me than a trip to a gallery, or a visit to an art fair. I try to expose myself to the best art I can as a way of developing my taste level. Many years ago a friend of mine who is a professional artist specializing in large-scale canvases taught me how to paint my own abstract work. At first it was hard for me to express myself with paint on a canvas. I had never done it before. I just gave it a try with no judgment attached, and to my surprise found I really liked it and had so much fun. Painting has now become a hobby, a creative release, and a soothing escape for me.

Is there something you have always wanted to try or learn about? Jewelry making? French history? Interior or fashion design? Eighteenth-century antiques? Photography? Screenwriting? Acting? Ballet? Don't let fear that you won't be good at something stand in your way. An interest doesn't have to lead to a new career. It can, of course, but that's not the reason why you should or shouldn't explore the possibilities. The fact that I will never be a famous painter (at least I don't think I will be) doesn't stop me from painting. Developing our minds is about satisfying a deep, primal need to be creative and to create.

YES TO YOUR SOUL

Quiet time spent in spiritual contemplation offers boundless opportunities for refreshment and reflection. Some of us connect with our spirituality in traditional ways, by going to church or synagogue. For others, spiritual practice means spending time outside in a natural setting (the mountains, a lake, a hiking trail). Unfortunately, more than a few of us have mixed feelings about spirituality, perhaps because we've been disillusioned by our childhood religion. Still, we yearn for a connection to something greater then ourselves. Call it God, a higher power, the universe, whatever you like. It's there and we need to get in touch with it.

"Without a conscious spiritual life or practice, life becomes so superficial that it loses meaning," says Jonathan Sonnenberg, a spiritual healer and codirector of The School of Vibrational Healing in New York. "Without a spiritual life, the world seems scary and you protect yourself from it by reacting to events with fear, instead of going out into the world with confidence."

Our spiritual life is there whether we consciously accept it or not, according to Jonathan. Those who don't get in touch with their spiritual life when things are going well are sometimes forced into it through emotional pain or disease. "We can all find a sense of spiritual joy simply by affirming the desire to do so. Once you open your heart to the spirit, it fills you right up," he explains.

The sense of joy that comes from a spiritual inner peace gives us a strong sense of ourselves. It grounds us. Troubling world and personal events don't affect us as emotionally as they do a person with no spiritual foundation. Jonathan compares spirituality to a sailboat. "The centerboard of a sailboat keeps the vessel from shifting to one side or another when a strong wind comes along. It will not go side to side with the waves but continues forward. Spirituality is the centerboard in life; when things go bad the joy allows us to keep going without being knocked over."

My friend Bonnie is a very talented and busy jewelry designer who makes time to meditate for fifteen minutes each morning. "I get up every morning and head for the gym. When I get back home I meditate and read affirmations. After a healthy, organic breakfast I go out in the world and see what happens. The discipline and deep relaxation of meditation prepares me for whatever the day brings."

Morning and evening rituals like Bonnie's are a very doable way to connect with our spiritual side, especially for those who may feel a bit "rusty." Consistency is key. Sip a cup of tea while observing the birds out your window before you get ready for the day. Or get up ten minutes early and take a mind-clearing walk and ask for inner guidance. Likewise, partake of an "active meditation" while you are on the elliptical machine or treadmill. In the evening, lie down for ten minutes and think about the day. Enjoy a mug of herbal tea or warm milk in a quiet room. Spend fifteen or twenty minutes reading prosperity literature. Two of my favorites are *The Game of Life and How to Play It*, by Florence Scovel Shinn, and *Dynamic Laws of Prosperity*, by Catherine Ponder (both are still in print and available online).

Jonathan recommends designating a specific place for your spiritual time or practice, such as a comfortable chair in a quiet room, or the same path on a hiking trail. "It will be a comfortable, familiar place imbued with spiritual energy."

Yes!

Yes is a mighty word, and putting it in your life literally, with a pretty little sign, is a positive and powerful thing to do. And it's so easy! Take a piece of paper (choose your favorite color) and draw or write *YES* as prettily as you can on it, copy this one, or download one of several YES signs from my Web site, liveitloveitearnit.com. Place it in a beautiful frame, one that makes you smile, and hang the sign where you can see it often (in your bedroom, bath, kitchen, on your desk, etc.).

When we women say yes to ourselves, we attract the flow of prosperity and abundance and are on our way to becoming rich, happy, and fabulous. By affirming our self-worth and our future through both thought and action, our efforts to improve our finances and create wealth will be met with success. Imagine, then, if you could also experience life through a lens of fun and joy? You can. It's the next tool in our box.

Say Yes to Yourself Summary:
- Find balance in your life.
- "No" is a complete sentence.
- Follow your instincts.
- Respect yourself.
- Maintain good health and seek help when you need it.
- Incorporate movement into your day.
- Get a good night's sleep.
- Develop interests that stimulate your mind.
- Get in touch with your spiritual side.

2.

Have Fun!

I TOOK AN informal poll, asking a group of women to tell me what they liked to do for fun. Some answers were predictable and pleasant: "shopping," "catching a movie with friends," "going out dancing," "taking a long afternoon nap with my boyfriend." Others were more unexpected. One woman told me that her idea of fun was hanging upside down on an inversion table. Another said playing poker with the guys was a blast. Even though the answers were different, they did have one thing in common: they all had to do with discretionary activities; not one had anything to do with work.

When you are having a blast, you are a bright light
and a target for great things to come into your life:
new ideas, people, places, and passions.

■

Let's do a 360 on our definition of *fun*. I want you to be excited about going into work on Monday. When you are working around the clock to reach an objective, you may tend to feel as if you're missing out on life. You can enjoy what you do if you see your work as a way of achieving goals. Believing work is only a means to pay bills makes any job or obligatory task seem like drudgery. On the other hand, thinking things like "I'm building a wonderful future and creating a great life," "I'm excited about what I do," "My work is my dream; I like doing what I do" turns work on its head and makes it more fun. Looking at your job this way may bring to light previously hidden feelings, and—if you do not believe these statements—it may mean it's time for a change.

This theory can be applied to anything, including a job that is a stepping-stone to something better or a necessary chore. We can approach our "serious" side (work, paying bills, running errands) with a fun attitude. Several years ago I read an interview with pop icon Madonna, who said she really enjoyed taking the fluff out of the lint trap in her dryer. Imagine, a big star like her finding pleasure in an insignificant household chore. Fun can be made out of anything. That's the attitude we're after!

You also have to make room in your life for laughter and silly stuff (as I write this it's snowing outside and I am about to make snow angels with my young son), and little indulgences (a pair of pink undies with "I'm happy" printed or embroidered on them, perhaps?). What meaning does material wealth, and the effort to create it, have if you don't enjoy what you are doing or take time to stop and smell the roses? Here's how to make the fun happen every day.

Reframing how you see what you are doing now is part of preparing for your potential and your future. It takes energy, faith, and a sense of adventure to get ahead.

THE FUN OF FLOW

Many women I've coached believe that external objects or events will bring them happiness: "If only I had that new purse, I'd be on cloud nine"; "Once I get that promotion things will be better"; "I'm just thirty pounds away from sheer bliss"; and so on. Once you achieve these desires, you have a "happy high" for a while, but if you are not living in a state of joy, that high disappears quickly. You go back to your not-so-fun daily life, and seek out the next object, event, or person that can feed your desire for a jolt of joy.

Everyday happiness is elusive for those who believe it can't come from their daily lives. It's almost as if fun and joy were somehow outside their routine. Not so! Fun and happiness are right where we live, inside all of us. Authentic happiness, says spiritual healer Jonathan Sonnenberg, is a constant calm and reassuring sense of love. He says, "An attitude of fun is achieved when you are at peace with your environment—you have the ability to enjoy whatever is going on around you, wherever you happen to be."

Science confirms what Jonathan says. When you are deeply absorbed in an activity, you reach a level of pleasure called "flow," a term coined by positive psychologist Mihaly Csikszentmihalyi in his book by the same name, which benefits both your soul and your body; being in a flow state improves heart rate, circulation, and blood pressure. Even more reason to "get happy." Athletes call the state of flow "being in the zone." I call it focus or full immersion in an activity, feeling totally energized and unconcerned about outcomes—even if it is challenging or difficult (like mountain climbing, or learning a new language).

When we are in a flow state our minds are free, and we are able to reach a place that Csikszentmihalyi describes as a combination of effortless concentration and enjoyment. I feel this way when I am teaching a motivational class, working on a financial issue, reading a favorite book, or playing a good game of tennis. Flow brings us "in the moment" pleasure. In time, living in a constant state of flow leads to a steady stream of overall happiness and creativity.

SUCCESS SECRET

Don't Force Happiness

Life is not always pleasant. We don't have to sugarcoat the ebbs and flows of life. We will actually be happier if we allow time to recognize and embrace the bad times. Giving the impression that we are in a constant state of "it's all so amazing" bubbly, buoyant, grinning enthusiasm when that's not the case is being dishonest with ourselves and with others. We all have been around someone who behaves like this. Sometimes she may be wearing a happy face because she fears revealing her true feelings. A fun attitude is not meant to hide or paint over your true feelings. If you are sad, give yourself time to feel it, accept it, then let it go and move on.

FRUZSINA'S STORY

When my friend Fruzsina Keehn found her passion for jewelry, an entirely new, fabulous career opened up for her. She is a very adventurous woman, the epitome of someone who embraces life with a fun attitude. After studying architecture and interior design, Fruzsina was ready to pursue a career in those fields. As it happened, she fell in love along the way with a man who was transferred to Geneva by his company. Fruzsina moved with him, wondering if she could find work once they had settled in.

Because she was a foreigner, it turned out that Fruzsina was not able to work because of Switzerland's restrictive employment policies. Fruzsina enjoyed Geneva, continued her studies, and spent many happy hours immersed in contemplating intricate design motifs in a sketchbook. "My birthday was coming up and my boyfriend wanted to buy me a piece of jewelry. I never found anything that was appropriate. Instead, we had one of my ideas for earrings made. They were exactly what I wanted: completely unusual and one-of-a-kind."

A week or so later, Fruzsina and her beau attended a dinner party and she wore her special earrings. "The woman seated next to me went crazy for my black diamond earrings. I told her that I had designed them myself." It turned out Fruzsina's dinner companion was the accessories editor at a well-known society and fashion magazine. "She told me she wanted to feature those earrings, took them off my ears, and had them shot for the magazine the following month!"

Her boyfriend encouraged her to take what she most obviously had a passion and talent for far more seriously. It was not until after a painful separation with him, and her move back to London, that Fruzsina really started to think about what he had said. "Designing was just magical for me. Time seemed to stop when I was designing; when I'd look up from my pad sometimes several hours had passed. It really got me through what turned out to be a rough breakup," she says.

Over the next few years Fruzsina built her business, FK Designs, and a loyal global following for her stunning jewelry. She has also created a far-reaching network of editors and stylists who admire her work and feature it regularly in a number of magazines. "It has been easy for me in a way because I love what I do so much. Many people understand my designs and respond to them well."

*Serendipity has a way of happily imposing itself
when you are engaged in an activity that you love
and following your passion.*

■

This "coincidental" meeting with an influential editor at a dinner party may seem serendipitous—and certainly it was. That's what happens when we choose not to use our time fretting about not being able to do one thing or another (in Fruzsina's case, getting a job in a foreign country), and instead put our energies into activities that we love. The fun and happiness is doubled whenever Fruzsina sees women wearing her jewelry. "It's the greatest feeling, knowing that you've inspired and pleased someone else," she says. Jewelry design has opened Fruzsina's life even more than she dreamed it could: she has had great fun traveling, exploring big cities, and meeting interesting people from all over the world. She is constantly inspired by vintage jewelry and estate sales; and has learned a great deal more about history and art than she had at school.

Exercise Your Fun Muscle

Increase your daily flow: identify simple activities that put you in a flow state but don't depend on favorable external conditions. For example, it does not matter whether it is raining or snowing, or whether you're at home or traveling, you can still paint your toenails, sketch shoe designs, practice yoga stretches, or learn how to make a new recipe. Then try to incorporate as many of these activities into your day as you can. I like to sit at my computer and read news stories, read a book, and sort photographs. The list can include pursuits from every part of your life. Here are a few flow activities my clients have shared; perhaps they will remind you of your own:

- ◆ Reorganize closets and drawers
- ◆ Talk on the phone
- ◆ Create song lists on my iPod
- ◆ Style my friends' outfits

- ◆ **Apply individual false eyelashes**
- ◆ **Research antiques**
- ◆ **Make a perfect sauce**
- ◆ **Groom my Persian cat**
- ◆ **Make scrapbooks for friends and family**

PRACTICE ENTHUSIASM

We all have to do things we do not like or want to do. From taking out the trash to filling in a monthly management report, the flow value of many everyday tasks is not immediately apparent. Some of you might be in a job that does not put you in the zone. We can train ourselves to make even the most tedious work more interesting, and more fun. I am very good at amusing myself, and you can be too. Making "fun" out of whatever we have to do, in whatever situation we find ourselves in, is the best way to clear our desk of dreaded tasks and do just about anything better. When we're having fun, outcomes are of less concern but usually of a higher quality.

It's a matter of approach. Just say, "This is going to be fun." Oh, so simple, but oh, it *really* works. For instance, perhaps you work in a job that involves cold-calling or making calls to clients you dread. When I was making cold calls, which are difficult and can be downright awful, I would turn it into fun by giving myself a time frame in which to complete a list of calls. Say, ten calls in twenty minutes. I would tell myself that every person I was calling was an old friend, and they would be surprised and happy to hear from me.

In my job as a hedge fund marketer I would engage the other person in a conversation by asking him open-ended questions; "yes" or "no" answers usually didn't work. I'd ask, "What kind of investments are you looking for?" instead of, "Are you looking for investments?" If they replied, "I am not looking for an investment," I would ask, "When will you be looking for investments?" as a way of getting around the no. The object would be to see how many people I could get into a conversation, which more often than not resulted in a sale or at least a valuable sales lead. My boss at the time would always remark on how cheerfully I made these unsolicited sales pitches. "I never saw so much enthusiasm with good results to match," he'd remark in wonderment.

There are other not-so-fun moments in life that can be made into pure pleasure—and we may well look forward to formerly dreaded tasks when we practice enthusiasm. Take, for example, the common office scourge: the grouchy coworker who is always in a bad mood, the one who has a chip on her shoulder the size of the Grand Canyon. We could spend our time ignoring her, but this doesn't help much if we have to collaborate on projects together. We can try returning the favor with an equally unpleasant attitude, but that's not good for anyone.

Such an individual is often in some sort of emotional pain (or she could just be a pain in the you-know-what). Why not dare, your own creative way, to make that colleague crack a smile and cheer her up? This could be one of the funniest things you've ever done. Respond with a big, cheerful thank-you when she answers a question with a smart remark. Tell her she looks stunning in that purple pants suit, bring her a flower, or present her with a pack of multicolored sticky notes. Anything that adds amusement and charm to your environment is bound to pay off big dividends, if not for a forlorn colleague, then certainly for you.

Ultimately, practicing enthusiasm is a way of not letting life's challenges, mishaps, or mistakes get the better of us. We women have to give ourselves a big break and stop criticizing that girl in the mirror. Beating up on ourselves is of no help whatsoever; it accomplishes nothing. The truth is that life is comprised of good times and bad; thrilling and tedious tasks; interesting and bright, or boring and bad-tempered, people. These are all part of the ebbs and flows we experience each day. I'm not saying that every day needs to be a source of excitement. But we can have a sense of joy on a daily basis. I truly believe that we can, even if the only thing we have planned is a day of work and a quiet dinner at home. Delight is what you make of it.

There's a well-known Buddhist saying that advises (you might have to read this twice to understand it): "Act always as if the future of the universe depended on what you did, while laughing at yourself for thinking that whatever you do makes any difference." I like the idea of playful seriousness embodied in this saying. It tells us that we can be absorbed by and sincere about what we are doing, but also lighthearted about it at the same time. For instance, we can approach a project with all of our attention and wisdom— think of it as the most important job at that moment. But at the same time, we don't let the challenges, mishaps, or mistakes get the better of us.

Tamara Mellon

FOUNDER OF JIMMY CHOO

Tamara Mellon is founder and president of Jimmy Choo, a complete luxury lifestyle accessory brand with women's shoes, handbags, small leather goods, sunglasses, and eyewear—and a fashion powerhouse. Jimmy Choo was launched in 1996 when Tamara Mellon, accessories editor at British *Vogue,* realized the potential demand for stylish but wearable shoes and approached Mr. Jimmy Choo, the couture shoe-maker based in the East End of London, and recognized for his excellent craftsmanship. Tamara partnered with Jimmy Choo to start the ready-to-wear shoe company, sourcing factories and production in Italy, and opened the first stand-alone boutique on Motcomb Street in London along with a strong wholesale business.

In 1998, Jimmy Choo opened its first boutique in New York, followed by one in Los Angeles in 1999. Sparking an immediate success among young Hollywood, Jimmy Choo became synonymous with the "red carpet" and was hailed the lucky charm for Oscar winners such as Cate Blanchett, Halle Berry, Hilary Swank, and many other Hollywood actresses. Tamara continues to extend her creative excellence to other projects, including the revamp of the iconic Halston line.

What advice would you give a young woman starting out trying to make it in your business today?

The most important thing you have—especially when you are young and female—is your intuition. It's something that you should get in touch with, trust, and follow. Whatever you are interested in—that's your intuition speaking to you, so go with that. Develop it. That combination (intuition-information-trends) gives you the best shot at knowing the right direction at the right time. But you also absolutely have to keep up with and become an expert in what's going on in your area of interest; you need knowledge and current information. Keep up with trends.

(continued)

Do you think that finding an existing brand or company that could be expanded is a good way to start a business? How can you spot a brand that's poised to break out?

Either approach—finding an existing company or starting your own business based on an original idea—can work. However, if you see a brand that was once iconic and has a great history, or one that offers something unique, and identify that it is a brand or idea that is missing in the marketplace, then there's a good chance that you can relaunch and expand it. You can also have your own creative vision. The most important aspects of either approach are your passion and a strong sense of business.

It's not enough to look for something that you think will simply make money. That won't work. If you have an emotional connection to a brand or product that is visceral, then you have found something with potential. If whatever it is leaves you feeling dead, then it is not going to work. And remember, if something you create or find evokes a strong emotion in you, you can be sure it will evoke that same feeling in other people.

What was the toughest challenge you had to overcome in starting your business?

The toughest challenge was being young and female. People always underestimate you; they are quick to tell you, "You don't understand,"' or, "You have do it this way, you can't do it that way." Don't listen! That takes strength, especially when you are starting out. You have to be very confident and incredibly disciplined and focused. You must believe in your vision—do not let other people come in and muck it up.

I broke all the rules, and I did what was best for the products I planned to create. For instance, in the very beginning, I was working with factories in Italy that were used to producing ten thousand pairs of identical black pumps. We wanted to produce smaller numbers of much more unusual shoe designs than these factories were used to manufacturing.

My orders were split, and the numbers per style were much lower than they were accustomed to, because we wanted to use interesting colors, fabrics, and accessories on the shoes—and because we were starting out. We didn't want huge inventory. I convinced them to push the boundaries of what they thought they could do. When the manufacturers saw that they could produce something special, and they saw the market reaction to it, working with them became easier and more collaborative. Persistence pays off—that, and believing in what you are doing.

What was your vision for the business when you started? How has your vision evolved or changed over time?

I've been consistent. From the beginning, my idea was not to have one shoe shop. It was to develop a global luxury brand. I knew that if I wanted to do that, I would have to expand relatively quickly, while at the same time keep the integrity of the brand's innovative design and very high quality. I wanted to grow, expand the collection cycle and product offerings while still keeping the product very precious—and we've succeeded, while still looking toward further brand extensions and product development, and ultimately achieving the right balance of fashion, price, and function.

Was there one thing that happened or one moment in the beginning of your career that made you sure you were onto something big—and on your way to success?

Yes. It was when the collection of '97 came out. It was like opening a candy store for a kid. The product was so innovative and so beautiful. I knew it would work—and in few weeks we had lines of women around the block trying to get into the store. It was a very powerful, real moment.

Make Room for Joy

The best way to create more space in your life for fun, prosperity, wealth, relationships, whatever, is by purging what's taking up valuable room in your home, closet, office, car—even your handbag. Make a date with yourself *today* to tackle one room or area of your home or office for a good purge. Get rid of anything that you don't use or wear—that's broken, ugly, outdated, or has outlived its usefulness. Recycle unnecessary papers, and donate clothes that no longer fit or flatter. Make a promise to yourself to give one belonging away at least once a week. It's unbelievably liberating to unburden your life of stuff. While you're at it, go ahead and cleanse yourself of friends and business projects that are not working. You do not have to cut them off with an ax; just gently let them go. Follow this five-week schedule or create your own with your abundance group or buddy:

WEEK 1: Clean out socks and underwear drawer.

WEEK 2: Organize closets and donate clothes that have not been worn in two years, don't fit, or you no longer care for.

WEEK 3: Sort through makeup drawers and purses—toss any products that are dried out and beyond their expiration date.

WEEK 4: Clean fridge and cupboards.

WEEK 5: Declutter office desk and drawers.

JUST FOR THE FUN OF IT

Whenever I hold a workshop I ask the participants to come up with a list of ways they can bring simple joys into their lives every day. We owe it to ourselves to incorporate pure relaxation, wholesome frivolity, and un-adulterated indulgence into our lives. Like a good night's sleep and excel-lent nutrition, time for pleasure—be it getting a pedicure in the middle of the day or getting dressed up for dinner—feeds your soul and ultimately is good for your health, well-being, and creative efforts. Let's all take a five-minute vacation, a half-hour breather, a weekend retreat. Even bet ter, how about giving ourselves the gift of an entire pleasure week? Why not pretend that every day is our birthday?

What follows is an annotated list of some of my workshop members' favorite pleasures. Some cost a bit of money, many are free, and all are totally accessible. The results are always unanimous. When the women come back the following week they relate many amazing miracles that happened when they made room for pleasure, including feeling better than ever, meeting a new man, succeeding at a challenge they were previ-ously worried about, and experiencing less stress. Use the following sug-gestions to inspire a personal list, and try to incorporate at least three of these ideas into each day.

Be completely unexpected.

Liberate yourself from routine. Buy a bouquet of flowers and send them to your office. Turn down invitations to events that are not enjoyable and see a movie instead. On the weekend wear a dress and stilettos as an alternative to the usual jeans and sneakers. Surprise a friend by making dinner for her.

Walk down the street as if you were on your way somewhere very exciting.

Conjure up the anticipation of a really exciting event—or of going to meet a wonderful new friend. Giddiness and confidence fill you up and you have an extra spring in our step. Put yourself in that kind of mood when you go off to work or run an errand. Your posture will be a bit better, you'll feel prettier . . . you may even turn some heads.

Smile at strangers and see how many smile back.

I was once making a speech and noticed one man in the audience who was very focused on what I was saying. When I caught his eye I gave him a great smile, and continued with my talk. After the meeting he introduced himself, and offered me a valuable business contact. Taking the initiative to smile instead of looking down or away or, heaven forbid, frowning may lead to a remarkable encounter. How many people, from businessmen to the dry cleaner to the sales clerk to little old ladies, can we make eye contact with, and smile at? How many return the favor?

Curl up on the sofa and read a magazine.

Fun doesn't have to be profound. Sometimes it's nice just to make a cup of tea, get cozy on the couch under a comfy blanket, and relish the latest issue of *Vogue* or *Harper's Bazaar*.

Wear a flower in your hair, or put one on your desk or in your bathroom.

I love this one. Why not brighten up . . . with a blossom?

Get a foot massage.

Sheer bliss! And after you've had your twenty minutes of ecstasy, ask for a pedicure too (perhaps with a daring shade of deep pink polish?).

Let someone else pamper you.

Every now and then we can treat ourselves to an afternoon at a spa or salon. Having an expert fuss over us, even for an hour, is such a relaxing mood booster (plus we look great afterward). "When a woman takes the time to accentuate her beauty on the outside, by indulging in a spa session, makeover, hair treatment, eyelash extensions, whatever, her inner beauty shines through," says Colette Draut, eyelash specialist and makeup artist at Pierre Michel Salon in New York City.

Dress to look "extra pretty."

Set the alarm twenty minutes earlier tomorrow and take extra time to put on a beautiful dress or suit appropriate for the day ahead (whether for work or socializing). Buff your nails to a natural gloss. Curl your hair (or straighten it if you're already a curly girl), put a bit of oomph into your makeup, and add a bit of shimmer. And have a glimmer in your eye, as if you know a really fantastic secret.

Dance.

Put on your favorite music and dance around your living room. No one is watching, so let loose! Creative, unstructured movement releases pent-up energy and at the same time lifts your spirits.

Take a long walk with a friend.

Instead of talking to the friend for forty-five minutes on the phone, go out for a walk or to the gym together. After an hour in the fresh air talking with a companion, you'll feel more relaxed and inspired.

Shop for fresh produce at the farmers' market.

Getting fresh food right from its source makes healthy eating even more meaningful. Besides, it's fun to stroll around the market, chat with the farmers, and trade tips with other customers.

Go for a drive.

There's nothing like being on the open road to clear your mind. Why bother with a specific destination? Make it a surprise.

Jog in the park for thirty minutes.

Nature and movement together—it doesn't get any better. I love that tired, happy feeling that comes from a good run. And you can follow it with the very next suggestion.

Take a bubble bath.

This is a reliable old-fashioned feel-good strategy. Light a few candles, add salts, scented oil, and bubbles, get in, close your eyes, and relax. Heaven!

Play and cuddle with your—or a friend's—pet.

What is it about an animal that makes us feel so good? Perhaps it's their unconditional love and affection, or their sweet innocence. Whatever it is, we need to get some of it as often as possible. Even ten minutes of playful pet play can be enough to improve your day.

Meet a friend for tea.

There's something special about having a cup of tea as opposed to coffee. Meet a friend at a favorite restaurant and order a pot of herbal tea (and perhaps a few sweet biscuits or a scone). Afternoon tea provides a welcome break in the day and a quiet, stress-free time to catch up with friends.

Go window-shopping without credit cards or cash.

Have fun catching up with the latest styles and trends without spending a dime.

Drink a tall glass of mineral water.

Perhaps with a slice of lemon or lime as a garnish, or a splash of cranberry juice? I don't know what it is about sipping fresh, clean cold water, but it always makes me feel slightly virtuous and wholesome.

Light a scented candle.

Enjoy this classic way to unwind every day. A soft fragrance and the gentle flicker of a flame are hypnotic.

Get absorbed in a romantic novel.

There's nothing wrong with a little escapism, especially when you need a break.

Stretch.

Touch your toes, or get in the cobra or child pose (classic yoga moves), to relax tense muscles and keep you limber and flexible.

Write a poem or a love letter.

Writing is such a release—be as creative and whimsical as possible. The more flourishes the better.

Keep a Brilliant Little Things Journal

Life is magical. So many tiny miracles and happy accidents occur every day. Why not make note of them? You'll see soon enough that Brilliant Little Things happen all the time. When you are conscious of the gifts the universe constantly bestows, a joy perspective is easy to assume. Do it for a week to see what I mean. Get a little notebook that fits in your purse, and every time something nice transpires jot it down. Coincidence, providence, fate, luck—call it what you will. Your Brilliant Little Things notebook will soon be filled with reminders of how your life glitters with the gold of good fortune. Here are some miracles that have happened to the women in my abundance group:

- I found a parking spot right in front of my office.
- I was invited to a special charity event.
- A friend loaned me a book I wanted to read.
- A stranger gave me his cab even though it was raining.
- My "skinny jeans" fit.
- I ran into a colleague I'd been meaning to make a lunch date with—and we were able to grab a quick bite together.

At the end of the day, seeing your life—every aspect of it—as a journey that's fun even when it's tough or boring, exciting or absurd, is a way of paying respect to all that you've been given. Tackle life with a fun attitude and life will pay you back with positive energy.

Have Fun Summary:
- Identify and practice activities that put you in flow.
- Exercise your fun muscles every chance you get.
- Practice enthusiasm.
- Get your tough jobs done first and save dessert for last.
- Give joy space in your life by purging what you don't need.
- Make time for fun, plain and simple.
- Do something nice for yourself every day.
- Keep track of small miracles and happy accidents.

3.

_____

Unshakable Belief

UNSHAKABLE BELIEF IS an unwavering certainty and confidence in our dreams and our ability to achieve them. Unshakable belief comes from identifying what we truly love and following where it takes us. Once we're aware of our passion, our journey to success may be smoother and calmer. This is the fun of flow, which we talked about in chapter 2, taken to its logical summit. By giving yourself permission to pursue your genuine interests you will learn to meet any obstacle that needs to be overcome with enthusiasm, not dread or fear.

Professionally, I followed what I have always been most drawn to and what was easy for me: working with numbers, finance, and marketing. These distinct preferences were evident since childhood. Instead of playing house, my sisters and I played "office." My father owned a small bookstore, and during the summer my siblings and I, along with neighborhood kids, created an imaginary town in between the tall shelves that lined the shop. Each one of us played a role, from the mayor to the sheriff to the beauty parlor owner, and I always played the banker. I doled out money, determined raises, and granted or denied loans—which had to be paid back promptly and on schedule, plus interest. My natural talent for running the "bank" and directing my playmates in their financial affairs sparked an entrepreneurial spirit and interest in finance that has stayed with me.

My interest in finance and marketing (although I would not have described it that way at the time) continued through the years. For example, as a preteen, I managed two successful paper routes simultaneously. One was for the then-fledgling *USA Today*. I would go door-to-door by myself, and quickly became the top salesperson in my New Jersey territory—including the adults on the force. Every subscription I closed earned a commission, giving me an early taste of what making money was like.

When occupied with financial and marketing activities, or anything else that I really enjoy, I am focused, engaged, confident, and self-assured. However, when I am working in areas that I don't feel comfortable with, or that aren't especially interesting to me, doubt begins to plague my mind, and I begin to drift. Frustrating!

We are happier when we follow our inner guidance.

■

Confession: *creating and maintaining* unshakable belief was not always easy for me; I had to fight the urge to give in to my own insecurities, fears, and uncertainties. Belief in myself made it possible to resist surrendering to those feelings, as well as to the skepticism of others. I learned how to stay grounded, get rid of lingering worries, and look past the people who scoffed at my ambitions. My success secrets and tested techniques that follow will help you do this too. Capitulating to reservations and fear (our own or others) is what makes most people fail to achieve a goal, get out of their comfort zone, or try something new. Don't let that happen to you.

PASSION LEADS TO BELIEF

Something happens when a woman uses her unique talents and knowledge to achieve her dreams. She is happier, richer, and, well, more fabulous. Each of us has unique talents and experiences. It's time we rediscovered them, honored them, and started using them. It's okay if you feel unsure of exactly where your talents lie and how they fit into your life scheme. My solution is self-reflection. It is amazing how meditation (and I mean that in the broadest sense of the word) allows the right ideas to bubble up to the surface.

Consider Leslie. She worked for *ten years* in an accounting job she hated. It was a path she followed because her family thought it was sensible and secure. Her lifelong passion was for people and psychology, not numbers. Can you guess how much her dislike for this career impacted her life? Leslie was tired all the time, and consequently had no energy to enjoy extracurricular, social, or intellectual activities. Her unhappiness was evident to her supervisor, who more than once passed her over for a promotion.

A nagging voice in the back of her mind would occasionally tug at Leslie: "Quit the job. Go back to school. You hate this." Yet every time this happened she shushed herself, allowing self-doubt ("I'm too old to go back to school") and family skepticism ("You'll never be able to set up a successful practice—there's too much competition") to stop her from taking the steps necessary to get a degree. All of that changed when she spent purposeful quiet time looking inward.

In assessing her daily routine at work, Leslie saw how much psychology she used at her job as an accountant for a large business. In fact, it turned out that Leslie had a gift for solving people's difficulties by talking with them. Her coworkers always came to her when they had a sticky issue, and she was always able to help. Leslie seemed to effortlessly understand situations from the other person's point of view; she had natural empathy. This is a gift the best psychologists have. So, it turned out she actually *was* a psychologist—who had somehow stumbled into the wrong building. After devoting several hours over a few weeks to solitary contemplation, Leslie had an unshakable belief that she could go back to school, get a degree, and counsel patients. Seven years later Leslie's therapy practice is thriving, and she is flourishing and happy.

Outcomes like Leslie's are very common, which is why I have never stopped taking quiet time. It is a regular part of planning and especially crucial when starting new ventures. For ten years I have known that I was going to write this book, but until I spent some quiet time thinking about it, I wasn't ready to pursue it. During my regular quiet time sessions I asked my inner self if the time was right for my book. I sat still and meditated over a two- to three-week period and the answer came: yes, the moment had come. Women would be ready and eager for the information I have, and they would learn from it. My quiet time had revealed that the moment was right. I had an unshakable belief that I could, would, and should write this book.

After that, I went along with my life, all the while affirming positive statements about my book ("Women's lives will be enriched by my message"; "*Live It, Love It, Earn It* will reach thousands and thousands of women") and visualizing the end result (the lively pink cover of the book; stacks of *Live It, Love It, Earn It* on the front tables of bookstores). I also talked to a few trusted people about my project, followed a few leads, and very easily found a literary agent and a cowriter in a matter of weeks. Doors began to open easily and quickly.

I do not have this kind of certainty about everything—cooking and water-skiing are not on my list of personal skills. Yet I also know that confidence in any endeavor, as long as it is realistic, can be developed and doubts erased with patience, effort, and strong belief. If there comes a time when I want to learn to cook, I am sure I will be able to do so. For now, I'm satisfied with eating healthy, fresh, and uncomplicated dishes that I can make easily on my own.

Uncover Your Strengths and Skills

It's time for a reality check. Have a half hour heart-to-heart with yourself. Who do *you* want to be? What do *you* want to do? This is your life, not someone else's. Women in particular have a tendency to do what their family wants them to do, or their boyfriend or husband. Are those people's interests the same as yours? Take the time to discover the answer to that question. Give yourself credit for your accomplishments, abilities, and unique skills. What are your strongest skills? It's surprising how much power and aptitude we have at our fingertips.

Take some time to write down exactly what talents you possess. For instance, say you are an excellent cook. You can whip up a delicious meal quickly with what's on hand and without a recipe. Clearly, you:

1. think on your feet (making something good, fast).
2. are resourceful (using what's around).
3. have creativity and knowledge (you don't need a recipe).

You can transfer these talents into other areas of your life. Use them to get a project done at work (you probably already do); start a side business; increase wealth through creative investment—and a financial expert's help—and much, much more. What other skills do you have that you might be hiding in the pantry?

IN HER OWN WORDS

Tory Burch

CO-FOUNDER AND CREATIVE DIRECTOR OF TORY BURCH

Tory Burch created an attainable, luxury, lifestyle brand in February 2004. The brand is defined by classic but eclectic American sportswear, which embodies Tory's personal style. She perceived a void in the market for a sophisticated American aesthetic at an accessible price, and she successfully launched a line of stylish, wearable clothing and accessories for women of all ages. She counts Cameron Diaz, Oprah Winfrey, Jennifer Lopez, Uma Thurman, and Hilary Swank among her fans.

How did you take creative action to start your business?

In 2001, after September 11, I gave a lot of thought to what I wanted to do with my life and career. I kept seeing a commercial over and over on CNN about starting a small business, and its main message was to be brave and follow your dream. It may sound odd, but the commercial truly inspired me to take a risk and begin the process of launching our brand.

What success tips do you have to women who want to start a business?

The most important thing that I can say to anyone facing the tremendous task of growing a business is that you have to have confidence in your vision and an incredibly focused point of view. You need to have a strong sense of what your product will look like, but also carefully consider how it will be packaged, as well as what the retail environment will look like. I thought about the music I wanted to play in the store, the candles I wanted to burn, and even about the importance of having comfortable couches for people to sit on while they waited. But most important, my vision was about giving women something they couldn't find anywhere else.

What about balancing the business with a busy personal life— you're a mom!

My mother and father always taught me that you have to keep it all in perspective. One of the biggest challenges I face personally is balancing being a mother and running a business. The only way it is possible to do both is by always putting my family first and then letting the rest fall into place. It can be very easy in this business to get caught up in the drama of it all—whether a shipment of clothing gets stuck in customs, a model doesn't show up for a fashion show, or there is the possibility of missing an event. It's always something. However, I always try to remember how lucky we are to be along for this exciting ride, and how at the end of the day, the most important thing is the health and happiness of my family and friends.

What's the most important thing you've learned while growing your business into the success it is today?

Surround yourself with people who are talented, creative, and strong-minded. Making sure that those people are comfortable sharing their opinions and disagreeing with you when they feel strongly about something is also incredibly important. Our company's success is the result of a collaborative team effort. Everyone who works in our office is so passionate about our brand, and I value their input so much because I know their goal is to make our brand more successful, not to simply make me happy.

ENVISION YOUR OWN SUCCESS

A tool that I have used successfully for more than ten years and recommend for every woman is the power of the vision board. A vision board is comprised of meaningful pictures and words that represent what you deeply desire pinned to a 24 x 18 inch cork bulletin board. It is a creative and effective method of seeing desired results, and jump-starts the active manifestation of ideas by tricking the mind into believing they are already realized. We see the results in front of us, therefore they exist. Whenever I look at my current board, I receive a jolt of self-assurance. How could I possibly doubt myself when my entire fabulous life is staring me in the face?

Eight years ago I showed one such collage to a friend. It depicted the life I was striving for—a successful business (a picture of a big brown desk and a leather office chair); beautiful homes, including one on the beach (images torn from magazines); rewarding relationships with family and friends (snapshots of loved ones); a fantastic, loving boyfriend (a portrait of a blissful couple); financial freedom (green play money, and large amounts written with a green marker); and travel and fun (a picture of a girl skiing, swimming on the beach, and walking in Paris). He rolled his eyes then, but eight years later it's all mine.

Bonnie, whom you might remember from chapter 1, is a very successful jewelry designer. She had been in the interior design business for twelve years and left the company where she was working to follow her passion for jewelry. She created her business with the help of a vision board. "My first step was to cut out the front cover of every single magazine I wanted my jewelry to be featured in, and I cut out pictures of an office I wanted to have, and printed out the address I wanted to be on in Manhattan, on Central Park West, and I put them all on my board." It happened. On the press page of Bonnie's Web site you will see every magazine and more that she had originally cut out—*Vogue, Harper's Bazaar, Lucky, InStyle, Elle, Town & Country.*

Now Bonnie has a new board, which she recently completed in a magazine clipping session we had together. "I cut out pictures of happy couples and houses and children because I feel I am ready to get married now. I also added pictures from the two major home shopping networks because I am ready to expand my business in that direction. I expect it all to happen soon!"

Create a Vision Board

Magazines are the best and most accessible source of imagery for your vision board. The more pictures you tear from their pages that represent what you want, *the more you receive*. So keep tearing! Write and print out your own affirmations, messages, and power words, such as *money, love, travel, promotion,* and pin them near the related pictures. Small objects (a toy shoe if you want to be a shoe designer, a small baking cup if you want to be a professional baker, an Eiffel Tower ornament if you plan to live in Paris) make charming "3-D" reminders of your dream. Corkboards are easy to add on to, so your "vision" becomes living and very organic. Hang the board in your bedroom or home office—a place where you will see it many times a day—*this is very important*. The board has to be in front of you on a daily basis; the more you see it, the quicker your dreams will manifest.

Once or twice a week, engage your senses with the images on your vision board: What does the front door of your store look like? Imagine the design and size of the sign. Are the displays and shelves made from wood or glass? How do the candles smell? See how lustrous the beeswax looks under the store's unique lighting. Feel the smoothness of the pillar candles. Imagine how much fun it is to chat with customers. See yourself offering beautifully designed business cards to your customers. It won't be long before you have your store.

Take a Trip to the Candy Shop

This is a great exercise to do with a group of friends or with your abundance group. Imagine yourself as a little girl walking into a huge sweet shop brimming with favorite treats. You can have anything and everything you want. In your mind, start gathering all the kisses and lollipops and Tootsie Rolls and licorice sticks. Each candy represents something that you desire: an

MBA, your own shoe store, your own gallery, a beautiful apartment with a fantastic view, a house at the beach, a fabulous guy, a huge promotion, lots of money in the bank, children, a happy family life, and on and on until you can't carry any more candy. Then tell the group about some or all of the "items" you grabbed. The group should respond by saying, "Yes, it is yours!" This fun exercise creates optimism you can turn into usable creative energy.

FOCUS ON IT

An unwavering focus on having my own business and becoming financially free helped me make the right career decisions and quickly correct mistakes. This is not to say that the path I took was a blemish-free, newly laid freeway. It was riddled with potholes and sharp rocks, which *focus* helped me to avoid or at least get over.

After graduating from Rutgers, for example, IBM offered me a position in its accounting department, which I took even though I wanted to sell financial products. Twenty years ago, every freshly minted college graduate wanted to work for a big corporation (as opposed to these days, when everyone wants to run their own personal empire), and IBM was one of the top companies to work for, along with GE, Xerox, and Coca-Cola. In short, IBM was a great brand name for my résumé and a valuable introduction into work life.

IBM was a perfect case study in how a big company operates. I considered it business boot camp. I learned so many valuable business lessons. IBM culture taught me how to dress and act professionally. I learned what to say at meetings and how to make presentations to management. Best of all, the company had a much-admired eighteen-month intensive marketing program that covered everything from how to deal with clients to how to handle rejection. I figured that at some point a position in marketing would open up and I would fill it.

The "Work smart, not hard" motto IBM espoused taught me to focus even more sharply on my daily to-do list: I would get any job done in half the time it took my peers to complete similar tasks. I already knew that time equaled money, so it was not hard for me to incorporate IBM's corporate philosophy into my office routine. Despite the fact that accounting was not where I wanted to be, it was a stepping-stone. The job would eventually lead me to my goal, so I made it a point to never take out my disinterest on the actual job I was doing.

While my colleagues would interrupt a project with coffee breaks and lunches, I worked straight through undistracted until an assignment was complete. As a result I never missed a deadline, and I had time for career-enhancing opportunities, such as pursuing graduate school after hours. As I left my office for class on Mondays and Wednesdays, I'd pass my work-mates, who were still burning the midnight oil on projects they could have finished between nine and five.

I continued to knock on every door—and I mean *every* door—to get into IBM's reputable marketing program, but for reasons beyond my control it wasn't meant to be. Tenuous market conditions in the early 1990s forced IBM into organizational changes and staff and department cutbacks. A third of its workforce took "early retirement" and others were simply laid off. Some units closed completely. Moreover, the company was top heavy with managers, and there just was never any open head count. Marketing department executives would say, "We like you, Marianna; however, we have no openings." The refusal didn't quash my dream. I took every internal education course IBM offered as well as many outside marketing and sales classes. At least I was able to sharpen my marketing skills, even if I was still stuck in the accounting department.

Almost two years later, I was still in accounting and the company was still in trouble. A new CEO came in and continued to make cuts and shrink units. Around that time, my boss offered me another position in accounting, complete with a promotion, an impressive title, and at almost double my salary. While it was an incredibly tempting offer, I had to say no. She was upset when I turned down the offer, but her emotions did not deter me because I knew in my heart that I did not want to continue in accounting.

Instead, I made a lateral move—meaning no promotion, no title, and no raise—into the company's pension fund department. The IBM pension fund invested $30 billion, half managed by outside firms and half managed internally. It was a chance to learn how a major company invested money and learn about different financial products. While IBM's pension fund was one of the largest in the country (including large state pension funds, like California), the department running it was actually quite small. Only thirty to thirty-five people were in the group, so I was able to move around and do everything from assisting portfolio managers to working in private equity to doing back-office work (duties not directly involved in sales or trading, including administrative jobs, accounting, and record keeping).

I was only twenty-four years old and was not yet a portfolio manager, and not senior enough to manage money, but the job taught me how the investment world worked. The company name gave me a certain amount of clout when dealing with outsiders. When you work for IBM's pension fund, people take your phone calls. So while the job did not offer a lucrative salary or an extraordinary title (come to think of it, I didn't even have a title), it was getting me closer to my goal of selling financial products. Advancement is not always about money or position; it's about getting closer to your true purpose. Of course at the time I had no idea how much the job would help me later on. Learning about investments and financial products gave me the experience I needed to start selling financial products and later start my own business.

What you focus on expands.

■

It's tempting to accept a big raise in exchange for a job you don't want. I know many people who wake up one day ten or even twenty years into a job they dislike and think, What have I done?, Why am I here?, or even, How did I get here? If we have unshakable belief, then we are not going to make that mistake, even if it involves a bit of suffering in the process (doubling my salary at that time would have been a bonus). It was a blessing to follow what I wanted to do, instead of chasing a promotion and a raise into a field I did not want to be in. By following my heart and the career I was most happy with, incredible opportunities opened for me; I was beginning to live the life I always wanted to live and the money did come.

After five years at IBM I worked for a short period of time in the marketing department of Bloomberg LP, an influential financial information provider (founded by Michael Bloomberg long before he became mayor of New York City). I wasn't directly selling financial products, but I *was* in marketing and sales. Plus, I was learning even more because Bloomberg covered all the financial markets. I kept dreaming my dream of selling financial products, and very shortly an opportunity came along that literally opened up the world to me.

THE MAGIC OF NETWORKING

I networked constantly in order to meet as many people in the financial world as I could, wherever and whenever I could. One evening, during a cocktail party, a friend introduced me to a man who recently started a financial business and he asked me what I wanted to do. I said I wanted to sell mutual funds. "What about selling hedge funds?" he asked. And I said, "Yes, I'm interested!"

Every time the universe opens a door, walk through it. I was unsure about selling hedge funds at that point, because it was an esoteric business back then and I didn't have much experience in that area. (Just so you know, in very plain English, a hedge fund is a pool of money that can be invested in many different ways—stocks, bonds, other financial products, countries, currencies.) Nevertheless, the opportunity offered me a chance to get closer to my goal of selling financial products, and so I went on the interview.

Once he saw my enthusiasm and desire to be in the financial marketing field, along with evidence of my hard work and persistence in school and in my previous jobs, he offered me a job. I accepted it even though it was at half the salary I was making at Bloomberg and had no perks, such as health benefits. What difference did it make? I would finally be living my dream of selling financial products and on my way to financial freedom.

The job was exciting. It required me to travel widely to industry conferences and investor meetings around the country and the world. Those meetings helped build my Rolodex of potential investors throughout America, Europe, Japan, and Asia. I took advantage of my position, and focused my energies on networking and meeting as many people as possible. After a few months of working with hedge funds, my eyes really opened to the potential of the industry and I realized how much money I could make on my own. This, in part, motivated me to start my own business. I had unshakable belief that I could do it.

In the midst of following your dream you have to enlist the help of others, especially if you want to assemble a roster of high-quality clients. There's nothing you can't do yourself that isn't improved by the counsel and advice of others in your field. I talked to everyone I could in my field whenever an opportunity arose. I did not call two people for advice; I called six. I did not call one broker-dealer about holding my license; I called eight. I didn't attend two conferences a season; I went to six.

Aida Khoursheed is the founder of Estarise, a fashion consulting company that provides strategic advice and brand development to designers at various stages of their growth. Aida had a successful stint as vice president and head of the U.S. sales office for Alexander McQueen, where she rebuilt a solid team and turned the business around. Her mantras for doing well are "Believe in yourself and you will find that your leadership qualities emerge" and "Do what is necessary to generate work which you are proud of, and that you can always stand behind."

When I met her I was anxious to know how she found so many great clients, because her business is service-based. Yes, she has confidence, know-how, and leadership skills—but how did she convey that to clients who may not know her work? "It's all by referrals," she said matter-of-factly. The three most important ways to earn referrals are by networking, keeping an open mind, and staying in touch with people, she says.

"At one time I might have dismissed going to a meeting, talking to certain people, or attending a particular luncheon. I don't do that anymore. I keep an open mind. Every opportunity *is* an opportunity." Aida also shared that you should always make an effort, even briefly, to learn more about someone who is interested in what you have to offer, particularly if you have a service-based business. "Don't prejudge a situation. If someone wants to talk to you, it may turn into an important project or a great contact. You never know, and it does not take that much to be polite, and to find out what someone's inquiry could lead to."

Make a plan on your own or with your abundance group to network each week by doing the following:

1. Call at least three people in your field or the field you want to be in and scheduling informal meetings to talk.
2. Register for at least one industry conference in the next month.
3. Ask friends if they know anyone in your field they can introduce you to.

4. Introduce yourself to at least five people you don't know at the next event or party you attend.

5. Ask colleagues to refer you to anyone who might be interested in your services.

SUCCESS SECRET

Two-Pocket Rule

Have you ever gone to a networking event such as an industry conference, returned with twenty business cards, and had no memory of which business cards to follow up with and which not to? The simple solution is my two-pocket rule. First, promise yourself not to leave the event until you have met more than half the people in the room. When you introduce yourself to a person, ask friendly and pointed questions that will reveal whether the person is someone you want to follow up with or not. In my case, I would listen politely to the person's answers; if he seemed as if he could be a potential investor I would put his card in my right pocket. I put the cards of those I deemed not worth following up with in my left pocket. After the conference, I would toss the cards in my left pocket and follow up with my right-pocket prospects.

DO WHAT IT TAKES TO GET WHAT YOU WANT

We better like what we do, because succeeding requires enormous time, energy, and sweat equity. The financial companies that took a chance on me when I first opened my marketing company did so because I was eager and known for going the extra mile. One of my earliest clients told me recently that he always knew I would be successful because I was extremely driven and persistent. "It was very easy to hire you because you were so hungry," he said. Another former boss used to say, "It's better to hire someone with a fire under his or her feet, and tone them down, than try to start a fire under someone who has none." Many employers and people who invest in businesses have the same attitude, so if you want to move forward you have to show them your fire.

My business motto has always been "Do whatever it takes." No task was too large or too small if it helped to move me closer to my goal of meeting clients, getting contracts signed, and selling financial products. I involved myself in many tasks that went beyond my job description—such as marketing funds to potential investors—because it would build both my reputation and my relationships. I copied reports, mailed packages, made coffee, ordered lunch, created full marketing presentations from scratch, wrote oral presentations, and arranged and organized speaking engagements for managers at hedge fund marketing conferences.

I had to say yes to eighteen-hour days, inconvenient travel, and working through weekends and holidays. For example, a British client wanted me to work over the Thanksgiving holiday. He didn't celebrate the holiday and it didn't even occur to him that it was an important day to me. It was, of course, but at that stage in my career, it was not as significant as pleasing this client and helping him. I didn't even hesitate to put my nose to the grindstone on that Thursday—the turkey would have to wait.

My first client was a well-known private bank. I really wanted to work with them because it would open many doors for me in terms of contacts and business experience. Their goal, without going into too much detail, was to market their financial product like a hedge fund and, in doing so, charge higher fees. This meant they would have to change the structure of the fund.

Many people would have said this kind of structure change couldn't be done because the group was primarily handling a traditional asset-based investment structure. At the same time, the group was doing everything that a hedge fund would do. After a considerable amount of research, talking to my mentors, respected people in the business, and other hedge funds, I developed a workable plan for the company. Working with their legal counsel, accountants, fund administrator, and other advisers, I helped create the separate structure for new monies coming into the hedge fund—it was a nightmare, but we got it done.

None of what I did for this firm was technically a part of my marketing job, but I did what it took to get to my goal, which was an exclusive contract to market the hedge fund once it was established. The hedge fund manager was so impressed with my ingenuity, problem-solving skills, and persistence to find and implement a resolution to every dilemma, he gave me the exclusive contract to sell his hedge finds. He thought, "Wow, Marianna really wants this job." The fund was a diamond in the rough and so was I!

My friend Bobette Cohn has been a fashion stylist for twenty years, and was pretty polished by the time she started a unique vintage fashion line. She has styled for *Vogue, Glamour, InStyle,* and many other national and international publications, as well as dressed celebrities such as Molly Sims and Ralph Fiennes, and worked for brands like La Perla and Nike. "I love styling, but at times I felt like I could do something more with my talents and imagination," she told me. Bobette had always been interested in vintage clothing, and for longer than she had been a stylist, she was collecting one-of-a-kind pieces from secondhand stores and antique markets. "I would re-create them, change the lines, and embellish them with other vintage details like buttons and trim."

So many people, including myself, would fall in love with what Bobette was wearing, and wanted to know where we could buy similar pieces. "I always had to tell them that they were one-of-a-kind vintage pieces and not available anywhere. But not long ago a lightbulb went off in my head. I loved taking something old and worthless and turning it into something fresh and new. Why couldn't I create a business from something I love to do?"

Bobette took the plunge, hired a seamstress to help realize her vision, and created a small but complete collection of unique vintage dresses, coats, jackets, sweaters, blouses, and skirts.

She named her line Bobette, in honor of her überstylish and inspirational grandmother. Her unshakable belief in her instincts and style allowed her to take the risk to start her own business. As soon as some pieces were completed, she made appointments to show the collection to fashion-minded friends and colleagues, both one-on-one and at private trunk shows. Right away she sold several pieces. "Kara Ross, the jewelry designer, was my first customer. I sent her a range of pieces to try on and she bought a stunning brocade coat. It was such a thrill that she loved what I loved."

In what seemed like no time at all, she got her first big break, a high-profile trunk show at Henry Bendel New York, an upscale department store, through a good friend she had known for years. Since then she has been getting referrals from friends of friends, requests for more trunk shows and private appointments, and is in the process of securing permanent placement in prominent retail stores worldwide.

It's not surprising to me that the line was an immediate hit because Bobette has great taste and an innate eye and passion for fashion. She also really believes in her fashion talent, and has the goods (literally!) to back that confidence up. "I just decided to go for it. My line started out as a way to express my love of fashion and design, and as a way of diversifying my business model. My clothing line has really eclipsed the styling, as least for now," she says.

It has been easier for Bobette to launch her line because she has been able to use her contacts that she has built up over twenty years. She has paid her dues in the fashion world. Bobette is well respected in the industry and had an unshakable belief that her reworked vintage pieces would fill a niche in the marketplace. One of the ways Bobette describes and sells her line is distinguishing it as "the low end of high end" because the pieces are affordable and unique. "Women want to go out in the evening and not see themselves coming and going. No one likes to show up at a party where two other girls are wearing the same dress."

Tremendous support from friends and colleagues came in handy. Bobette advises anyone who wants to start a business or get ahead in any industry to make, nurture, and keep contacts because you never know when you will have a chance to connect. "I have a meeting with the fashion director at a high-end department store because a few weeks ago I ran into her at my neighborhood nail salon. I told her about my line and she said she wanted to see it. I had met her a few times before at fashion shows and social events. You never know where or when you're going to run into your next big break. My fingers and toes are crossed."

Bobette's most important words of wisdom: "If you gravitate to what you are passionate about and what you're good at, it's much easier to feel confident and clear."

IN HER OWN WORDS

Elaine Crocker

PRESIDENT OF MOORE CAPITAL MANAGEMENT

Elaine Crocker has spent more than thirty years helping to launch some of the hedge industry's most talented portfolio managers, and is one of *Crain's* 100 Most Influential Women in NYC Business. She joined, in 1970, Commodities Corp., a new trading company, and eventually became its executive vice president. Elaine Crocker is now the president of the flagship firm, Moore Capital Management, where she has global responsibility for the day-to-day operation of the organization, including direct management of the trading business, research, finance, operations, technology, legal, and human resources, as well as taking a leadership role in sourcing and developing portfolio managers.

What was the most valuable skill you had for your success at Commodities Corp.?

Listening is an important skill. Both common sense and listening skills are underrated in today's marketplace. There is a great quote that there is nothing common about common sense, which is all too true. I was fortunate that my career began in a demanding, but forgiving, environment—meaning my managers and mentors understood that if one demanded perfection at all times, one could never be as creative or act outside of the "box." I also learned through my own errors, and the errors of others, that complexity often ensures failure. It is much more difficult to find a simple solution. Commodities Corporation was an amazing learning environment with an unusual blend of academics, pragmatists, superstar trading talent, and truly decent people. It is difficult not to succeed when exposed to such an environment. And joining Moore with its demanding and dynamic investment environment has continued my ability to grow and learn.

When you first started out in business, what was your attitude?

I was there to work and learn. I may not have liked some of the tasks I was given, but I did them. And I created good relationships so

(continued)

that when there was spare time, the portfolio managers helped me understand aspects of trading I would never have learned by reading books. And I will say that a great work ethic is always noticed, and mostly it is rewarded with more responsibility—if it is not, move on.

You were promoted three times in one year. That's an incredible vote of confidence.

Luckily I had tons of common sense, and I was intuitive in a business where no one has very much time to mentor. I worked hard, and I liked what I did so it never seemed tedious. Still, it may take a number of years to be rewarded by being given larger responsibilities or autonomy, so in the meantime, one should always be in a learning situation. The minute you're not learning anymore, go do something else. Time is the most important commodity so it makes no sense to waste it. And by the way, even though I was promoted three times in a year, I worked as an assistant for many years after joining Commodities Corporation.

You find talent and nurture it, and you have a great track record. In terms of managing people effectively, what can you share?

I began in an environment where mentoring was a strategic part of the culture. Personal contact, listening skills, and directly taking care of issues in a timely manner with sensitivity are so important to managing well. Today, we all use e-mails frequently to communicate instead of personal interaction. A useful tool is having one-on-ones with people across the organization. There are times when communication in a team setting is best, as well as times when it makes sense to gain information from individuals in different areas across the companies. I regret I use e-mails as much as I do—today there is such a sense of immediacy, and technology supports immediacy over thoughtful response. And we forget how much we learn when we actually sit down face-to-face and discuss issues.

There have never been a lot of women in hedge funds, or in important positions on Wall Street. Yet you have made a name for yourself. What's your advice to women who want to go into male-dominated industries?

(continued)

Don't lose your femininity. Women are different from men. We do things differently, and we think differently; we have better memories. Often we are more detail-oriented and are willing to be direct but not confrontational. I don't think females are always supportive of one another. That's a shame. I like to see individuals succeed, and if they work for me, frankly I feel good about myself when I see them grow in their careers. Great girlfriends often help each other through life's twists and turns, and women working with women in an office should use the same skills with their female coworkers that they use to support their friends. It is not a competition—at least in a hedge fund environment. There are plenty of opportunities for all. The best advice I can give anyone is love what you do and be selective so that you join a firm whose culture plays to your strength. If it doesn't, learn what you can, then move on. Then it is easy to excel at your career. For those starting their careers, you will have to prove your worth. We have become so good at providing positive feedback to our children, often they continue to expect it when they start their careers. You don't want to be the person who doesn't know what he doesn't know, or the person who needs to be applauded for every action, because in our fast-paced environment, there is little time for applause.

FIND SANITY IN THE CHAOS

From the minute I opened the doors of my office in Rockefeller Center I dealt with one challenge after another. The best way to handle problems was to step back from them, do nothing for the moment, weigh my options and reactions carefully, and then, *and only then*, respond.

One such obstacle was finding a broker-dealer firm to hold my Series 7 and Series 63 licenses (these are licenses some financial salespeople need to practice, much like a real estate agent's license is required to broker property transactions). It's not easy to find someone willing, because broker-dealers do not want to take the risk of being responsible for someone who does not work directly for them. They are ultimately accountable if something goes wrong.

I networked and met every person who knew broker-dealers. I was not having much luck and was starting to feel as if the licensing issue could be my undoing. Finally, one broker-dealer who I was introduced to by a good friend agreed to hold my licenses. I was grateful and relieved, but he did not make it easy for me. I had to sign a complex contract, pay him five hundred dollars each month (a great deal of money for me at the time), and he supervised everything I was doing to the point of looking over my shoulder. Even so, it was worth it, because without his help very early on I could not have started my business. He didn't have to offer to help me, but he did, and I am forever grateful for his generosity.

SUCCESS SECRET

Get Physical

When fear overwhelms you, take a break and do something physical. It will distract you from your fears and will in turn help you to refocus on your goals and whatever challenges you are facing. When I am anxious it helps me to run in the park for thirty minutes, work with weights, take a yoga class, ride a bike, or swim. It clears my head, calms me down, and makes me feel strong, healthy, and ready to deal with anything that comes my way.

One woman in the broker-dealer's office was kind enough to help me go through the process of applying for my own broker-dealer license. The women in the hedge fund business really stuck together and looked out for one another because there were so few of us. It took eight months to secure a license because of the mountain of paperwork required, the testing involved, and the interviews with industry regulators. After that I was finally, truly, on my own. I no longer owed the broker-dealer a monthly fee, and I could fund my own office.

One of the hardest times and lowest points for me was after I had been running my business for about a year. It was the early months of 1999 and market conditions were not the best. The infamous collapse of the hedge fund Long Term Capital Management (LTCM) exposed the dark side of the hedge fund world to the general public. It's an interesting story. John Meriwether, the former vice chairman and head of bond trading at Salomon Brothers, founded LTCM in 1994. Noble Prize-winning economists sat on the fund's board of directors. During the first few years after it was established the fund was wildly successful, but then in 1998, in less than four months, it lost $4.6 billion, and it folded a few years later, in 2000.

The spectacular failure of LTCM (which now seems ridiculously small compared to recent collapses and frauds on Wall Street) was widely reported in the mainstream press. Suddenly hedge funds and their high-risk potential were "out." Add that to the worry left over from the crash of emerging financial markets of developing countries (such as Latin America and Eastern Europe) a year earlier, and the financial landscape looked bleak. Money dried up on Wall Street. No one was interested in buying hedge funds and that was what I was selling.

I was sitting in my office reviewing paperwork one evening in December around eight o'clock. It was cold and dark outside. The market down cycle was in full swing. Suddenly, a fax came through from my silent partner, the person I counted on and trusted the most, saying he wanted to discuss his investment in my business. Because the financial market was bottoming out and business was so slow, he wanted to rethink our strategy. Maybe our business wasn't the right one to be in at this time.

My heart sunk. I would do anything to keep the business alive, even if everything on the outside seemed to be collapsing. I was working eighteen hours a day, seven days a week; everything I had was invested in my new business. Walking home to my tiny one-bedroom apartment that night, a million thoughts were running through my mind.

I realigned myself with my goals, and reminded myself of how far I had come. I couldn't back down now. I visualized the company becoming successful. I couldn't change market conditions, but I could visualize meetings with clients, attending conferences, and selling financial products. These were all things that I could realistically see myself doing.

Lesser men would have closed their doors and sold the furniture at this point—and some did. Not me. Even though the market conditions were sour, money had dried up, and my business partner was rethinking the sustainability of our business, I still had an overall feeling of optimism and success. The next day my partner and I had a long talk about the business, the pros and cons of going forward, and we both realized that the bad times would pass and the business would survive. Showing his unwavering support in the business and in me, he invested another thirty thousand dollars to get me through the next couple of months. I am forever grateful for his taking a chance on me. I will never forget his kindness.

> *Words are powerful:*
> *positive words give positive results;*
> *negative words give negative results.*

■

A few months later, the sun did come out, shining strong and bright, and my business started to take off. The dust cleared and investors started looking at and investing in hedge funds again. I was becoming known in the business and raising a lot of money. I even joked with one of my clients that one day we would raise so much money we wouldn't know what to do with it. Watch your words. That statement came true. One year later, the hedge fund manager I was working with *was* turning away additional contributions because he had an overabundance of money!

IGNORE NAYSAYERS AND NARROW THINKERS

There's no doubt you'll come across pessimism and disapproval on your journey. I cannot tell you how many people were right-off-the-bat negative when I told them I was starting my own business. After mailing announcement cards stating the name of my business, my title as founder and president, and contact information, I received many gracious congratulatory calls. However, there were a few exceptions. A longtime client called and actually chuckled into the receiver. "Oh, you're the president, ha, ha," he chortled. "The president of what, a one-person business?" Other people laughed in my face—so you can only imagine what they were saying behind my back.

Pessimistic and discouraging advice came my way disguised as caring concern. "If you start your own business you won't be able to take in or appreciate a sunset for three years," one friend said. A relative told me,

"You'll be eating, sleeping and dreaming the business 24/7; you will be burned-out and exhausted in two years." Colleagues tried to dampen my spirits with dire predictions such as, "You will never make it in a man's world"; "You will never make it in hedge funds"; "You are a young, inexperienced girl in a tough industry, so forget it"; "Don't be silly, it's an unattainable dream"; and "You don't know the first thing about starting a business." Others were even more direct: "You will fail"; "Don't waste your time"; and "Nine out of ten new companies collapse."

When we have an unshakable belief in ourselves and our aspirations, disregarding these people is close to effortless. I learned how to bypass cynics and detractors, those who had skepticism around money and ambition, including longtime colleagues and even a few friends who didn't think I would be able to market financial products on my own. If I listened to them I would be *nowhere*. Whenever someone offered me a dismal piece of "advice" I would nod and smile politely. I was always gracious and never bothered arguing or getting defensive. What would be the point? I went about my business.

Once my business was up and running, there were still people who actively tried to stop me. I was now an expert at turning obstacles into challenges. By embracing and accepting roadblocks with a happy attitude, negative comments ricocheted right back to their senders. I quietly dismissed the people who lacked belief in me and hoped that someday they too could develop my ability for boundless self-belief. The real power of unshakable belief comes from *certainty*, a clear *focus* on the end result, and a *willingness* to do what it takes to make the result a reality.

REJECTION IS YOUR PROTECTION

For such a tiny word, "no" has a lot of clout. Most times, I advise finding a way around the "no". However, there are times when we have to stop and listen to see if "no" is ringing in our ears. If you keep getting resistance, I have to believe there is a reason for it. Try to accept that it might not be clear to you now, but that you will understand the reason in time. Consider this a blessing.

Aida Khoursheed, founder of Estarise, is a master at reframing rejection for her clients. "When your work involves advising brands and companies, as mine does, you will at some point be faced with a client who has a strong desire to work with a certain retailer, or to partner with a particular firm. If something doesn't work out, I don't beat myself up. It means there is a better fit someplace else. Rejection always leads to something good—it means that you will evolve your product or brand and make it better; or find a better marriage elsewhere—a company that is a better fit and who understands what you have to offer."

Aida speaks truth to power. You can't keep beating your head against the wall if you aren't getting anywhere. For instance, right before I started my own firm, I worked for one of the few companies that marketed hedge funds at that time. A man who had historically refused to make his top salespeople partners in the business ran the company. It would have meant splitting more of his profits, which he wasn't willing to do. I thought I could change his mind and he would make me a partner. It would certainly have been an ideal situation for me, or so I thought.

Whenever I broached the subject with my boss, he would say, "I'll think about it," or, "Maybe," or sometimes he would just say, "No." There was another marketing person who had worked in the office for several years without making partner. So the writing was on the wall. Still, I kept at it, thinking I'd be different. One day after I asked my boss yet again to make me a partner, he looked me in the eye and said, "Marianna, it's never going to happen. I don't want a partner." Final answer. This turned out to be one of the seminal moments in my life, because I realized at that point if I wanted a bigger share of what I was selling, I would have to sell it myself, through my own business. My boss's rejection to make me a partner in his company was the catalyst to start my own. Almost immediately after his definitive refusal I began to formulate a business plan.

Once my business was up and running, there was one company in particular that I wanted to sign as a client. While the man who ran the firm took numerous meetings with me and asked me for a lot of marketing advice, he would never formally agree to work with me. After nine long months of trying to convince him to sign a contract, and doing everything possible to show him that I would enhance his company, I finally let my efforts go. I had turned over every stone. There was really nothing left for me to do. A year and half later his company went out of business. If I had worked with him, it would have been short-lived, most likely unprofitable for me, my reputation would have been soiled because of a bad association, and my business could have gone sour, as his did.

Rejection can also protect our personal lives—the fellow you so wanted to marry but who left you turns out to be a deadbeat; a friend who betrays a trivial confidence forces you to end a relationship that could have done more substantial damage; the organization you wanted to be a part of didn't work out and in retrospect it would have been too much of a commitment; and so on. If we can remove the emotional power that hearing "no" has on us, we become better at discerning when "no" means no, and when "no" means try again. The following exercise should help in this regard.

"No" Means Nothing to Me

Elizabeth Webb and I use this exercise in our workshops, and it always receives a very positive response. Below is a list of statements that you should read with your abundance buddy. Take turns reading the A and B statements (if you're really brave you can print a longer list from liveitloveitearnit. com). Try to go through the list three or four times with your partner in one sitting. When you are done with this exercise, "no" will mean nothing to you!

A: Do you think I am smart?
B: No.
A: "No" means nothing to me.
A: Do you think I'm pretty?
B: No.
A: No means nothing to me.
A: Do you think I have a nice house?
B: No.
A: "No" means nothing to me.
A: Do you think I have a great job?
B: No.
A: "No" means nothing to me.
A: Do you think I am kind?
B: No.

A: "No" means nothing to me.

A: Do you think I have good taste?

B: No.

A: "No" means nothing to me.

A: Do you think I am rich?

B: No.

A: "No" means nothing to me.

A: Do you think I have nice friends?

B: No.

A: "No" means nothing to me.

A: Do you love me?

B: No.

A: "No" means nothing to me.

THE CREATIVE POWER OF UNSHAKABLE BELIEF

I heard a story about fifteen years ago that resonated with me because it is such a great example of unshakable belief. A little girl wanted a dog, and she asked her father, who said, "No dog." She used her allowance to buy a small dog dish and some food. Every morning, she laid out food and water for the dog she really wanted. Her father saw and smelled the food, and still said, "No dog." The next day she bought a leash, which her father promptly tripped over. However, he still said, "No dog." Then she found some dog toys. Her father stepped on the dog toys, heard them squeak, and finally said, "Okay, I'll get you a dog." This little girl had no doubt she would someday have a dog to love and care for.

It's the same childlike imagination, persistence, and anticipation exemplified in this tale that can help frame our own efforts to create and manifest our desires. Our thoughts can become things. When you have the dream, the desire, the vision, and the unwavering belief inside your core, you can shift the world.

Unshakable Belief Summary:
- You're really good at something—pursue it.
- Create a vision board so the future results of your efforts are visible today.

- Focus on your goals.
- Do what it takes to get where you want to go.
- Find sanity in the chaos.
- Ignore naysayers and narrow thinkers.
- Rejection is your protection.

PART TWO

Embrace Financial Freedom

Financial freedom is the key that helps unlock nearly every door we want to enter. From a practical point of view, economic independence affords us the ability to learn, advance, and do what we like, unfettered by worry and punishing debt. Psychologically, having "enough" alleviates worry, pain, and fear. How much money each of us needs to design the life we want is personal, and based on our unique circumstances and aspirations. Yet no matter what the number is—$20,000, $200,000, or $2,000,000—it can be achieved.

Unfortunately, many women have blocks around money that stop us from attaining financial freedom. In part 2 of *Live It, Love It, Earn It* we will cut through the confusion, talk objectively about money, and discover the exciting possibility of financial freedom. It can be yours! Chapter 4 shows how to neutralize feelings about money, look clearly at your money situation, and clean up debt. Chapter 5 provides tools that protect and grow your money. Money can be fun! I'll show you how.

4.

Love Money

"Life in abundance comes only through great love."
—ELIZABETH HUBBARD, AMERICAN EDITOR AND WRITER

YOU CAN HAVE a love affair with your money. That's right, just like a man you're head over heels about, you will come to love keeping track of where your money is going, when it is coming back, and how it is spending its time when you're apart (in the bank, on your credit card statements, etc.). Best of all, when you love your money, it *always* loves you back. To that end, this chapter is all about making dates with your money, getting to know it well, and . . . falling in love!

Loving money, to me, means nurturing it, treating it well, and never taking it for granted. There's no love when a woman says, "It's only money," or, "Who cares; it's just paper," right before she plunks down hundreds of dollars for a piece of clothing or books a vacation she cannot afford. Think about it: how many times do we say, "He's just my boyfriend," or, "Who cares, it's just my apartment?" Not very often, I would think.

Such a careless, cavalier attitude toward money is part of the reason many of us find ourselves in a financial pickle. Compound that negligent behavior with a fear of finances and mixed messages around money, and we drastically diminish our chances for creating wealth. We are short-changing our potential when we neglect to develop a loving relationship with money.

Let's nurture and treat our money well, and stop taking it for granted. That way, we can have the shoes, the vacation, and the quality of life we want and also have money to save for retirement and our future without putting ourselves at financial risk.

My four-step plan for falling in love with money pays big dividends:

1. Neutralize money feelings.
2. Be clear about money.
3. Do away with debt.
4. Use cash.

STEP I:
NEUTRALIZE MONEY FEELINGS

Like religion, sex, and politics, for most of us, money is a strongly charged issue that results in a variety of reactions: anxiety, fear, worry, greed, anger, jealousy, giddiness, embarrassment, humiliation, love, even exultation. It's not especially surprising that money causes emotional mayhem within ourselves as well as in our relationships. Many of us grew up surrounded by a swirl of confusing money messages, like "It's a necessary evil"; "I want more even though I know I shouldn't feel that way"; "Why would you want to be rich? They take advantage of other people."

It doesn't really matter whether money was scarce or plentiful, it was how your family regarded, used, and treated their money that has likely determined much about how you view and treat money today. Many women in my coaching sessions tell me they grew up feeling tension in their house surrounding money, or, on the other hand, that money was never discussed. Their parents were often at odds with each other over how money was spent. Others tell me that money was their father's domain, and they were told not to worry about finances. Still others tell me it was either not proper or looked at badly if the topic of money was brought up.

Even the idea that money is dirty has filtered into our psyches. Google "money quotes" and dozens of maxims appear, admonishing us for wanting money, from the biblical "Money is the root of all evil" to the musical

"Money can't buy me love." It takes a bit more digging to find verses that are complimentary toward money.

I'm not a psychologist, but I know from experience that mixed money messages make people do inappropriate things—from overspending to cheating and stealing. Coming to grips with our negative feelings about money and releasing them drains their power over us. We can then see money for what it is—a facilitator that allows us to live richly and fully. Let's neutralize our feelings about money so that we can manage finances with calm reason and work on wealth creation without guilt.

SUCCESS SECRET

No More Mixed Money Messages

When a mixed money message, or MMM, creeps into your financial thinking, recognize it for what it is and correct it by saying, "This is an MMM, and not a rational thought."

My money hang-ups centered on two things: fear of scarcity and not feeling as if I deserved prosperity. In the back of my mind, I believed that making money was justified only if it was hard to earn (as in working multiple jobs, or staying up until all hours to get a job completed). When I first started earning large profits from my own business, I actually questioned whether I deserved it. I had to do substantial work on my money history, uncover my old patterns, understand them, and finally change them in order to release the negative charge around money. I had a breakthrough when I received a particularly large commission from a client. Acknowledging that the check represented money I had earned fair and square was a turning point in my life. It was the first time I really believed I was worthy of a rich and abundant life.

While our experiences may differ from one another's, the thread of fear that ties them together is the same. The following are four women's stories that represent how fear and uncertainty around money play out in diverse ways.

TINA TAKES ACTION

Freelance film costumer Tina turns down jobs with small production companies because she thinks such positions are beneath her. Maintaining a certain reputation by working on only A-level films produced by major studios was central to her identity. "I can't take a job with a company that is not up to my standards," she would tell me. The reality is that no one in the film business judged Tina on her clients; they are interested only in the quality of her work. Meanwhile, Tina was in debt by tens of thousands of dollars. Because of her dissatisfaction with her work, she tried to fill the void by spending money on expensive meals, clothing, and jewelry.

Tina openly admitted to her dream solution: "I'd like to find a rich guy who can pay off my debt and bankroll my business." Okay. Well, eighteen months after sharing this with me Tina was still waiting for that guy, her debt had doubled from what it was when I first talked to her, and she was continuing to turn down work. Needless to say, she was very depressed, but she refused to look at her money situation and acknowledge that her financial picture was within her own power to change. Tina created her troubled financial life, and it was within her power to re-create it into something better.

Tina needed to go back into her personal history to understand her unrealistic view of how money works. It turned out that no one really talked about money in her house when she was growing up. Her mom stayed home and her dad earned the money and "took care of everyone, and always told us we needn't worry about money." She would go to the store with her mom, who would "charge it" or tell shopkeepers to "put it on [her] account." Tina continued the habit of putting items and services —her entire life—"on account" because of the magical quality it had for her.

Once Tina saw she was continuing the patterns of her mother—who actually did have a bill-paying husband—she was able to put a stop to her reckless charging. She also stopped turning down work and in the process made valuable new contacts, leading her to other contacts and more and better work.

CAROL'S COVER-UP

In the course of reviewing her money history, Carol realized that she absolutely hated everything about money. Financial disagreements were at the root of the anger and animosity between her parents, which ultimately led to a painful divorce. Carol witnessed many "knock-down, drag-out fights" between her parents, "and they always involved credit card bills," says Carol. As a result, she found it difficult to make a commitment to creating a healthy relationship with money *or* a man.

The divorce was even more painful than the money fights had been—it was one of the largest (in terms of actual money) and most public separations in the history of Carol's home state. Carol was embarrassed by newspaper accounts and idle gossip. "I just looked at money as a cause of misery and humiliation." After she released her money history, and realized that it was not so much the money she was angry with but her parents, she regained her power over money. For the first time, Carol began paying attention to her finances in a reasonable and unemotional way. Carol had previously tended to go out of her way to avoid men who made a good living. Now she understands that she can evaluate potential mates in many other ways.

JODY'S WEALTH TAKES A TOLL

Jody has a $2 million trust fund, a fabulous-sounding arrangement. But it really isn't if, like Jody, you are focused on spending it as quickly as possible. Jody has a good job with a lot of potential and makes about $65,000 a year. The first time Jody "borrowed" $200,000 from the trust was shortly after a bad breakup with a boyfriend. She thought it would be a one-time occurrence and spending the money would help her feel better and lessen the pain around the breakup. "What's the point of having a trust fund if I can't use it?" she thought. Soon taking advances from the trust became a habit. Jody first came to me in a state of anxiety because even though she had access to money, she had also piled up debt, and was afraid of losing what remained in the trust.

In reviewing her money history together, we realized that Jody was doing two things. First, she was trying to use money as a way to fill the "emotional hole" she had from the breakup. "I didn't know what to do with all my feelings, so I went shopping," she says. Jody saw her mom spend recklessly and buy whatever she wanted when her mom and dad had an argument, so it was not surprising that Jody also used spending as a way of alleviating the pain her boyfriend had caused her. "I saw my mom buy clothes and shoes whenever she and my dad had a fight," she wrote in her money history, and "that seemed natural to me. That's what you do when you get upset—you go shopping. Right?"

Second, Jody was trying to create a lifestyle she learned about from her mother, who felt that a particular level of comfort was necessary to live "the right kind of life." Yet this life was always out of reach for Jody and her mom. Jody told me that she felt entitled to designer clothing, a large apartment in a fashionable part of town, first-class travel, furs, jewelry, fine dining, and lots of other luxuries. "I believed it was my birthright to buy whatever I wanted, anytime I wanted, even if it meant breaking into my savings and living beyond my means."

Jody—all of us, in fact—can have a glamorous life with all the trimmings. I'm all for it. However, we need to go about it in a responsible way. In Jody's case, she had to first see that her spending was an attempt to fulfill her mother's dreams and wishes. It was actually a burden on Jody to try to create the fantasy life her mother wanted. She looked around and saw that she was already living a great life that she loved. Jody paid back her debts, slowly cut back on purchasing without eliminating it entirely, discussed ways to make the money in her trust grow with a financial adviser, and learned to live beautifully on the money she earned. Because of her improved self-esteem, Jody was able to focus more energy on her job, and in the process she increased her income.

At times, all of us try to fill an emotional hole with some kind of indulgence—overspending, overeating, drinking to excess, overexercising. But sometimes you need to acknowledge and experience your feelings and then deal with what's behind them. This is the most effective (as well as least expensive and least harmful) solution to addressing our money issues. Spending money you don't have on shoes, clothes, purses, vacations, dinner out is only a temporary fix. Jody needed to acknowledge her feelings about the breakup, take some time to really get in touch with things, and work them out.

ANNA'S AMERICAN DREAM

Anna emigrated from Romania to America in the late 1990s when the economy was strong and there were many opportunities for newcomers. Money and resources were so scarce in her country that she had to spend hours waiting in food lines, never knowing whether there would be anything left when she made it to the front. Through hard work, determination, and sacrifice, she was able to save enough money to buy a plane ticket to New York and start a new life. When she first arrived, Anna found work as a waitress. She took the job seriously and became quite accomplished at it, making good tips. Then she landed a better job, this time in a boutique, working as a salesperson.

Anna is very eager to keep growing and expanding her earning potential. Even though her five-figure salary is not what most people would consider high, especially in New York City, she manages to save and wants to learn more about how to grow her investments. She is not afraid of hard work, and understands that sometimes you have to get in the back of the line and wait, and work, before you get to the front.

However, Anna's money history makes her tentative about placing money into a savings account or investing it. "When I have money I tend to keep it locked in a drawer, because I still think I may end up on a breadline tomorrow." Her challenge was to expand the eagerness she has to work and improve herself while diminishing feelings of scarcity she had long known in her home country. "Now I realize that as long as I keep working toward my goal, I will be fine. I still stash some cash, but I have opened a secure savings account. Right now that's a big step for me."

WHAT'S YOUR MONEY HISTORY?

Like Tina, Carol, Jody, and Anna, you can neutralize your money history by facing it head-on and releasing it. Until you understand where your faulty ideas, overwhelming emotions, and bad patterns come from and accept them, you can't change negative money behaviors into positive ones. In my classes, after discussing our money histories we use biodegradable red balloons to release them. Try this at home with your abundance buddies:

Using a marker, write "My money history is *history*" on balloons (one for each of you). Then have each person release her balloon out a window. It's a powerful visual, watching your old money history float away.

Putting your money history down on paper is also liberating. Set a timer for fifteen minutes and type or write down every childhood money memory you can think of. Place the history in an envelope and label it "That Was Then." Hold up the envelope and say out loud seven times, "I release this and let it go," taking deep breaths between each declaration. Afterward, tear up the envelope into small pieces and toss them away. It is amazing how effectively this ritual cleans the slate and makes room for new money behaviors. Here are some questions that can get the memories rolling:

- What did your parents spend money on?
- Who was in charge of the money in your house?
- What does money mean to you today?
- What money stories do you remember—pleasant, unpleasant, or neutral (saving change in a piggy bank and buying yourself something special; your mom cutting coupons; your dad spending extravagantly)?
- Were there family fights about money?
- Do you save money now? How?
- Do you ignore money? If so, in what way?
- How does the way you relate to money either reinforce or react to any behaviors you saw as a child? For instance, if your mom saved change, do you save change? If your dad splurged to make you happy, do you splurge when you're stressed-out? If your mom clipped coupons and used cash, do you instead buy everything at full price, on credit?

Change Negative and Anxious Feelings about Money

Visualization techniques and affirmations can help you improve your relationship with money, break old money habits, and release negative money feelings. The following are four

things that you can do either on your own or with an abundance group.

1. *Write down your new desires about money and abundance.* When you put down your desires and goals in
   black and white, and read them once a day, you are
   much more likely to do what it takes to reach them. I
   promise you will reach your goals faster. For instance:
   a. I want to pay off all my credit card debt.
   b. I want $280,000 in the bank by the time I am forty-
      five.
   c. I want my own successful business and to live com-
      fortably and worry-free.
   d. I want a new job that pays $135,000 a year.
   e. I want a promotion.
   f. I want to travel to Italy.
   g. I want to buy an apartment and own it free and
      clear within ten years.
   h. I want to send my children to college debt-free,
      stop working before I am sixty, and enjoy my
      grandchildren.

2. *Picture many actual dollar bills coming toward you,
   and see yourself reaching out and grabbing them.* If
   you do this for a few minutes every day over a long
   period of time, money will actually come to you. Practice this visualization when you are getting ready for
   bed, taking a bath or a shower, stopping at the bank,
   driving your car, or walking down the street.

3. *Read abundance affirmations daily.* An affirmation can
   be as simple as writing "$100,000" on a piece of pa-
   per and saying it out loud once or twice a day (I read
   affirmations in the morning before starting my day and
   once more at night, as the beginning of my evening
   ritual). You do not need to know exactly how the affirmations will manifest, just know they will. Start with
   any or all of these:
   a. "I live in abundance."
   b. "I have all the money I need."

  c. "Money comes into my life easily."

  d. "There is room in my life for plenty of money."

  e. "Money is attracted to my bank account."

  f. "My prosperity is overflowing."

  g. "I expect a surplus of money miracles today."

  h. "I am rich, happy, and fabulous."

4. *Add an extra zero onto the amount in your savings or checking account.* This technique is both a visualization and an affirmation. If your checking account indicates that you have $200, the trick is to add another zero and move the comma so that it says $2,000. If you have $1,000 in your savings account, turn it into $10,000. This is very powerful. "Whoa, hold on," I bet you are saying right now. "What do you mean by that? I can't just turn $200 into $2,000 or $20,000." As a matter of fact, you can. I'm not saying that you should add that zero and then go out and spend it—or try to withdraw it from the bank. Absolutely not. The idea is to get used to seeing a lot of money in your bank account, so that when you start manifesting money you are ready for it.

STEP 2:
DON'T BE VAGUE ABOUT MONEY

Let's be honest. Learning to love money requires you to know exactly how much you have, precisely where it is, and how you are spending it.

Without knowledge, fuzzy emotions and inaccurate information control our money behavior when information and common sense should be guiding our decisions. The best way to educate yourself about your money is to:

■ Put your numbers down on paper and look at them.
■ Keep a money diary.
■ Create a Fun Spending Plan.

Some of us would rather clean the bathroom, sweep the floor, or take out the trash before opening their bills or examining their checking account. Quite frankly, I do not always want to review my finances, but I make myself do it on a regular basis, just as I have committed to exercising and eating well. Tracking what you own and owe cannot be done accurately in your head. You need to sit down and pour out the numbers on paper, where you can look at them. Start by looking at your calendar and making a money date with yourself to do just that. It is an eye-opening and liberating experience. That dark cloud overhead disappears, and the relief of clarity takes hold. Remember that the numbers can't harm you; they only help you become clear about money.

Lead your money; do not let it lead you.

■

Choose an afternoon that will be uninterrupted for your money date. Gather bank and credit card statements, bills, receipts, checkbook, and any other financial documents, a calculator, a legal pad, and a pencil. Make a soothing cup of tea and light a green candle (for money) and a white candle (for abundance). Or you can make a pot of coffee or pop a big bowl of popcorn, throw on your most comfortable sweats, and settle in. Either way, start the date with a pat on the back and a reminder of what is wonderful about your life: "I have a great job, an apartment, a steady income, supportive family and friends, and I am making an effort to get clear about money." Or, "I have a loving network of friends and family, and even though I'm out of work right now I can take control of my own financial future." Get comfortable and know this is a huge step toward a Live It, Love It, Earn It life.

SUCCESS SECRET

Balance Your Checkbook

It's important to balance your checkbook so that you know how much money is going out (expenses) and how much is coming in (income). It tells you if you have money in the bank (positive balance) or if you're overdrawn (negative balance). Let's face it—how many of us balance our checkbook on a regular basis? Sometimes I don't do it every month; I do the best I can. It's so easy to do, and once you establish a routine, it takes very little time. Here's how:

1. Place returned checks (or statements with copies on them if your bank does not send you back the originals) and ATM withdrawal slips into two piles.

2. Put your returned checks in numerical order and compare them to your checkbook or use a computer program like QuickBooks by putting a check next to each figure that matches a canceled check.

3. Put your ATM withdrawal slips in order by date and compare them to your ledger book by checking off every figure that matches an ATM withdrawal.

4. Make final changes in your ledger after comparing your deposit receipts with your bank statement. Put a check mark on each figure that matches a deposit receipt on your statement.

5. Calculate your balance. Write down your checkbook's current balance at the top of a piece of paper or on the back of your statement (many banks provide a worksheet on the back of each statement for calculating your balance).

6. Subtract amounts for the deposits that have not yet cleared, as well as bank fees, and subtract that figure from your calculated total.

7. Add in any checks that have not yet cleared and any interest you have earned to this figure.

8. Compare the final figure to your bank statement. If you notice any discrepancies or unfair charges, call the local branch of your bank

(continued)

or, better yet, go there in person to discuss your statement. They will be more than happy to go over your statement and your figures with you. In fact, I encourage you to do so—it could well be the beginning of a long and fruitful relationship with your banker.

TODAY'S ASSETS AND LIABILITIES

A personal assets and liabilities sheet is a simple two-column catalog of what you own (assets) and what you owe (liabilities). When completed it represents a clear snapshot of what you have at this particular moment in time.

Assets are what you have in your favor. It's like looking in the refrigerator and seeing what's on hand right now—four eggs, one pound of hamburger, a carton of milk. There are two kinds of assets, *liquid* and *nonliquid*. Some of them you can consume right away (milk), and others you have to cook in order to eat (eggs), so it takes a bit more time to address your appetite. Likewise, liquid assets are cash on hand and anything that can be easily and quickly converted to cash, such as money in a checking or savings account, money in a trust or that has been inherited, stocks and bonds, mutual funds, or gold and silver coins. Nonliquid assets take more time to be converted to cash, and include real estate, life insurance policies, furniture, fine jewelry, artwork, vehicles, and businesses you own.

Liabilities are the money or property you owe to people, banks, or businesses. This can include credit card bills, mortgages, personal loans, student loans, car loans, or other debt. The difference between the value of your assets and all of your liabilities is considered the equity you have today.

Use the worksheet here, or download Asset and Liability worksheets from liveitloveitearnit.com, to calculate a personal own-and-owe assessment.

ASSET AND LIABILITY WORKSHEET

ASSETS (OWN)

Liquid

Cash _____

Checking _____

Savings _____

Investments

Mutual funds _____

Stocks/Bonds _____

Other _____

Non-Liquid

House/apartment _____

Other real estate/land _____

Retirement accounts _____

Life insurance account _____

Car value _____

Artwork _____

Jewelry _____

Other _____

Total: _____

LIABILITIES (OWE)

Mortgage balance _____

Credit card balances (total) _____

Personal loans _____

Car loans _____

Student loans _____

Other debt _____

_____

Difference (Total Assets minus Total Liabilities): _____

KEEPING A MONEY DIARY

Writing down how you spend your money day-to-day is enlightening. Do you really know where the two hundred dollars you withdrew from the ATM went? A money diary shows exactly where your money is going, penny by penny, dollar by dollar. Use a purse-sized notebook to record expenditures, no matter how small— even a one-dollar package of mints. When paying a phone bill, ordering takeout, shopping at the grocery store, or buying a cup of coffee or bus fare, write it down. Do this for one month, or longer if you're willing.

After thirty days of scribbling, my coaching clients usually come to me wide-eyed and amazed. "Wow, I can't believe I spend x amount on coffee, gum, and gas in one month," is a typical shocked reaction. One client's cash drain turned out to be drugstore beauty products. "I realized that I was not even using all the lip gloss, body lotion, and mascara I was buying, and I was spending at least fifty dollars per week on this stuff." At the same time, don't beat yourself up about your spending or put too much pressure on yourself to change old habits overnight. Simply becoming aware of spending habits is the first big step in changing them gradually and for the most lasting results.

MAKE A FUN SPENDING PLAN

When I first mention the Fun Spending Plan, or FSP, to women, they are often worried that unbreakable rules and a strict "money diet" are involved. Where's the fun in that? I assure them, and you, that this is not the case. A spending plan is not a rigid directive that requires sacrifice, skimping, or deprivation. Rather, it is a simple and flexible way of determining how to pay bills, get out of debt, and afford everything you need and want, including that vacation you've been dreaming about. The FSP does not judge or scold; it is completely neutral. You have the power to tweak it at will, according to shifting needs and priorities. It's a way of viewing your financial life as a series of fun savings and expenditure projects, as opposed to a set of obligations and drains. This strategy puts what is important into focus and proves that dreams for a house, a car, and a graduate degree are worthwhile and that getting there is half the fun.

Use your thirty-day money diary and the worksheet on page 90 (or liveitloveitearnit.com) to create a personalized FSP. Financial obligations such as rent, mortgage and debt, car loan or lease, utility bills, and food are fairly predictable expenses. This does not mean they cannot be thought of as fun. In fact, I suggest you start thinking of more of your expenditures as fun. For instance, move mortgage payments into the Fun column if you absolutely love your house.

Once established, keep track of your FSP by noting what you actually spent next to the allocated amount for each category. At the end of one month it will be clear what needs to be adjusted: actual spending or the FSP. Making changes to the FSP is a way of having more of the things that are really important. For example, if eating out is cutting into a vacation fund, a simple adjustment is in order: revise the monthly restaurant allotment and allocate the difference to the vacation fund.

Don't devise a heavily restrictive plan, which would be similar to going on a very strict food diet. It might work for a few days or even a few weeks, but if the deprivation is so great, there will be a break and you will start consuming (i.e., spending) more than you ever did before. A strategy that is reasonable has a far greater chance of succeeding than one that is confining.

One client says, "I enjoy doing my spending plan in a beautiful pink leather ledger book. I find it empowering." This is a terrific idea. Why not make a date with your FSP, say, every Monday from seven P.M. to eight P.M. Put on a pretty dress, light a candle, and pull out the lovely ledger. You and your money deserve the royal treatment.

Other women tell me about small miracles that started happening after creating and using an FSP. "Every year I would go to Provincetown, Massachusetts, for a summer vacation. This year I thought it would be impossible because of the expense," one says. "Lo and behold, a friend said I could use her house for free." Another describes unexpected perks: "Unexpected checks show up in the mail. My friends chipped in to pay for the tuition of a class I wanted to take. I truly believe this came about because I started to pay attention to how I was using my money."

SUCCESS SECRET

Start on Monday

Start using your FSP on a Monday instead of a Friday. You will be less tempted by weekend social events or afternoon window-shopping excursions and more likely to get your new approach to money off to a good start.

MONTHLY FUN SPENDING PLAN (FSP) WORKSHEET

Here's a simple sheet for you to keep track of your FSP. Copy this page, or download additional sheets from liveitloveitearnit.com. It's a little different from others you may have seen in the past. Under the column "Fun Money," you will notice that there are several uncommon items— that may not seem like fun. That's because the term *fun money* has been used to describe discretionary income used for items that are not "necessary" to living. I want to change all that by getting you to look at money and its uses as fun—even savings, retirement (don't you want to have a lot of fun when you're sixty-five?), and car payments.

INCOME (MONTHLY MONEY COMING IN)

Salary (after taxes) _____

Interest income/Investment dividends _____

Child support _____

Gifts from family _____

Bonus/royalties (after taxes) _____

Rental income _____

Retirement/Social Security income _____

Other _____

Total monthly income _____

EXPENSES (MONTHLY MONEY GOING OUT)

Fixed and Predictable

Mortgage/rent _____

Property taxes _____

Home maintenance _____

Monthly utilities _____

Insurance _____

Home _____

Health _____

Car _____

Child care/tuition _____

Loan payments _____

Credit cards _____

Student loans _____

Other (list below) _____

Fun Money

Monthly savings _____

Emergency fund _____

Investments _____

Retirement/401(k)/IRA _____

Car loan/lease _____

Education _____

Food _____

Groceries _____

Takeout _____

Cocktails _____

Restaurants _____

Entertainment (movies, sports, parties, other) _____

Clothes/shoes/purses _____

Beauty (hair, nails, makeup, spa treatments) _____

Jewelry _____

Charitable giving _____

Gifts _____

Vacation _____

Pet(s) _____

Other (list below) _____

_____ _____

_____ _____

_____ _____

_____ _____

Total Monthly Expenses _____

Barbara Stanny

FINANCIAL EDUCATOR AND AUTHOR

Barbara Stanny grew up relying on a wealthy father (the "R" of H&R Block), then her husband, to manage her money. A devastating financial crisis was a personal wake-up call for Barbara—she had to get her money life in order. And she did. She has since devoted her life to helping women become financially independent. Barbara is an accomplished inspirational speaker and author who empowers women to live up to their financial and personal potential. She is the author of *Secrets of Six-Figure Women*, among other books.

What was the biggest challenge you faced surrounding money?

My challenge was getting out of denial. I grew up in a wealthy family and my father did not believe women should make or manage money. Anything to do with finances was out of bounds for women as far as my father was concerned. Whenever I brought the subject up, he'd say, "You don't have to worry about it; don't think about it."

When did you first realize that you had to take control of your finances?

I married a financial adviser. I realized in the third year of our marriage that my husband was a compulsive gambler and he was losing my inheritance. Despite this knowledge, I continued to let him manage my money and investments, and pay bills, for fifteen years. One day I went to an ATM to withdraw something like sixty dollars and there were insufficient funds in the account. That's the moment I came out of denial. It was as if someone threw ice water on me. I knew I had a problem so I got rid of the problem. I got divorced.

What happened after that?

I started getting tax bills, which I gave to my accountant. He turned white when he saw them—the first was for over $500,000, and the second was for over $800,000. My accountant said, "I think you need a lawyer." My ex had left the country (I knew where he

(continued)

was, but the IRS couldn't touch him). My father would not lend me the money. It was then that I realized that no one could fix this for me. I was in sheer terror. I had three daughters to think about.

How did you pay back the taxes?

I hired lawyers to help me work with the IRS and I used just about all the money I had to pay the amount we settled on. I had a portfolio of bonds, and real estate. My husband had gotten to most of the bonds while we were still married but not the real estate. My lawyers got the tax bill reduced significantly. I had enough bonds left to sell and used the proceeds for back taxes. People need to know that you can work with the IRS and creditors to figure out a way to pay off debt.

Why wouldn't your father lend you the money if he still believed women shouldn't worry about money?

I really can't tell you that. I can say that I have thanked my dad many times for not lending me the money. Hearing him say no was shocking. The weird thing was, at that moment, there was a solar eclipse, and as I hung up the phone, I looked outside and saw the daylight turn an eerie green. I was sure my world had come to an end. I think God knew I had a job to do. I am sure it was divine intervention that my dad did not give me the money because it forced me to grow up.

How did you get smart about money?

In the beginning of my journey my eyes would glaze over when it came to money. Reading a financial book was like reading Swahili. I was working as a freelance writer and was hired by an organization to research women who were smart with money. Those interviews changed my life. I realized that it was not so much what these women did with money, it was how they thought about everything, not just money. When I shifted my thinking everything changed.

I've come to see that financial success is a three-pronged process: the inner work of wealth, the outer work of wealth, and the higher work of wealth. Most everything we read about finance is about the outer work—savings, investing, planning. That's great. But so often

(continued)

we stay stuck if the inner work and higher work are neglected. Inner work is dealing with your fears, beliefs, and attitudes about money. Higher work is how we can use the money to help others.

What should people do differently during an economic downturn? Do you have any tips?

There are no new rules for this economy, as some have suggested. I believe that one of the reasons for the economic downturn is that people were not following the old rules. The old rules are as sound today as they were one hundred years ago: spend less, save more, invest wisely, and give generously, in that order. I actually believe that the current crisis is the universe taking us by the shoulders, shaking us, and saying, "Pay attention!" This is not a good time to ignore money—it is a time to get educated so you can make it from a place of knowledge. Most of us make decisions out of fear, and that rarely works. Remember that severe contractions always lead to big expansions. The downturn will not last forever.

STEP 3:
DO AWAY WITH DEBT

Debt is a major symptom of money confusion. If you have allowed yourself to rack up thousands or tens of thousands of dollars' worth of debt, you are not being clear about money. In fact, the bigger your credit card debt, the less you love money. I say this because I have seen what big debt does to people—it's debilitating, paralyzing, and depressing. Women tell me every day, "I just can't get out from under it." It creates hopelessness and helplessness. There is a solution. I am going to show you how to get out from under it in the easiest, fastest way.

For years, cheap money (money lent with few preconditions and at very low interest rates) meant people could borrow vast amounts of cash very easily. Even more damaging, many women (and men) have a tendency to live a debt lifestyle, meaning they use credit to pay for essentials such as groceries, utility bills, and household supplies.

In consumer terms, there are two kinds of debt: *secured* and *unsecured*.

Secured debt is backed by collateral, such as a house and a car. Lenders can repossess the house or car if there is a default on the loan. Credit card debt is an example of *unsecured debt,* or debt that is not secured by collateral. If a credit card balance remains unpaid, the issuing bank cannot seize the items bought with the card—designer dresses, shoes, vacations—but they can and will ruin the borrower's credit rating.

If some of you are breaking into a cold sweat at the thought of going without "fun stuff" like clothes, shoes, or restaurant meals because of credit card debt, calm yourself. You can get out of debt, save money, *and* buy a great pair of shoes. There's no need to feel deprived and depressed. You do, however, have to rearrange your FSPs to reflect the fact that you are improving your financial situation by putting more of your fun money into eliminating debt. That is cause for celebration.

First, check the interest rates of all your credit cards. A bill was signed in May 2009 that does not allow companies to punitively raise credit card rates for nonpayment, late fees, or buying habits, called the Credit Card Accountability, Responsibility and Disclosure Act (or Credit CARD Act). Moreover, the law says that consumers whose interest rates have been increased can reduce their annual percentage rates to previous levels if they've been good and paid their bills on time for six months. If you've been paying your bills on time after a rate increase, call the bank and ask for the interest reduction.

If you are in a bind with high, old (more than a year) balances that have nearly reached the point of litigation, you can, in some instances, negotiate down those old balances. The credit card companies just want to be paid something, so they may, depending on the circumstances, take off up to 40 percent from your balances and remove partial or all interest and penalties from those old accounts.

More than likely, retail or store credit cards will carry the highest rates, often exceeding 23 percent. However, you should call all your card issuers and try to negotiate lower interest rates across the board. They will say one of two things: yes or no. Card companies want to be paid, especially in a tough economy, so you may be pleasantly surprised at how many issuers will agree to work with you.

Whatever you settle on with your creditors, work on paying off the highest-rate cards first with the highest payments you can afford, even if their balances are lower than other cards, because they are costing the most amount of money. Don't stop paying off the other cards. I suggest paying the minimum amount due on the other cards while you pay the largest amount possible on the high-interest cards. When the high-interest cards are paid off, work on eliminating the balances on cards with the second highest interest rates, and so forth, until all credit card debt has been erased. Then put as much as you can every month into paying back loans by making extra payments, except for those with very low interest, such as a 2 percent student loan, or a fixed-rate mortgage debt.

Some of you might be wondering why paying off the balances on credit cards is so important. "After all, I always make the minimum payments on time every month." The problem with minimum payments is compound interest. One two-hundred-dollar pair of shoes can turn into a pair of four-hundred-dollar shoes in three years if only minimum payments are made to a credit card that charges 21 percent compound interest (meaning that interest accrues on the principal, or cost of the shoes, *and* on the unpaid interest).

Even more troubling, studies show that chronic credit card debt lowers self-esteem. Credit card debt reduces our control and power over our money, which in turn leads to money anxiety, frustration, and anger. Eventually our debt starts to control our lives, much like drugs control an addict. What follows are stories that two of my clients were generous enough to share, which clearly illustrate how racking up debt can become a dangerous pastime, and getting out from under it is a powerful and life-affirming adventure.

CARA'S MONEY MARRIAGE

Cara is like a lot of women in their late twenties: college-educated, great job (she's in public relations), above-average salary. Cara is engaged to be married and wants to buy a house with her husband-to-be. Sounds good, except that Cara is a self-admitted "bad saver" and emotional spender. "A lot of times I shop out of boredom," she says. As a result, Cara found herself with substantial credit card debt before she even had her first job.

"I was still working off credit card debt from college, mostly racked up from clothes shopping and going out when I first started working," she says. The debt was exacerbated when she moved from New York to Virginia. "I moved south with a boyfriend who was in the navy. He was away all the time, and I had no friends and a crappy job. There was a nice mall near me so I went shopping all day to compensate for my loneliness and discontent."

SUCCESS SECRET

Don't Shop When Emotions Are High

Do you go shopping when you are depressed or angry? How about when you are excited and happy? Emotional spending is similar to emotional eating. Some people eat a pint of ice cream when they're under stress; others charge an expensive outfit or jewelry. Some people go out for a big meal when they are happy; others treat themselves to a few pairs of shoes. Don't use shopping as medication to cheer you up or calm you down. Curb potential impulse buying and postpone shopping until you are in a neutral mood. Following are a few tips that I use when I get the urge to splurge:

+ Go window-shopping, and leave your purse at home; it's fun and a lot less expensive.
+ In your wallet, keep a small card on top of your credit card that says "Buy it later."
+ Before you make a purchase, write it down on a three-by-five-inch index card and keep it in your purse. Promise yourself that if you still want it in one week, you will buy it as a special treat.
+ Ask a friend to be "on call" to help you face reality when you find yourself at the checkout counter with a pile of items. Stop right there and call her: "Hi, Audrey, I'm at the checkout counter ready to buy five pairs of jeans, three tops, and four pairs of shoes."

After Cara had split from her boyfriend and moved back east she decided to get serious about her finances, starting with calculating her assets and liabilities. "My credit balances totaled twelve thousand dollars. Most of the debt was from store credit cards with very high interest rates, more than twenty percent," she says. Cara used a free online debt calculator to see how long it would take to pay off the cards making minimum payments of six hundred dollars a month. "I was stunned when the calculator estimated that it would take *thirty-one years* to get rid of the balances on my cards! That's a big chunk of my adult life."

Cara's grandparents were willing to secure a small, low-interest (5 percent) home equity loan to help clean up her debt. She respected that gift by meeting her obligation to her grandparents. "I paid them $375 a month and in three years I was debt-free. I could have moved out of my parents' house during that time, but having my own place would have been too expensive." Cara was able to clear the slate, maintain a good credit rating, learn to be more careful about spending, buy a house with a 20 percent down payment, and feel very optimistic about her future.

"I no longer shop during my lunch hour, and I usually eat at my desk and then go for a walk," says Cara. She avoids the mall on the weekends to reduce the temptation to impulse shop. "If I have to buy something, I park near where I need to go, and get in and out without extra browsing. I still love shopping, but focusing on what I need helps curb my spending. Having bought a house helps me stay the course as well, since it represents a tremendous responsibility."

Cara is making positive strides, but she still has some issues to resolve. For instance, she and her husband are facing three thousand dollars in debt from their wedding and honeymoon. "Paying that off is our first priority, along with building our savings and emergency fund." Cara says she could have spent a lot more on her wedding, but she knew she could plan a gorgeous celebration without racking up more credit card debt. That can-do attitude and attention to her finances will allow Cara to succeed.

If you have large credit card debt like Cara did, a family loan or a home equity loan (if you qualify) are two good ways to consolidate debt into one reduced-interest loan. Making the difficult decision to live at home until your debt is paid off may also be necessary. If this isn't viable, lower your cost of living another way—by moving into a less expensive apartment, or finding a roommate to share expenses.

SUCCESS SECRET

How to Spend Less

When you are trying to spend less there are so many creative and resourceful ways to reach your financial goals. Don't be afraid to use your imagination to get what you want. The following are a few suggestions to get you started:

+ Barter—trade a service or product for one that you want: Watch your friend's children two nights a week in exchange for her cooking you dinner two nights a week. I have a friend who does PR for her gym, and the gym gives her a free membership in exchange. I have another friend who's rebuilding a fashion designer's Web site in exchange for free clothing from the designer.

+ If you get a mani-pedi every week, skip a week instead or do your own nails or have a spa night at home with your girlfriends.

+ Meet friends for coffee, tea, or lunch instead of a full dinner.

+ Instead of subscribing to magazines, read them online, at the library, or at the gym.

+ Instead of getting shirts and skirts pressed at the dry cleaner, iron at home every other week.

+ Skip buying the bottled water; filtered tap does the same job (check the water in your area first).

+ If you're still using a travel agent to plan your vacations, start researching and buying your airline tickets online using CheapTickets, TravelZoo, TripAdvisor, and other similar sites. You can save money on both the agent fee and the overall cost of the ticket.

+ Cook at home. Make it an event by shopping with a friend, and spending time on creative meal planning.

+ Shop in your closet and then have a clothes-trading party with your girlfriends, swapping clothes instead of buying new ones.

+ Instead of buying a cup of gourmet coffee every morning, pick out a cute travel mug and make your own coffee at home—a cup of home brew costs about thirty-five cents a cup.

(continued)

✦ Instead of paying full price at a hair salon, volunteer as a hair model at a beauty school and get cuts/color for free or a deeply discounted price.

✦ Rather than driving alone each day, walking, taking public transportation, and carpooling are all less expensive ways to get to work.

GABRIELLE'S FRESH START

Gabrielle, a divorced teacher with two master's degrees, makes more than $85,000 a year. Sounds great. But when I met her, she was at a low point in her life and was facing bankruptcy. Gabrielle's problems began because of her vague knowledge of her own money. "I did not pay attention to how the money in my house was managed while I was married, and that continued after I was on my own. I did not have a clue why bills had to be paid on time, how to balance a checkbook, or how to plan for necessary expenditures or future needs. One day not long after my divorce I went to my accountant, and he told me that the $200 in my checking account was the sum total of my holdings. I had never looked at my bank statement once in my life so this news came as quite a shock to me." Gabrielle maintained a calm front in the accountant's office, but as soon as she got home? "I freaked out."

Gabrielle had no idea what she had in her bank account, what was going into it from her salary, and how much was going out of it for regular expenditures such as rent, food, and utilities. Nor did she pay attention to what she was spending on clothes, household items, and luxury purchases. "After my second divorce I went into a tailspin of shopping. I racked up $30,000 in credit card debt in six months. My ex-husband and I sold our house, and I used some of my share of the proceeds, $170,000, to pay those bills off. But then I charged another $40,000 on my cards and maxed them all out. I spent the remaining $140,000 from the house sale on clothes, charity donations, dinners out, vacations, and other things I can't even remember. I would walk into department stores and charge hundreds and hundreds of dollars and think, "What's the big deal?"

The big deal was that after her divorce, Gabrielle found herself flat broke and owing $40,000 to credit card companies. Not only had Gabrielle burned through the proceeds from the sale of her house, she borrowed $25,000 from her tax-deferred annuity—a retirement account she had been building for years. "I thought the money would tide me over until I figured out how to pay back my debt," says Gabrielle. Instead, she used the money on a lavish vacation to Miami and to buy more clothes and other items. What was she thinking? She wasn't thinking very clearly, that's certain.

"I was completely aware of the fact that I had this big debt, but I just did not see it as a real thing. I thought, 'Oh, I'll get a raise at work and use it to balance out my bills.'" That was incredibly unrealistic, because Gabrielle's pay increase was only about 5 percent, not enough to cover what she owed on one credit card. "My blindness was laughable," she now admits. "I applied for a zero-interest credit card as a way of solving my credit crunch thinking I could transfer my high-interest balances over. I was denied."

Adding further to Gabrielle's painful problem, the interest rates on her cards were raised to a whopping *33 percent*. "Every time I was late with a payment they would charge me forty dollars and there was nothing I could do about it." Then, on New Year's Eve before 2008, Gabrielle realized she was virtually penniless. Her salary barely covered her expenses and the enormous monthly payments to her creditors.

"I was desperate and hopeless. I finally understood why people jumped out of windows during the 1929 stock market crash. I did not have a party, as I usually did, and I did not go out. There was nothing to celebrate. I stayed home in my flannel pj's alone, my dog by my side." Around nine P.M., a friend who knew about Gabrielle's predicament called to check in on her. The two women talked for a while. "I leashed up my dog, put a jacket over my pajamas, tugged on a pair of boots, and walked down the street to her house for some company."

As they sat on the couch chatting, Gabrielle's friend confessed that she too had a debt problem and was attending Debtor's Anonymous meetings. "I felt such shame about the situation I had gotten myself in, so I told her I would think about going to a meeting with her." When Gabrielle got home that night, she checked out the organization online, and thought she had nothing to lose (she had lost it all already). "Something happened as I sat in that room with people who were in similar situations to mine. There was reason for optimism, especially when I heard the words *prosperity* and *abundance*."

Gabrielle started keeping a money diary and stopped using her credit cards. One day a few months into her new routine, the superintendent of her apartment knocked on her door. "He told me my rent check had bounced. I had not put my paycheck into my account right away, and so there was no balance to draw on." Gabrielle was so embarrassed, panic set in. "I charged a couple of hundred dollars of merchandise on my credit card."

Gabrielle went back to DA shortly after that incident. It took six more months before she was able to grasp the gravity of her situation. "It was not until the end of June that I realized I did not have enough money to pay all my bills. Minimum payments on my credit cards were one thousand dollars a month, five hundred dollars of which went to interest and penalties. I tried to borrow from my pension again, but was denied. I went to a credit counselor, who analyzed my situation, ran some numbers, but all the restitution plans the counselor tried to get me into were denied. He told me to declare bankruptcy. That really hit home—there was absolutely no way I was going to do that. To me bankruptcy was more than just a financial assertion, it was a very negative spiritual and psychological admission."

Thoughts of suicide crept into Gabrielle's mind, but one thing stopped her from going through with it. "I have a daughter, so I just could not let myself fall that deeply into the abyss. Instead, I continued to go to DA meetings, and I prayed. A lot. I called my brother, who is an attorney, to ask for help in requesting another withdrawal from my tax-deferred annuity." The annuity manager denied Gabrielle's request. "At that point I was hysterical. The next day my brother and father both called and said they would lend me the money. That was big, because after my first divorce, I had asked my dad for a little financial help and he had refused."

A $40,000 family loan wiped out Gabrielle's credit card debt, and she continues to pay $500 a month toward the $25,000 she borrowed from her tax-deferred annuity. "It should take three and a half years to pay back. I am fifty-five, so in four and a half years I will be able to withdraw the money from my tax-deferred annuity and pay my family back every penny, and still have money left for my retirement," she says.

If any of you are in a situation similar to Gabrielle's, don't give up hope. Family members might be able to provide a loan at a very low in-terest rate, or no interest rate at all. However, not all of us have families with money or the inclination to extend a loan. Even if that is the case, I recommend against bankruptcy. It is damaging not only financially, but it is also devastating to self-esteem, pride, and dignity. I encourage every woman to do everything possible to get herself out of debt and on to a better life. It's quite simple: if you got yourself into debt you can get yourself out of debt.

If you are in serious debt trouble, be very clear about how much needs to be repaid. Purposefully change your attitude from "I cannot get out from under this" to "I *will* get out from under this." Surround yourself with people who support your attitude and goal, and consider attending Debtors Anonymous meetings or joining an online support group. Seek the help of a financial coach, and with her help devise a debt elimination plan that spells out monthly contributions and a final payment date. Find a money group in your area or form an abundance group using the suggestions in this book. Having positive support and knowing when a debt will be paid off are the lights at the end of the tunnel.

CLEAN UP YOUR CREDIT

The previous two stories highlight why living a debt lifestyle can be so risky and demoralizing. Dangerously high debt is a sure way to damage your relationship with money. It can also damage your credit rating even if you eventually pay back the debt. A credit rating is a snapshot of how responsible we've been with loans, which lenders use to judge whether someone is a good credit risk. A perfect score is 800, any number in the mid to high 700s is considered an excellent score, and anything less than 620 is considered very risky. A high score is more important now than ever because lenders have become more cautious about which borrowers they will do business with.

You may wonder why a good credit score is so important. What does it mean for you? A good score allows you to be approved for a mortgage, secure another credit card, buy a car, go to school, gain access to any kind of loan at a favorable interest rate, and maybe even find a new job. Many employers can look at a potential hire's credit ratings as part of a general reference and background check.

The three major U.S. credit bureaus—Equifax (equifax.com), Experian (experian.com), and TransUnion (transunion.com)—provide lenders with credit information. You have the right to look at your credit reports. Doing so four times a year does not affect scores as long as the reports are ordered directly from credit-reporting agencies or through an organization authorized to provide credit reports to consumers, such as annualcreditreport .com, which is run by the three aforementioned U.S. credit bureaus. Checking your own score, even if you do it often, will not lower your score.

It's only when banks or lenders make many inquiries about your score over a long period of time that you have to be concerned. Banks do this when you apply for new lines of credit, or when you are making a large purchase, like a home or a car. All inquiries are recorded, and many inquiries over several months (usually more than six) can be a red flag to future lenders.

No one piece of information or factor alone determines a score. Lenders look at many things when making a credit decision, including the following:

- *Income* and *length of time* at a current employer
- *Payment history* (length of established credit, timely bill payments, debt, and delinquency or default on a loan)
- *Amounts owed* (balances on mortgages, credit cards, and other loans; portions of credit lines used)
- *Length of credit history* (time since you opened an account; activity on the account)
- *New credit* (number of recently opened accounts; number of recent credit inquiries potential lenders have made; reestablishment of positive credit history following past payment problems, such as missed or late payments)
- *Types of credit used* (number of cards, frequency of use, and recent information on various types of accounts such as credit cards, retail accounts, installment loans, mortgages, or consumer finance accounts)

The bottom line is that lenders want to see a responsible history of paying off credit on time.

Get Your Abundance On

If you're in debt and having difficulty getting in touch with an overall feeling of abundance and richness, this exercise will help you. By concentrating on an area of your life that is plentiful, you become familiar with the feeling, and are able to shift it to other areas of your life where you may feel lacking in abundance. The big bonus is that when you feel abundant you have less of a need to overspend. Follow these steps to getting your abundance on:

1. Choose an area of your life that makes you feel wealthy right now. This could be your friends and family, a talent like piano playing or tennis, or your collection of beautiful scarves.
2. Focus your attention on this area, and get in touch with the bountiful feeling it gives you.
3. Transfer those positive, hopeful feelings to other areas of your life.

INCREASE YOUR SCORE

Everyone can increase their credit score, high and low scorers alike. The following ten tips are guaranteed to up your number:

1. *Pay bills on time.* The longer bills are paid on time, the better the credit score. Delinquent payments and collections can have a major negative impact on credit scores. Missing one or more payments can lower a score, so get current with bills immediately, and then stay current. Note that paying off a past-due account doesn't automatically remove it from your credit report. It stays there for approximately seven years.
2. *Keep balances and limits low on credit cards and other revolving credit.* High outstanding debt on numerous cards can negatively affect a credit score, even if you make regular minimum pay-

ments. Spending limits tell a lender how much credit a potential borrower has access to; a high amount can raise a red flag. That's because a person with a $2,500 credit balance could have a $25,000 balance if credit card limits allow. A bank may feel this could put their loan at risk.

3. *Have credit cards—but manage them responsibly.* In general, having credit cards and installment loans (and making timely payments) raises credit scores. Someone with no credit cards, for example, tends to be a higher risk than someone who has managed one or two credit cards consistently.

4. *Pay off debt rather than moving it around.* The most effective way to improve your credit score in this area is by paying down your revolving credit. In fact, owing the same amount but having fewer open accounts by consolidating cards to one low-interest card may lower your score. This does not mean constantly transferring debt from one card to another—this practice sends up red flags to creditors and lenders.

5. *Don't close unused credit cards as a short-term strategy to raise your score.* Canceled cards don't disappear from your credit report automatically. You still have to request that closed accounts be removed from your report and you must contact all three reporting companies—Equifax, Experian, and TransUnion—because each one does slightly different reporting on your credit history.

6. *Don't open new credit cards that you don't need as a way to increase your available credit.* This approach could actually lower your credit score. We need only a limited number of cards. For instance, I have one personal card, one business card, and one for my favorite department store.

7. *If you have been managing credit for a short time (less than a year), don't open new credit accounts too rapidly.* New accounts lower "average account age," which will have a substantial effect on a score if there is not a lot of other credit information to go on. Rapid account buildup might appear risky to a lender.

8. *Shop for interest rates for a given loan within a focused period of time.* Credit scores distinguish between a search for a single loan and a search for many new lines of credit, in part by the length of time over which inquiries occur. For example, when shopping

for a mortgage, do it over five or six months, not two years, to reduce the number of bank inquiries that are recorded on credit reports over a broad span of time. Multiple inquiries over a long period of time may signal to other lenders that you may have been turned down for loans.

9. *Reestablish your credit history if there have been past problems.* Opening new accounts responsibly and paying them off on time raises your credit score in the long term.

10. *Write to each credit company to remove errors.* Credit reports often list long-closed accounts and other inaccurate information. Adding to this, each credit-reporting company can have slightly different information. Disputing information and requesting that old accounts be removed is a straightforward process, but it does take time because all three credit bureaus must be contacted. Each reporting company offers clear instructions on how to file disputes and request report revisions on their Web site. If the bureaus do not respond in thirty days, they must grant your request.

STEP 4:
CASH IS QUEEN

The fourth and last step in learning to love money is recognizing the power of cash. If you are unclear about money, in deep debt, or can't stop spending money, living on a cash-only basis can help. Even if you don't have a problem with debt or spending, using cash is a self-corrector because *you are physically spending money.* Exchanging actual money—bills and change—for goods or services is very immediate. Counting out tens and twenties gives you a feeling that is very different from pulling a credit or debit card out of your bag. Paying with cash also creates a feeling of true abundance for the very same reason. You feel rich when you have cash, so you are rich. It's a self-fulfilling prophecy.

Try an experiment: next time you visit a favorite boutique and want to buy an item that costs more than one hundred dollars, use cash to pay for it. Instead of whipping out a charge card, count out tens, twenties, fifties, dimes, nickels, and quarters. Look at the pile of cash on the counter, and then look at the item. Is the item worth exchanging for an empty, or at least much lighter, wallet? When women in my coaching classes do this, eight out of ten of them put the money back in their wallets and walk out of the store.

Something similar happened to me the other day. As I was counting out cash to pay for a pair of shoes, I ultimately just could not justify the purchase. They were *so* expensive. I put the bills back in my wallet, said, "Thank you very much, I've changed my mind," and left the shop. If I had really loved those shoes I would have bought them, so I did not feel deprived in the least. One thing I've learned is that stores and designers never seem to run out of good ideas. If you can skip buying something you aren't really enamored with this week, you'll be able to afford the fabulous "It" shoe or bag next week—the one you'll truly want.

Women in my classes who use cash for purchases tell me that their spending on nonessentials is reduced by almost half. "Living on a cash-only basis does not make me feel I have less; it has given me tremendous courage. I feel rich, I feel real, I feel truly independent," says Gabrielle of her cash-only lifestyle. More important, my clients continue to buy the beautiful things they really want, and don't feel deprived. Try it yourself. Designate a specific amount of cash each week, based on your FSP, for fun purchases and little things. Limit yourself to that amount only. See how your consciousness shifts about spending. Don't be surprised if you think twice before buying a five-dollar coffee or that cute top that's on sale.

YOU DID IT!

I'm sure that for many of you, this chapter brought up some strong and perhaps previously hidden emotions. Congratulations for taking the first important steps in knowing your money better and cultivating a beautiful relationship with it. Loving your money is not a tool to be used once and then forgotten. I am at the point in my life where I understand my feelings about money, but I still continuously look at my money, regularly review and revise my FSP, and keep tabs on my credit rating. I urge everyone to do the same—print out as many Asset and Liability charts and FSPs as you need from liveitloveitearnit.com. In the next chapter I will show you how to respect your money by learning how to keep it safe, and how to make it work for you.

Love Money Summary:

- Neutralize money feelings.
- Be clear about your money—what you have and where it goes.
- Calculate your assets and liabilities.
- Keep a money diary.
- Create and stick to a reasonable FSP.
- Do away with debt.
- Clean up your credit, and improve your credit score.
- Use cash.
- Congratulate yourself for taking the steps to love money.

5.

Respect Money

WHEN YOU RESPECT money you tend to treat it more carefully, protecting it and helping it grow by saving, through financial planning, and by investing wisely. In the last chapter we talked about how to become clear about your money, recognize what you have and where it goes, and begin to reduce and eliminate debt. If you haven't started to feel better about your life already, you will when your finances are in order, and slowly your respect for money will grow and mature.

Despite the many straightforward and relatively safe ways to save and grow money, it's surprising how many women, including those with MBAs and six-figure salaries, seem uninformed or uninterested or just can't find the time to learn about the basics of saving and investing. Many women aren't familiar with the principles of money, investments, paying the proper amount of taxes (and not overpaying), buying real estate, contributing to a retirement account, creating a will or a trust, and making other financial decisions.

Yet incorporating these practices and habits into your financial life will make you richer and more secure. There are investment, tax, and estate experts who can help you out—there is no need to go at it alone. In fact, you should not make big financial decisions or take risks without a reliable pro by your side. Once you become deeply involved in creating a strong financial life you'll be hooked. Not to worry, I'm going to explain the basics of saving, investing, and estate planning in plain English, using real-life examples you can relate to. Watching money grow is *fun*; it's *exciting*. When we're done, I know you will think so too.

SAVING MADE SIMPLE

Do you save as much money each month as you'd like? You may have the false perception that you cannot afford to save because your monthly expenses take up every dime you earn. Or maybe you've been so focused on the items and activities you want to buy right *now* that saving for your future wants and needs comes in a distant second.

So where to start? The secret to saving is to develop a strong saving habit that is very hard to break. It can be as natural as brushing your teeth. It's not the amount of money you put away each week; it is the act of doing so that is important. Everyone can put some amount of money in the bank on a weekly basis. How about twenty-five dollars? The only way to accurately determine how much money can be put into a savings account every week is to look back at your FSP (page 90). How much have you allocated to savings? Is it possible to increase the savings amount a little more each month, maybe to 10 or 20 percent of the fun money allocation?

I promise that once you start saving you won't be able to stop. Women tell me it feels good when they save. "I never saved money before because I needed to pay my credit cards off. Then, when I actually started to save, and I saw my money accumulating and getting interest, it felt good. I look forward to every month putting x amount into savings; it's weird, but it's empowering." And another woman: "Saving makes me feel more independent and more confident. If anything were to go wrong I have money in the bank."

SUCCESS SECRET

Saving by Half and Half

Remember Gabrielle from chapter 4, who just barely avoided declaring bankruptcy? Once she had solved her catastrophic debt problem she used the "half-and-half" approach to saving. "Aside from the money that is going back into my retirement account, which is taken directly from my paycheck, I put twenty-five dollars a week into a savings account to build up a rainy day fund, and I place twenty-five dollars a week away in a jar for splurges. It is a very humble gesture, but I have a couple of hundred dollars in my jar now, and I plan on using it to go to a bed-and-breakfast for a couple of days." We all need to keep some funds on hand for spontaneous fun, and the half-and-half plan is a realistic way to do it.

Once saving becomes a habit, and it will (watching a bank balance grow is quite addictive), consider categorizing your savings. As I see it there are five basic reasons to save:

1. Retirement
2. Emergency fund (loss of a job; health crisis)
3. Major goal (down payment on a house; education; starting a business)
4. Dream fulfillment (cruise around the world; build your dream)
5. Build wealth

Through the next five sections of this chapter we will discuss these savings goals, retirement planning, the basics of investing, and estate planning.

RETIREMENT: IT'S NEVER TOO EARLY TO PLAN

"Why do I have to think about retirement?" Women in their twenties and thirties ask me that question all the time. They don't see the value in placing a portion of their paycheck into an account they won't use for thirty or forty years. Those who are a little older might recognize that retirement planning is important, but younger women sometimes neglect to consider their future. If you are one of these young women you might be thinking, "But retirement is so far away"; "I don't need to think about that yet"; "I have time." Believe me when I say it's hard to "catch up" and save what you need for your golden years if you wait too long to begin.

Please don't operate under the assumption that a Social Security check and Medicare will be enough. It is far better and safer to make your own retirement plans. Besides, there are tax advantages (for the time being) to retirement planning. Here are the retirement basics:

401(k)

You've probably heard of or participate in a 401(k) plan offered through your company. Public employees such as state workers and public school teachers have a similar plan, called a 403(b). For many of us, a 401(k) or 403(b) employer-sponsored retirement plan represents our first serious savings. These plans offer two advantages. The first is that the contributions are tax-deductible and the accumulated earnings are tax-free until withdrawals are made at retirement.

The second is that some, but not all, 401(k) accounts have an employer-matching feature, meaning that if you put one hundred dollars in your plan, the company will put one hundred dollars into your account and will continue to do so until a certain preset threshold is met. That's free money. Normally, companies that match do so with cash or stock contributions. Not every company offers a matching feature and small firms or start-ups often can't afford to make such an investment. Be aware that company-sponsored plans do bear the same investment risk as investing on our own. However, if an employer goes bankrupt, the employer or its corporate umbrella cannot, by law, take the money in the employee's account, nor can it be taken away in the event of a termination or layoff. In this sense, a 401(k) is "safe," but that does not mean the investment itself can't lose money in a market downturn.

You can get a car loan, a home equity loan, a business loan, or a student loan, but you cannot get a retirement loan.

■

Tom Sherwood, a certified public accountant, says, "In 2009 you can contribute $16,500 into a 401(k) retirement account tax-free. If you're over fifty, you can contribute an additional $5,500 in what is called catch-up contributions." The theory is that when you begin to use the money at retirement you will be in a lower tax bracket than you were when you earned the money. Therefore, you won't pay as much taxes on the 401(k) distributions in retirement as you would have had you not put it into the 401(k) but used it while you were working. "But the real bonus is you have paid no tax on the earnings while it's in your 401(k)," says Tom. "Using round numbers, let's say you put in $15,000 a year; fast-forward just ten years—that's $150,000, but with earnings it could be worth substantially more. The potential to build a huge retirement nest egg for someone who is twenty-five is tremendous."

I made $33,000 at my first job at IBM. It was difficult to make ends meet, especially because I had student and car loans that I wanted to pay back as soon as possible in addition to rent and other expenses. Still, I arranged for money to be taken directly out of my paycheck every month and placed it into my company's 401(k) account. It was so simple and painless, because I never saw the money and therefore never missed it. I became fully vested in IBM's pension plan after five years, which simply meant that I was eligible for a full percentage of IBM's matching contributions. At the end of those five years I had a substantial amount of money in my account because as my pay increased, so did my contributions and the matching funds that IBM supplied.

I've never been tempted to touch the money. My retirement money is for just that—my retirement. However, some people think that it is okay to use retirement funds to solve current financial problems or pay off credit cards bills. Plainly speaking, and I will go into greater detail about this later in the chapter, this is a bad idea and I strongly advise against it except in extremely extenuating circumstances. The taxes and government penalties could wipe out a large percentage of your retirement savings if you make what is called a hardship withdrawal. Even if the government allowed access to the funds without a stiff penalty, I believe doing so would create a precarious financial position because it's highly unlikely that you would replace the money you took from the account. Besides, the idea that there's a retirement fund quietly waiting (and growing) provides such a warm and cozy feeling. Why would you want to tinker with that?

Muriel Siebert

Muriel "Mickie" Siebert is known as "the First Woman of Finance" and rightly so. She was the first woman to own a seat on the New York Stock Exchange (NYSE) and the first woman to head one of the Exchange's member firms. Her struggle to obtain that seat—and join the 1,365 male members of the Exchange—culminated successfully on December 28, 1967. Ms. Siebert has been a vocal advocate for women in finance and industry throughout her career.

When did you know you were a success?

I realized I was a success when I started to do the business I did as my own business. That happened in 1967, when I bought a seat on the Exchange and started my own company, Muriel Siebert & Co., Inc. That was a major accomplishment. The reason I did this was because at that time I knew I was not being paid the same as men who were doing the same thing I was doing.

I changed jobs a few times, but still I was not being paid equally. I asked one of my colleagues whom I trusted, "What large firm could I go to where I would be paid equally?" He said, "Don't be ridiculous, you won't be paid equally." This was in 1967. He said, "Buy a seat on the Exchange, work for yourself." I said, "Don't you be ridiculous, there are no women on the Exchange." To which he said, "I don't think there is a law against it."

I also felt very successful when I was appointed to be the first woman to regulate the banks in New York State. Governor Carey asked me to serve. He was very frank. He said, "I have made a decision to hire women. I want a woman as supervisor of banks and your name is the only one that keeps coming through."

How has business changed vis-à-vis women from when you started on Wall Street?

People now realize that both sexes can make money. Today many more heads of companies are women than in the sixties and seventies. This country is ready to continue changing. I hope more women become real leaders.

(continued)

What's the best way for women to approach risk and decision making?

Before going forward with a deal or a risk, I ask myself, Will it hurt anyone in any way? If a woman is afraid or not sure about taking a risk, I suggest that she take out a piece of paper and list all the pros of taking the risk on one side, and then list all the cons on the other. If you look at the risk in a less emotional way, you will feel more comfortable taking smart ones. The more experience you have with the risk involved, the more you will know about it and you will have more confidence.

How about handling rejection?

Keep going. When I was getting sponsored for a seat on the NYSE, I was looking for the highest-level person to sponsor me. After I was turned down by many men, I kept asking for sponsorship from other men until two agreed to help. I never gave up.

What would you say to a woman today if she was having trouble being taken seriously in her profession?

It depends on whether it is the profession or the company. If it's the company, consider taking another job with another firm. But don't quit a job until you have another job, because it will make you less desirable. If it's the profession, you have to keep fighting to prove yourself in a professional way.

What would you say to a young woman today who wants to conquer the world or start her own business?

Roll up your sleeves and start. If you get knocked down, pick yourself up. Don't get too discouraged; try again.

Have a goal. I have a goal. I started a program ten years ago that teaches kids in public schools about money, credit cards, and personal finance: Personal Finance in the Classroom. Too many young people don't know enough about money and personal finance. It's okay to make a mistake—but don't make the same mistake twice.

Do you have financial advice for women?

Many women come to me after their husbands die or they get divorced and tell me they have never written a check and don't know

(continued)

the first thing about money. I suggest they get a pad with columns and use one column to list each of their expenses, such as housing, medical, clothes. Then I tell them to go back two years and check bank statements, credit card statements, and receipts and list past expenses in another column. Then I advise them to go into their checking account to see how much income is coming in and where it is coming from. This way you know your total income and expenses.

Afterward, sit down and see if you are spending more than you should be. My savings tip is that each month you should try to save at least as much as you spend on the most expensive piece of clothing you buy that month. It doesn't matter how you save, either in an IRA, a 401(k), or a savings account (so you can take it out if you need it), or open a brokerage account. I suggest mutual funds and putting money in each month; you have the safety of diversification. Don't buy speculative stocks with money you can't afford to lose.

IRA and Roth IRA

It's not unusual to change employers, take a new career path, or choose the mommy track for a few years. When you leave a company to take a job elsewhere, start a business, or stay at home to raise children, you'll have to make a decision about your 401(k). Taking the money out of the account and paying taxes and penalties on it (unless you are 59½) is a bad choice, as I said earlier. One option is to leave the money where it is, especially if it is being managed properly (obviously, any matching-funds program ends). Another option is to roll the money into a new employer's plan. Or you can roll it into an individual retirement account, also called an IRA. That's the choice I made.

Rolling my IBM 401(k) into an IRA gave me greater control over how much money I added to the account, and how the money was managed. I chose a Roth IRA instead of what's called a "traditional" IRA because the Roth offered advantageous tax benefits at that point in my life. The fundamental difference between a traditional IRA and a Roth, in fact, is how they are taxed. An investment adviser, accountant, or personal banker can make recommendations on which of these vehicles suits your individual needs and situation.

If you earn $50,000 a year and put $5,000 into a traditional IRA, you can deduct the contribution from your federal income tax (meaning you will have to pay tax on only $45,000 to the IRS). At 59½, you may begin withdrawing funds but will be required to pay tax on all withdrawals (contributions and capital gains, interest, and dividends that were earned over the past years). If you put the same $5,000 in a Roth IRA, you would not receive the income tax deduction, which means you would have to pay tax on the money at the time you contribute to the fund, but all withdrawals (contributions and capital gains, interest, and dividends that were earned over the past years) are tax-free when you begin to use the funds at retirement.

The principal (the money you put in) can be withdrawn from the Roth at any time. Penalties apply when earnings (accumulated interest) are withdrawn before 59½. At retirement age, all monies, including earnings, can be withdrawn totally tax-free. According to Tom Sherwood, many statistics have shown that Roth IRA accounts are more profitable over time than traditional IRAs. Check with your tax accountant for details to see if a Roth IRA works for you.

My career path took me to Bloomberg, LP, which did not have a 401(k) plan at the time that I worked there. So I opted to invest the maximum in a traditional IRA, which was separate from my Roth account. Most people can set up a traditional IRA, and contribute a maximum of five thousand dollars into it annually. At age fifty, an extra one thousand dollars can be invested in the account each year (these rules and dollar amounts may change in the future). The earnings grow tax-deferred until withdrawn, meaning that you do not have to pay taxes on capital gains until you start to use them.

When I started working for a hedge fund I continued to make maximum contributions to my traditional IRA every year (the hedge fund I worked for did not offer a 401(k) plan). Sometimes it was a challenge to contribute, and there were years when I couldn't put anywhere near the maximum allowable amount into my IRA. Nevertheless, I made it a priority to put in as much as I could.

It's very easy to set up an IRA. I urge you to do so if you work for a business that does not offer a retirement plan. An account can be established with an initial investment of as little as fifty dollars at almost any bank, insurance or investment company, brokerage firm, or other financial institution. After researching a few banks and institutions (perhaps the one you are already using for your checking and savings account), complete the simple required paperwork, which your banker can help you with if need be, and make a deposit.

The only real challenge is in selecting specific investment vehicles for your IRA and designating a beneficiary. For investments, it's a good idea to consult the investment professional at your institutions. For retirement accounts, I suggest a diverse portfolio, one that includes conservative as well as moderately aggressive to higher risk investments. If you are relatively young, in your twenties, thirties, or early forties, and have many years before your retirement, I would suggest a bigger portion of your investments in aggressive or growth investments, which are structured to make more money over time but also have more ups and downs. Since the money is not going to be taken out for twenty or thirty years, your portfolio has time to make up for any unexpected downturns in the market.

I do not plan on withdrawing funds until I am 59½ (quite some time from now), so I am comfortable keeping my money diversified, with bigger allocations to equity investments. However, eight to ten years before retirement (late forties to early fifties), I strongly recommend that the bulk of retirement funds be shifted into noncorrelated, more conservative, and less risky investments such as money market, bond, and treasury funds. The closer to retirement you are, the safer you'll want your nest eggs to be, because you'll be drawing from this retirement pool soon. If the overall market goes down significantly, a large portion of your retirement investment could be lost if it was correlated to the market. At that point you would have a short window of time for the market and your investment to go back up. The above suggestions could help keep capital intact, even if the market becomes volatile shortly before you retire.

Keogh

A Keogh account is a retirement savings vehicle specifically for self-employed people (an IRA is for anyone) or those, like me, who own their own business. When I started my own business, I opened a Keogh account on the advice of my trusted accountant. "Self-employed people

TRADITIONAL AND ROTH IRA PROFILES AT A GLANCE

Here is a side-by-side snapshot of the differences between traditional and Roth IRAs.

Traditional IRA

The plan is generally available to everyone; there are no income restrictions if you are not covered by a pension plan. You must have earned income.

Contributions are tax-deductible, but deductibility depends on your income level.

Withdrawals can begin when you turn 59½ and are mandatory when you reach 70½.

Any funds withdrawn before the age of 59½ are subject to a 10 percent penalty, with a few exceptions.

Taxes are paid on distributions at withdrawal.

Funds can be used to purchase a variety of investments (stocks, bonds, certificates of deposits, etc.).

Roth IRA

Contributions are not tax-deductible.

There are no minimum distribution rules.

Principal contributions can be withdrawn anytime without penalty.

All earnings and principal (which you have already paid taxes on) are 100 percent tax-free if the fund rules and regulations are followed.

Funds can be used to purchase a variety of investments (stocks, bonds, certificates of deposits, etc.).

have a lot of options," says CPA Tom Sherwood, but if you are an independent person, "Keogh is the plan to have because the amount of money you can put into it tax-deferred is incomparable." In 2009, a Keogh allowed up to $45,000 per year in tax-deferred retirement contributions, $40,000 more than an IRA. At age 59½ the funds can be withdrawn, and are taxable. However, at retirement most of us will be in a lower tax bracket than when we were working full-time, meaning the taxes paid on the funds will be lower than they would have been had the funds been withdrawn while working.

SUCCESS SECRET

Make Friends with Your Banker

Online banking is certainly convenient, but a personal relationship with the banker right in your neighborhood is even better. Make friends and build a working relationship with her. She will be your advocate and partner in building your wealth, and can also advise you during times of economic uncertainty.

IN CASE OF EMERGENCY

An emergency fund is a cushion of protection against the unknown—job loss, the death of a loved one, a health scare, or even a national disaster (not an "I have to buy myself a new dress" emergency). I recommend building funds equal to at least six to eight months of living expenses in a federally insured savings account (check if your financial institution is covered by FDIC). Except for adding to it, the account should remain untouched unless there is an emergency need to do so. Never deplete a safety net even for debt elimination.

An easy way to calculate the amount needed is to multiply your fixed monthly expenses (rent/mortgage, utilities) and predictable fluid expenses (food, clothing) by six or eight. Those figures can come right from your FSP. Here are two real-life scenarios that show how doable building an emergency fund really is:

GRETA'S WAKE-UP CALL

My friend Greta, whom you met in chapter 1, realized it was imperative to have a fund to fall back on after living through both the 2001 terrorist attacks and the New York City blackout a couple of years later. After filling out her FSP, she saw that it cost her about $3,500 a month to cover her mortgage, health insurance (she now runs her own small business and buys her own insurance), child care, food, and utility bills. Those are her minimum monthly expenses.

Over a two-year period, Greta managed to put $21,000 (6 x $3,500) into a separate "emergency fund" money market account, which earns the highest interest available at her bank, but is still accessible twenty-four hours a day. If her business enters a slow period, she and her family can survive for a few months while they look for alternative sources of income.

How did she do it? She cut back on a few nonessential extras and reduced expenses. "We live very nicely without dry cleaning everything in sight or eating out twice a week," she says. Every time she did not spend money (on clothes, makeup, gourmet groceries), Greta consciously deposited that money into her emergency fund. She also diverted some of her fun money to her emergency fund until she reached her goal of $21,000. When Greta received a windfall of money from a project she had worked on, she used the half-and-half approach, putting half of the money into her emergency fund and then splitting the other half between her retirement account and her day-to-day checking account.

SUCCESS SECRET

Windfall Profits Are a "Savings Grace"

Earning a windfall in the form of a gift, inheritance, bonus, or royalty check is not that unusual for many of us. If you receive a lump sum of money, I suggest using 5 percent to spend on something special

(continued)

for yourself and your family—you deserve it! The other 95 percent should go toward paying off high-interest debt (such as a credit card), building an emergency fund, and adding to a savings or investment account.

WELL-MEANING MEG

Meg has made an earnest attempt at saving, and she wants to establish a seven-month emergency fund, or $12,950, based on her monthly expenses of $1,850. In order to do so, she needs to revise her FSP. Here's a snapshot of Meg's financial picture:

- Earns $120,000 in salary
- Monthly fixed (rent, utilities) and fluid but necessary expenses (food, toiletries) total about $1,850
- Contributes the maximum to her employer's 401(k) program (we'll talk more about this type of investment shortly). "I do the maximum, which is $16,000 a year, and my company matches it."
- Contributes $100 a month to a mutual fund
- Eats dinner and lunch out five times a week
- Buys a new handbag and shoes twice a month
- Takes a $12 cab ride to work every day
- Pays the entire balance of her credit card each month, 50 percent of which consists of dinners out
- Has no outstanding debt

Like so many young single women her age, Meg enjoys socializing, fashion, and having fun. Why shouldn't she? She works hard; the evenings and weekends are her time to relax and catch up with friends. I remember doing the same when I was a young, single girl-about-town. "My apartment is relatively cheap, eleven hundred dollars a month, which is why I have a lot of extra cash," explains Meg. "Fifty percent of the charges on my credit card bill are from eating dinner out at least five times a week. A quarter of the charges are for nice bags and shoes that update my classic wardrobe. The rest probably goes to incidentals and impulse purchases."

Meg is a liberal spender, to say the least, so it would not be difficult for her to make small changes, still have fun, and build a robust safety net. The fact that she is diligent about paying off her card each month puts her in an excellent position to start saving right now. Meg has no revolving debt to pay off. Dinners out in New York City, where Meg lives, can cost upward of $50 per person. Cutting out even two or three nights of those dinners, and eating for $10 or less a night at home, would enable her to put about $120 a week into an emergency account. That's about $6,000 a year.

"Pretending" she pays more rent would allow Meg to put an additional $500 a month into her emergency fund. That's another $6,000 a year for her fund. The average rent in New York for a studio apartment is $1,600. The average cab ride from her apartment to her office costs about $12 with tip. That's $3,120 per year. If she wanted to wake up fifteen minutes earlier and walk to work, she would save another $60 a week, and another $60 if she also walked home. She could save about $40 a week if she went to work and came home on public transportation.

Those few shifts in spending and behavior result in a savings of $15,120 in just one year, more than Meg needs for her seven-month emergency fund. The good news is that Meg is excited (and relieved) that the changes are not painful. "Totally doable," she says about her emergency savings plan. "Frankly, I'm getting a little tired of eating in restaurants every night." Once her emergency fund is tucked safely in the bank, Meg can shift her FSP to reflect new goals. "I am getting to the point where I want to be able to have the freedom to quit my job and do something different—if I'm cash-strapped I'll be stuck where I am," she says. Her next savings challenge: a down payment to start her own business.

GOALS WITHIN REACH

Like a lot of women, Meg wants to someday have her own business, take time off to pursue a new field, and perhaps even go back to school for an advanced degree. These are worthy goals, and they all take money to achieve. When we consciously start to save for such endeavors, they have a way of becoming real. That's why I recommend setting up a separate savings account at the bank that is dedicated to specific goals. Give the account a name that reflects its purpose: "Law School Account," "Antique Business Account," "Take a Year on Sabbatical Account," and so on. Use that trusty FSP to calculate how much can go into the account each week, and how long (weeks, months, years) it will take to accumulate what's needed.

Once you've established a retirement account and are on your way to a fully funded emergency account, saving money for dreams is a great way to acknowledge success and identify the lovely items and adventures that mean the most to you. Nothing is off limits for this kind of saving. You deserve to have what you want, and when you buy it on your own, trust me, it's an amazing feeling. The first time I walked into a realtor's office in Miami and bought an oceanfront apartment with money I had earned, it felt exhilarating. If an expensive purse or new car or is a long-held desire, go for it. How about spending August in Europe or traveling around Asia? Yes, you can. Anything you want to buy is within your reach with focused savings efforts.

WEALTH CREATION: INVESTING 101

Investing is not the only way to create wealth but it is a strategy that many people use to complement their earning and saving strategies. Like many people, I initially made the money I have by working hard and earning it. Now my money has grown through my investing, which has become more sophisticated as I have learned more about the markets. So I do encourage women to invest, but only *after* clearing substantial credit card debt, contributing to a retirement account, creating a six- to eight-month emergency fund, and saving additional discretionary income for other purposes.

SUCCESS SECRET

Acknowledge the Four Pillars of Wise Investing

1. *Investing is a head decision, not a heart decision.* Put emotions aside when putting money in the markets.
2. *Diversify is the golden rule.* Diversification helps spread investment risk by mixing a wide variety of investments within a portfolio.

(continued)

When one investment in a diversified portfolio fluctuates, the impact on overall investments is lessened. That's why buying one or two stocks is a very bad idea for a new investor. Like the saying goes, "Don't put all your eggs in one basket."

3. *If it sounds too good to be true, it is.* If someone promises to double your money or guarantees double-digit returns on a regular basis, it could be a scheme.

4. *Start small and safe.* When first investing, start with a small amount of money and invest in conservative products.

The best way to find a financial adviser is the same way you would find any expert. Start by first asking friends, family, and colleagues for recommendations. All of the people who help manage my money and business—accountants, financial advisers, lawyers—came on recommendation from colleagues who had used that person for four of five years and had seen how he or she reacted during various market fluctuations. Try to ask at least two or three people you know and trust to provide referrals. Interview at least two or three different professionals to see which one you feel most comfortable with (remember to pay attention to your instincts), and who seems the most informative, knowledgeable, and genuinely interested in educating you on investments and helping you achieve your objectives.

If you do not know anyone who can offer a referral, I suggest making appointments with two or three large and reputable institutions, such as Fidelity or RBC (I have no personal or professional stake in either of these companies), and talk to investment advisers and personal bankers.

Never invest in anything you don't understand.

■

Once you have chosen an adviser, build a relationship with her. It's important that she gets to know you so that she can better assess your needs and risk comfort level. Most financial advisers ask clients to fill out a form detailing their assets and liabilities (in which case you're way ahead of the game!) and financial goals. I suspect that an adviser will start by recommending relatively safe investments, treasuries, money market accounts, mutual funds, bonds, or municipal bond funds.

Mutual funds are investment companies whose job it is to handle investors' money by reinvesting it into stocks, bonds, or a combination of both. Mutual funds are divided into shares and can be bought much like stocks, which gives them a lot of liquidity, meaning they can be converted into cash with relative ease and certainty. I like mutual funds because of this liquidity, the ease of buying and selling them, and their diversification into many different securities. Money market funds, municipal bond funds, and bond funds are also generally considered conservative investments.

However, depending on market conditions, there can be more fluctuations in the underlying securities, which means the funds could have losses. I would suggest that every woman speak to her financial adviser or investment professional about the different options available to her for investing her money. Depending on her lifestyle, income, spending habits, savings, time horizon, and comfort level with risk, the adviser will help customize an investing and savings plan.

IN HER OWN WORDS

Jessica Einhorn

DEAN OF THE PAUL H. NITZE SCHOOL OF ADVANCED
INTERNATIONAL STUDIES AT JOHNS HOPKINS UNIVERSITY

Jessica Einhorn is the former managing director of the World Bank, the largest public banking institution in the world, which lends money to more than one hundred developing economies at reduced interest rates in support of community projects. Its primary focus is helping the poorest people and countries. She is now dean of the Paul H. Nitze School of Advanced International Studies at Johns Hopkins University. Prior to joining the World Bank, Einhorn held positions at the U.S. Treasury, the U.S. State Department, and the International Development Cooperation Agency of the United States.

(continued)

What's the most direct route to being happy?

If you have a passion for something, follow it and there will be a much greater probability of your succeeding in life. The other thing I say is that if you have the great luck of having health, education, family, and you live in a democracy, the world is all yours. Those things give you a choice of what you can do. Your life is yours to create. Not everyone has all those blessings. So if you have them, you have to hold yourself responsible for your own achievements. You only have one life, so you might as well enjoy what you are doing.

How did your passion manifest itself in your career?

In my case, I loved capital markets and found institutions where I could apply that interest, particularly the World Bank. I was able to do work for the benefit of developing countries. And because of the World Bank's size and distinction, I was privileged to work with some of the best minds in the world.

When I left the World Bank I thought about moving to the private sector. I made the decision, after having such a great life in the public sector, that going to the private sector was not likely going to feel that enriching. At a new chapter in my life, I wanted to do something new. When the opportunity to go to Johns Hopkins crossed my path, I initially thought educational administration wasn't something I was cut out for. With the encouragement of friends, I fell back in love with the school I attended.

Is money important for success?

I am not one of those people who says that money does not matter. I want to stress that I do not start with the notion that struggling to put food on the table is to be taken lightly. Being comfortable, generous, and able to provide education to young people are important goals. A certain amount of money is necessary for peace of mind. Being able to provide for your children is wonderful. I would not make money to give my kid a Mercedes, but I love the idea that a child can choose the college they want and be debt-free.

(continued)

On the other hand, if you look at career and choices, I truly do not think chasing wealth brings happiness. I always felt I was working on something bigger than money. It is really easy to go after money, but if you do that you quickly discover the relativity of wealth. You never feel wealthy if you chase money because you are always comparing yourself to the person who has more. I like clothing and a little jewelry, of course, but material things make demands.

A lot of people do want success, and if money is the metric they use to measure it by, then I say what they really want is to be as successful as someone else. Basing the desire to be successful on a relative measure (like another person's wealth) instead of a personal metric can be pretty self destructive. For example, if it's my metric to do something for the students at Johns Hopkins, then I will have satisfaction. If my metric is to be the hottest person in international affairs, then I think I'd be frustrated. How do I measure or compare outcomes?

How can we shape our own careers for optimal success?

Work for great bosses. Choosing the right bosses is very often on par with choosing the right job. Find someone to work for who will watch your back, someone who is not challenged by you and loves to see a young person flourish. That's really important. Absolutely make sure that you always do both the right ethical and the right legal thing. It does not matter who asks you to do something; you are accountable for what you do, so always do the right thing. I started my career during the Watergate scandal, so it was a good early lesson for me in the importance of working for people who insist on doing the right thing, because if you don't, you will have to walk or blow whistles.

Why don't more women invest?

I have not found, in my casual, anecdotal experience, that the average man knows any more about retail investing than a woman. They may be less timid about engaging in the stock market, they may be less worried about the outcome, but I have not found that they are more knowledgeable.

(continued)

> **What would you say to women to get them to invest?**
>
> For me it is always about reading. I actually think *The Playboy Investment Guide*, written nearly forty years ago, was the most-straightforward guide to asset classes and the great theory of index investing. *A Random Walk Down Wall Street* is a classic, and still in print. And I would recommend early books by John C. Bogle, the founder of Vanguard Funds, and David Swensen, the chief investment officer of Yale University, as good introductions. In our family we would give the young people Bogle and say to them, "Read it and then take one thousand dollars and invest it."

TALKING TAXES

Taxes are fascinating, controversial, and complex, just like a great novel. Here's an admission you won't hear many people make: I enjoy talking about taxes. At a party not long ago I met a tax accountant and ended up monopolizing her for the entire evening because it was so interesting to hear what was going on with tax rules. The rules change so frequently, there's always something new to learn. This fact also makes it impossible for me to pass along specific advice today because the tax landscape may be different tomorrow. However, I do think we should always see our tax bill as part of our overall financial strategy. After all, taxes are probably the most significant and consistent financial obligation we have. It's well worth paying attention to how much money we are contributing to the "common good" and consulting an expert as to how we might be able to retain more of it for our own good.

The 9-to-5 Tax Bill

Many people who work on a salary basis look at a tax refund as a gift or a bonus. It's not. It's your money, and it could have been deposited in a savings account or a certificate of deposit (CD) and have earned interest. That advantage is one reason why tax accountants want to get their clients as close to "break even" at tax time as possible, meaning come April 15th you don't owe anything, but you don't get anything back either.

There are limited ways for salaried people to put more money into their weekly paycheck. Determining the proper number of exemptions to claim is one of the most effective. According to Howard J. Samuels, CPA, a tax professional in New York City, "As far as planning goes for a salaried person, if she gets a big refund every year she should adjust the number of exemptions she claims. Exemptions represent people at the end of the year but during the year they are a legal way to adjust the tax dollars coming out of your paycheck." All individuals, trusts, and estates qualify for an exemption unless they are claimed as a dependent on another individual's tax return.

Those of you who own an apartment or a house will get a tax benefit based on the interest and property tax you pay. Technically, single homeowners should claim one exemption on an employee W-4 form. The reality is that they can legitimately claim more by estimating how much they are going to make in charitable donations and how much they will pay in interest and real estate taxes every year. Those amounts may be equivalent to the exemptions for three people. For example, Mary claims one exemption, for herself, on her tax return. She always donates a fixed sum to a nonprofit theater group she supports. She receives a twelve-hundred-dollar refund. If she had adjusted her exemptions by claiming two, she could have had an extra hundred dollars in her paycheck each month.

If you see that based on previous refund checks you are overpaying taxes throughout the year, you need to ask an accountant to help determine the number of exemptions you realistically should be taking. Alice is a single woman with no children, but she does have a very substantial mortgage on a recently purchased house. She claimed only one exemption so she will likely receive a big refund. One exemption means Alice has a job and only one person to support (herself), but it also means she has no mortgage, which in this case isn't true.

Alice consulted a tax professional who analyzed her situation and found, by looking at her expenses and income and consulting tax tables, that she could claim two additional exemptions because of that mega mortgage. She made a change to her W-4 form, which immediately put more money in her paycheck every week. She used it to help cover her monthly house payments.

Most companies reimburse employees for business-related out-of-pocket expenses. For those of you who work for small companies that don't reimburse expenses, they may represent eligible deductions. The government gives everyone a standard deduction; for a single person it is five thousand dollars. If your expenses total more than five thousand dollars, you can itemize the expenses by filling out Schedule A to demonstrate how they exceeded the five-thousand-dollar standard.

However, be sure to keep accurate records and documentation of expenses. It's wise to pay for such expenses, like professional publications, with a credit card because the IRS does not like to see cash receipts, says Samuels. "As far as the IRS is concerned, you could have picked up that cash receipt from the floor." There are two parts to every expense; one part is the receipt and the other is proof that it was paid. If you are a salaried person with numerous expenses, and you make many charitable donations and have questions about how you can adjust your exemptions, seek the help of a qualified accountant.

To be very clear, a refund check represents an interest-free loan to the government. The money you have been loaning to the government every year could be used to help establish your emergency fund or retirement account. You can also use the money to pay off high-interest debt, other than a mortgage or a student loan, says Samuels, who cautions to check student loan interest rates because the 2 percent window can close after ten years and go up to 9 percent. "If that's the case, consider using the extra money to pay it off sooner rather than later," he says.

Some of you might be saying, "Well, I would spend the extra money if I had it." On the other hand, how many of us spend our refunds as soon as we get them, and how many of us put them into the bank? In fact, many retailers depend on people to spend tax refunds, and often plan sales on home furnishings, kitchen appliances, and other high-ticket items to coincide with refund mailings to entice you to spend them. Bottom line: don't give the government an interest-free loan. It wouldn't do the same for you.

The Self-employed Tax Bill

Those of us who work for ourselves already know that our filing obligations are a bit more complicated than they are for those who receive a salary from a company. Schedule C, the tax form that allows itemization of business expenses that can adjust taxable income, is one distinguishing feature of tax preparation for the sole proprietor or self-employed. "You need to get fairly organized, and have all receipts that support your claims that exemptions are business-related in order and at the ready," says Samuels.

SUCCESS SECRET

Separate Business and Pleasure

It's wise to keep business expenses separate from personal expenses if you are self-employed. Although the IRS does not require doing so, establishing a second standard checking/savings account for the money you use for your business makes record keeping and filing easier and, frankly, safer. "The IRS is always favorably impressed by a person who is organized and serious, and who does not mingle their personal money with their business money," says CPA Howard Samuels.

The second account does not need to be a formal business account, which often comes with heavy service fees. A second personal account will suffice. Maintaining two credit cards, one used exclusively for business and the other for personal expenses, is another good idea and keeps records organized. "If you get audited, the auditor will ask for documentation of your Schedule C items. If you keep business expenses separate, they would generally not have the right to look at the charges on your second personal card," says Samuels.

To make paying taxes less of a burden on self-employed people, the IRS asks that they pay estimated quarterly taxes in April, June, September, and January of the following year. The IRS requires the self-employed person to pass one of two rules each year to avoid paying interest and penalties. The first is that you can pay 100 percent of the *previous* year's tax liability at any time during the year (if your income exceeds $150,000, you have to meet the test at 110 percent); the second is that you can pay 90 percent of the *current* year's taxes evenly (quarterly) during the year. As long as you have paid 100 percent (or 110 percent) of the amount paid last year, you do not have to pay interest and penalties even if your tax bill ends up being more than last year's. You do, of course, have to pay the difference by April 15. It's called the safe harbor rule.

Even with all the additional expense exemptions (taking clients out to dinner and travel) self-employed people are allowed to claim, those who run their own businesses always pay more taxes than other

(continued)

people. This is primarily because self-employed people must pay 100 percent of their Social Security tax. People who work for a company pay half, and their employer pays the other half, of the 15.3 percent Social Security tax. The remaining amount, 7.65 percent, is taken out of the employee's paycheck. This is one of many reasons why self-employed people need the help of a qualified tax specialist.

SUCCESS SECRET

Why a CPA?

Both of the tax experts you've heard from in this section are certified public accountants, or CPAs. If you need tax advice and planning help, I recommend that you seek the counsel of a CPA. Certified accountants are required by law to be up-to-date on all new tax laws, and they are specially trained to understand the tax implications of your financial decisions. In order to be a CPA you have to pass a nationwide exam that takes two days, or sixteen hours, to complete. On top of that, a CPA needs two years of experience and a certain amount of continuing education per year to maintain her status. New York is one of the toughest states to become certified in, and Florida is one of the easiest, so you might also want to check to see where your accountant is certified. You can use a CPA who is certified and works in a state other than the one you live in.

An accountant without a CPA could be very good, but remember that anyone can hang out a shingle that says "tax preparer." The noncertified person isn't required to demonstrate documentation of their up-to-date knowledge of tax laws. A non-CPA can't act on behalf of clients under various circumstances, such as signing extension forms on behalf of companies. Perhaps most important, a non-CPA has nothing at risk for signing as the paid preparer of the tax return. If the tax returns are incorrect and cause the taxpayer to owe money in penalties and interest, there is no real

(continued)

recourse against a non-CPA. A CPA, on the other hand, can be held liable for errors if he or she neglected to do the proper due diligence. If you can't find a CPA, the best advice I can offer is to learn as much as you can about tax preparation. This is important because individual tax preparers and large chain preparers don't usually ask any more questions than they have to and enter only the data they are given. Another option might be self-employed and small business software programs that could help you with your taxes if your situation is straightforward and uncomplicated. As your business grows, however, you may want to reconsider hiring a CPA.

Social Security taxes can be reduced somewhat if a portion of your total income comes from royalty payments. For instance, a writer who gets paid per project earns royalties when one of her books sells well. She would not have to pay Social Security taxes on those royalties. However, if a business is entirely dependent on royalties, the IRS considers that regular income and you have to pay Social Security tax on it. For instance, a designer friend of mine lends her name to a line of home products at a major retailer. That retailer pays her a royalty for the use of her name. She pays income tax on all those royalty earnings, because selling her name is what she does for a living.

Another, more complex, way a self-employed person can reduce her Social Security tab is by establishing her company as an S corporation, which allows her to pay herself a reasonable salary. The Social Security tax is based on the salary, not on the income, of the S corporation. However, an S corporation requires detailed book- and record keeping. It costs substantially more to incorporate than it does to remain a self-employed individual, and accountant fees are about three times higher because corporate-level tax preparation is complicated.

A simpler route is to establish an LLC, which is a business structured so that its owners are not personally liable for debts or other business liabilities such as damages from lawsuits. An LLC helps avoid double taxation. Double taxation is the result of certain tax laws too obscure to explain here that cause the same earnings to be taxed twice. An LLC does not offer any benefits in terms of Social Security taxes; however, the main benefit is that it keeps personal property safe in the event that a client or customer sues the business.

An LLC is now super easy to establish—I did it online in just a few minutes for a few hundred dollars. Sites such as llc.com, smallbiz.com, and ladieswholaunch.com guide small-business people through the process. The exact rules for forming an LLC vary by state, and online LLC services generally take this into account during the application process. An accountant or attorney can also set up an LLC.

Clearly, anyone who has her own business or plans to start one must have a good accountant, if only to help prepare annual tax returns. A good accountant also comes in handy whenever a question arises about the tax implications of any business decisions or purchases. When in doubt, ask a pro.

REAL ESTATE

Owning real estate, as I mentioned earlier, offers tax benefits in that mortgage interest and real estate taxes are deductible. But these advantages can be limited, depending on income and location. In New York, for example, if real estate and income taxes are more than a certain amount, deduction benefits may not be available. That said, there are two reasons to buy real estate. The first is as a place to live, and the second is purely as an investment (e.g., a rental property, land that you want to develop, or property you plan to resell at a profit).

If you are considering buying property to live in or build a home on, I have a simple rule. Do you plan on being in that location for four or more years? If so, then buying makes sense. Thinking of moving in less than that time? If your answer is yes, consider renting. The costs involved in closing on a house, combined with the mortgage, interest, and property taxes, could be so substantial that it may not make sense to relocate and have to sell the house in the near future. If buying is an option, check your trusty Asset and Liability worksheet (see page 86) to see if there is adequate money for a 10 or 20 percent down payment.

Don't forget to examine the FSP to ensure your ability to easily make mortgage payments every month. No one should be "house poor" and as a result struggle to pay the mortgage. In such a situation, a house becomes an albatross around your neck, and will adversely impact your quality of life. However, building equity in a family home is at once deeply satisfying (pride of ownership and all that goes with it) and practical (it's a place to live that, as long as payments are made, can't be taken away).

As you would for other kinds of investments, I suggest doing a significant amount of research, educating yourself about the market, and talking to your financial adviser before putting any money down on a real estate property, no matter how good a deal you may think it is at first glance.

ESTATE PLANNING: INSURANCE, TRUSTS, AND WILLS

How many of you are thinking, "Oh, Marianna, come on, *estate planning*? I don't have an estate!" Oh, but you do. I am not talking about a country manor with staff. An estate is everything you own, including all of your assets (house, land, investments, and personal property) and liabilities. Since you calculated your assets and liabilities in chapter 4, you know exactly what's in your estate. Now you can think about what to do with it to protect it, and to ensure that it falls into the right hands in the event of death or incapacitation. I know, I know, no one wants to think about something that gloomy right now. But I would argue that one of the most important ways to respect your assets and money is by protecting them and making them available to beneficiaries after you're gone.

It's true that extensive estate planning is not necessary for a single young woman with limited assets and no dependents. However, as you begin to earn, save, and invest money, accumulate or inherit property or other valuable possessions (jewelry, artwork), and start a family, planning for the future is essential no matter how old you are. Honestly, I did not adjust my estate planning until after I was married and had a baby. When my son was about six months old I knew I had to act and plan for his future. There are several ways for you to ensure a secure future for your family and protect the wealth you have built.

LIFE INSURANCE

How many of you have thought this about life insurance: "No, I don't need it"? Life insurance is important for most people to have, even young, healthy, single women with no dependents. In the event of our death, any financial obligations and funeral costs would be taken care of by the payout from the policy and would not burden family members who may not be able to afford these costs.

The advantage of buying a policy while young and healthy is its low price. It is much less expensive to buy a policy when you are in your twenties, thirties, or even your forties than to buy one as an older person. At that point you are catching up on your life expectancy, and you may have ailments that make it more difficult to find affordable insurance, or any insurance at all. "Term life insurance is so affordable, you'll hardly notice the yearly bill. And if you buy it when you're young, you don't have to worry about it later," says Nancy Curtin, an insurance expert and owner of SmartFuture, LLC, in New York City. It is best to work with a good insurance planner to determine current and future needs, and then lock in the best possible rate.

There are two basic kinds of life insurance, term and permanent. I suggest that most people buy term insurance that is good for a specific period of time, normally twenty or thirty years. This product is seen as a vehicle to protect minor children and any dependents you have or until your nest egg is big enough to take care of them if something unfortunate should happen to you.

Permanent (sometimes called whole life) policies have a savings component called cash value that builds over time and is another relatively low-risk, low-growth way to accumulate savings. However, Barry Zischang, an adviser with RBC Wealth Management, offers some caveats to consider before purchasing permanent life insurance. "The premiums are higher than for term insurance, so it is more important to have a retirement account established, along with basic savings and educational funds, before putting additional savings into a life insurance policy." Also, permanent insurance requires that you must pay premiums until you die, which, given longevity statistics, could be a very long time. "Women live longer than men, so you can get competitive term rates well into your fifties," says Barry.

So how do you find a term policy? Those of you who work for large corporations likely have access to basic, inexpensive, partially subsidized term policies. However, it may be a better idea to have your own life insurance policy. An independent insurance agent—someone who works with a variety of carriers—can steer you in the direction of a policy that fits your needs and pocketbook. He can help you determine how much coverage you need. Your financial adviser can also help you with insurance policies.

As always, recommendations from friends, colleagues, and family members are a good way to find reputable agents. When it comes to insurance salesmen, if you feel pressured to buy any particular product, steer clear. Insurance agents are compensated by a percentage of the premiums they write with an insurer the first year they write the policy and every subsequent year the policy is active. If an agent is pressuring you, they could be trying to sell you a policy that works for them (because it pays a high commission) and not for you. Work with someone you like and trust and always read the fine print. "There's no general right or wrong in terms of buying life insurance. You just have to know exactly what you are buying," says Barry.

TRUSTS

A revocable living trust is basically a contract in which you state that you (as "grantor") are transferring your property and assets into a living trust for the benefit of yourself during your lifetime (lifetime beneficiary), and after that, for the benefit of your heirs (remainder beneficiaries). Barry Zischang says that even though you may think a trust is only for wealthy people, or that, for example, young or single women are not in a position to think about setting up a trust, that's not necessarily true. If you have any assets that you want to protect, a trust is a valuable tool.

"We should all be thinking about it right now because we do not know in terms of our own mortality what will happen, and second, if you have assets of value you need to express your wishes about what happens to them through a trust or a will. Otherwise, the courts will have to rely on your state of residence's statutes, and those are rigid and may be contrary to what you want," says Barry.

When you establish a trust, you become its "trustee," meaning that you have complete control over its assets. The "successor trustee" that you name takes control of the trust if you are incapacitated or when you die. Because it is revocable, you can change or amend the provisions of the trust at any point in your life. A living trust is also confidential and the transfer of assets is kept from public view, unlike a will. On the other hand, living trusts, because they are a viable entity during the grantor's lifetime, can be expensive to draft and implement because there are many documents involved. Depending on where you live, and the value of the estate, a trust could cost hundreds or thousands of dollars more than a will to establish.

Despite the extra costs to draw the revocable living trust, I like the flexibility and many benefits it offers. All of my assets, including investments and property, are in a trust. Another benefit of a revocable living trust is that the assets are transferred to the beneficiaries immediately, leaving no room for arguments and no after-the-fact legal fees.

WILLS

A will takes effect upon the death of its author. You can create a will in several ways: write your own, create it online, or draw one up with the help of an estate lawyer. Wills do not need to be done by an attorney, but they do need to conform to state law and be witnessed. Most states require two witnesses, while a few require three. Likewise, some states require a notary and others don't. To find out the laws in your state, check the Web site http://law.findlaw.com/state-laws/wills/. It is generally advisable that witnesses *not* be beneficiaries of the estate. That could cause conflict-of-interest problems later on.

A will is usually less expensive to establish than a trust because there is less paperwork involved and no associated administrative obligations, as there are with a living trust. There are a few drawbacks to creating a will. One is that it is not a private document. The public has access to it, including creditors who may be looking for funds owed to them and family members who disagree with their inheritance or were not included in the will and feel as if they should have been. However, there is a very short statute of limitations period, which varies from state to state, for creditors and others to bring claims after your death. Once that period has passed, creditors cannot, by law, assert claims against heirs.

Second, most wills go to probate unless they are distributing a small amount of money (less than thirty thousand dollars). Probate is a court-supervised process that determines if the will maker's final statement is legitimate. It can take six months to two years to be completed, and generally costs about 3 to 4 percent of the value of the assets. Furthermore, a will can be contested (which means someone can make a legal argument that the will's provisions are not valid), which can take years to sort out. Disagreements among beneficiaries can make probate last even longer, and make dealing with the probate court system and bureaucracy a frustrating experience.

That said, even a simple will provides some sense of security. Even those with a trust must have a will to cover items not included in their trust, such as jewelry, artwork, and personal possessions. In such cases, a will can be a simple document, and any lawyer specializing in estates can create one. Wills are also a good option for people who do not have substantial financial assets or property, say, less than thirty thousand dollars.

The Respect Money Checklist

Think of ways to start respecting your money *right now* by saving more of it, for example, or by making an appointment with a financial adviser or putting away money for a down payment on a condo. Make a "Respect Money To-Do List" and bring some fun into this because saving, investing, and planning seem *so very serious.* For instance, why not dress up to go to your abundance group, and serve tea in beautiful porcelain cups. Or plan a potluck supper for after the meeting. Allow three to six months to complete the list, and then assess how you did. Here's an example:

1. Start a savings account with fifty dollars a week.
2. Ask friends and colleagues to recommend a good insurance agent.
3. Buy *Investing for Dummies*—and read it!

4. Ask your bank what you need to do to be preapproved for a mortgage.
5. Talk to financial advisers at three different financial institutions, choose one, and seek her help.

Whew! That really wasn't so bad, was it? It's true that when it comes to respecting money, there is so much to think about and so much to do. It may seem insurmountable at times, but it's not. If you address your money issues bit-by-bit, step-by-step, they can be resolved more quickly than you might have imagined. Now we are moving on to even more breathtaking activities because once you've made up your mind to be Rich, Happy, and Fabulous, and once you've taken control of your finances, every opportunity is open to you, every dream can come true, every goal is within your reach. I have *no doubt* about it, and neither will you when we're done!

Respect Money Summary:
- Make a habit of saving.
- Plan for your retirement needs—no time is too soon.
- Build an emergency fund to cover six to eights months of expenses.
- Save for long-term goals.
- Save for special items and adventures that give lasting pleasure.
- Learn the basics of investing and get involved at a comfortable, diversified level.
- Ensure that your tax liability is calculated accurately.
- Address estate-planning needs, including life insurance, trusts, and wills.

PART THREE

Make Your Dreams a Reality

$\mathcal{L}$et's move forward. Parts 1 and 2 showed you how to say yes to your well-being, rediscover the fun of living, and develop an unshakable confidence in yourself and your dreams to bring you closer to financial freedom and living the life you deserve. Learning to love and respect money creates a "can do" attitude that is important to getting on top of your finances. Your financial picture is coming into focus, and continued clarity about money keeps your abundance and prosperity goals on track. The dynamic set of tools in part 3 of *Live It, Love It, Earn It* will help you become even more empowered and self-confident about your money and your life.

6.

Claim Your Power

WE ALL HAVE incredible power to control our money, our lives, and our happiness. No one can take that power away unless we allow it to happen. When you choose *not* to use your power or when you give it over to someone else, your life becomes smaller and more constrained. If you have been giving your power over to a particular environment, parents, friends, a job, or your spouse by letting them (or it) dictate how you live and what you think, it is time for you to make a change and take your power back.

While it's true that we are all born into specific and unique circumstances, we are not bound to or by them. From the moment you were old enough to think for yourself, to reason, and to use logic, you could change, re-create and govern your world. For instance, before you came of age legally you were probably living at home and obliged to follow "house rules." On the other hand, you had the freedom to do well in school, find a job to earn extra money, and choose friends wisely. As an adult you can select whatever path in life you want—to study, to become a mother or an entrepreneur (or both), to climb the corporate ladder, to travel freely, to move from country to city or vice versa, and so on. There are a few house rules now—you have obligations to meet (paying bills, showing up for work), sole responsibility for your choices and actions, and complete control over your money and life. You have the power to choose, and your power is found in the choices you make.

THE POWER TO CHOOSE

You are the product of your choices. In other words, you have a tremendous amount of say over who you are, what you do, and where you end up. When you decide not to use your power or when you give it over to someone else, that's when life becomes sad and restricted. Even small annoyances rob you of your self-possession and productivity when you choose to respond in an unproductive manner. When you allow common matters—a mix-up at the dry cleaner's or a call to the phone company about your bill—aggravate you to the point of anger, you are forfeiting your power. If we make a habit of letting the little things get to us, eventually we become psychologically crippled.

I was in Whole Foods one Friday afternoon picking up a few items for the weekend. It was very busy, and the lines were long but moving. I love watching people, so as I waited for the next available checker I observed two women ahead of me. They could not have been more different. One was industriously checking her BlackBerry. When she was done, realizing that she still had a few minutes to wait, she calmly took a news magazine out of her bag to read an article. The checker actually had to call to her to get her attention. The other woman, right next to her in line, tapped her foot impatiently, sighed loudly, and shot dirty looks at any employee unlucky enough to enter her line of vision. She was fuming all because she was stuck on a line. When she finally paid for her items, she called her checker a jerk and stormed out of the store.

If I had asked these women if they thought the line was slow, I predict the first one would have said no and the second woman would have probably bitten my head off. Which one has more personal power? The woman who comes prepared for every eventuality, or the one who lets trivialities turn a perfectly nice day into a horrendous one?

*True personal power is the ability to take control of your life so
it works for you, not against you*

■

What about circumstances that we create ourselves? Not long ago my
friend Laura realized that she had given her power over to a charitable
organization. Members of its steering committee would call several
times a day to ask for one favor or another. "I would drop everything
and help no matter what else I was doing." Laura was neglecting things
that were important to her because she gave so much time to the charity and eventually started to get angry with the people there. "Then
I realized that it was *my* responsibility to set time boundaries in the
relationship." Because Laura hadn't done so earlier, naturally the people at the organization felt comfortable calling her without constraint.
"Funny thing is, when I voiced my concerns with the charity's board
members, they were completely understanding and accommodating."
That was an important lesson: if people really want our skills and time,
they are generally willing to wait for them and work around our other
commitments.

Then there are the many things in life that come with strings attached. They too can tie up your power if you allow them to. A young
woman I know, Jamie, is fortunate to have parents who give her money
and pay for all of her expenses as long as she works in the family's ar-
chitectural design business. This probably sounds wonderful to many
of you, but she is totally beholden to her parents and the many caveats
and restrictions they place on her. On top of this she has no interest or
passion for architecture. Her dream is to study dance. Still, Jamie told
me she plans to follow her parents' rules and stay in the family business, because she wants the money and because it's much easier than
starting over. I'm not so sure how happy she'll be. Only time will tell
if her decision was worth it. There can be strings attached to relationships with friends and lovers, family and employers. Do you have such
strings in your life? To which strings are you willing to be tethered, and
which ones can you untie?

Identify Your Power Drains

Make a list of the people, organizations, and things that you give more power to than you should (a job, a coworker, your sister, boyfriend, friend, husband, a volunteer commitment, the editorial page of a particular newspaper, etc.). Next to each make a note of why or how this power shift happens. Consider how giving away your power interferes with your ability to achieve what you really desire in your life. Go through the list and come up with solutions to take back your power: Commit to working on skills that help you keep your cool so that your buttons can't be easily pushed. Make a plan to extricate yourself from situations that are choking you. Make the time to focus on being true to yourself without being influenced by outside events, people, or situations.

THE POWER OF BEING A WOMAN

Being a woman is a great natural resource. Some of us have a tendency to shut down our femininity for fear that we won't be taken seriously. But when you cut yourself off from your own identity as a woman you run the risk of being thought of as one of the guys, becoming invisible, or becoming an aggressive bully. These are ineffective forms of overcompensation for what we mistakenly think is a disadvantage: being a woman.

Femininity is the sum total of your inner strength, poise, quiet determination, and gentle but firm resolve; it's your essence and your charm, not to mention your physical attributes—hair, eyes, skin. Yes, your physical attributes and interpersonal skills do have an impact on everyone you meet, and they are positive ones, especially in professional settings. Allowing your inner light to shine through will actually yield better results throughout the day. Being your best self is a great aid in navigating the world, inspiring others, negotiating for a raise, leading people, starting a business, or working up the corporate ladder.

My friend and colleague Elizabeth Webb, a private relationship coach and CEO of La Vida Femme (lavidafemme.com) defines femininity as a woman's characteristic sense of fun, spontaneity, and creativity. "Use your feminine energy to get noticed. Take pleasure in yourself in the presence of others. Women can get away with telling the boss he's sporting a great tie or that she's wearing a beautiful dress. We can laugh and show energetic enthusiasm and still be taken seriously," says Elizabeth.

There's no reason to shut down our femininity even if we find ourselves in corporate environments. "If everyone is wearing gray, that does not mean you have to wear gray," says Elizabeth. "You can still display your professionalism in a pink suit." Feel free to decorate your cubicle or office with fresh flowers, and never hesitate to offer genuine compliments or praise. Most important of all, by word and deed, give other people permission to enjoy themselves in our presence, says Elizabeth. That is truly feminine power. If you do so, people who are attracted to your inner light, who feel comfortable and happy around you, will do whatever they can to promote your cause. As Elizabeth sees it, and I agree, you get a zing of energy every time you have a pleasant exchange with a coworker or a superior. "Delightful interactions, which you have the power to give, help you survive and thrive even on the worst days," she says.

Free Your Femininity

Elizabeth Webb has a trick up her sleeve if you feel as if your femininity is on the fritz. Try her suggestion for at least one week, after which you will most likely be hooked for life. "Wear one piece of clothing or accessory every day that pays tribute to your femininity," says Elizabeth. "It's a physical reminder that you're a fabulous woman." This could be any of the following:

- Scented or sparkly lip gloss or lipstick in a deep, sophisticated shade
- A colorful watch—perhaps with a bright blue or patent leather red band
- A silky camisole under a satin suit or a work-appropriate dress or a pencil skirt instead of your usual suit
- A distinctive pair of glasses
- Funky-colored, patterned tights or silk stockings instead

of panty hose under a more formal suit or dress
+ A higher heel than usual in basic black or a classic shoe in your favorite bright color to put some sass in your step
+ A beautiful bracelet on your nondominant hand

DON'T RELY ON A MAN

All of us have the power and ability to create our own financial freedom. If you plan to rely on a man for your future financial security, think again; you could be taking a big gamble. Many of us at one time or another have secretly hoped that someone would come along for the rescue, and give us a life that we can actually give to ourselves. Even if Prince Charming does come along, sometimes it's not always what we expected. There are also, unfortunately, disagreements, divorce, death, or other factors and events that could leave us in a vulnerable position. None of us wants to think about such things, but they can and do happen. For those of you with great marriages or partnerships, you *still* have to do for yourself. It is unwise to leave your future and finances in someone else's hands entirely.

"A man should be an equal partner, not the CEO of the household," says Elizabeth Webb. "The best relationships happen when both parties are working together toward the same goals and hold the same values," she says. "You could be giving up a lot when you marry a man only for his money. A little piece of yourself goes along with it." Are you willing to give that up?

It would be unfortunate if we women gave up our dreams, desires, and a part of ourselves for supposed security. When Jennifer married Bob she quit a job she loved, one that gave her a sense of satisfaction, self-worth, and financial freedom. It was her dream. All that was gone, and when Bob became very demanding and controlling, Jennifer went into a tailspin of depression, feeling she was no longer in control of her life. Bob expected her to account for every penny she spent and every moment of her day.

Don't give up your dream for a "security blanket."

■

Jennifer barely left the house, and when she did it was only to run an errand. Whenever a friend asked to meet for coffee or see a movie, she declined. Spiritually diminished, Jennifer sought the help of an open-minded pastor, an old family friend. It took a lot of talking, quiet time, and inner work for Jennifer to realize that her so-called security was too "expensive." It cost her her self-esteem. Eventually, Jennifer left Bob, went back to work, and regained her sense of self-worth. It took time and there were many hardships along the way, but Jennifer did reclaim her power and says it was well worth it.

"I left a man who looked great on paper: Wall Street job, Ivy League pedigree, expensive suits . . . the whole nine yards. Unfortunately, he cheated on me," says my friend Anna, a real estate agent. When she finally ended the relationship she was able to look after her career and is fast becoming one of the most sought-after and successful agents in Manhattan. "The experience also crystallized for me what I was looking for in a mate. A trophy boyfriend is no longer important to me," she says. Anna is now happily engaged to a New York City firefighter, has tripled her earnings in the last few years, and has established substantial savings and valuable real estate investments.

Some of us relinquish our power to a man even when he doesn't want us to. Julia was a consultant to hospital administrators all over the country. It was a high-pressure, high-reward job, one that put her in daily contact with very smart and interesting people. "It was exciting," says Julia. "I wanted to be the best in the business, and I was."

When Julia and her husband, Ted, started a family, Ted was open to the idea of a nanny or day care, but Julia was less enthusiastic about leaving the care of her children in the hands of others. "Ted runs his own accounting firm with a large staff, so taking a three- or five-year leave of absence really was not an option. I was a one-woman show, so bowing out of the workforce would be less complicated for me." Even though Ted did not want Julia to completely give up her work, because he knew how happy it made her, Julia made the decision to stay home with her two children until the youngest was ready to start nursery school. "I never regretted the time I spent at home raising my children," she says. "It made a difference to their self-esteem, intellect, and socialization."

A few years passed. Julia and Ted had to make a decision about schooling and felt their only alternative was to move to a suburb where the public schools were considered to be as good as private schools. Julia did not want to leave the city she loved so dearly for its culture, excitement, and diversity. Ultimately, she made a compromise that left her feeling as if she were missing a piece of herself.

Then, about a year after moving, with Ted's urging, Julia figured out a way to make her new circumstances work for her. She would open her firm again, and use the city apartment as an office. This way she could enjoy the city during the week when her children were at school, and work on establishing herself in the hospital administration business again. "I realized that I was the only one who thought my situation was unchangeable," she told me. "My husband and children support me and my business is growing at a pace I can manage and enjoy." Each of us has the power to change our life at any time, and if something is truly important to you, don't let it go. Hold on to what you have, what you love. There are always ways to make it work.

Another possibility you have to consider is that unforeseen events, people, or relationships may take away your power in an instant. If we are not prepared for the unexpected we can be dangerously vulnerable. Stella, for instance, found herself at a crossroads when she lost her husband in a car accident several years ago. No one can be prepared emotionally for such a tragedy, but Stella had the added burden of not being equipped financially. She had been very happy in her life with George, but when he died she saw that she had neglected her own responsibility to make sure her children were provided for in case of an emergency.

"Before I was married and had children, I worked in the music business, and it was demanding," she says. "When I started a family I made a career switch and found a part-time job in a doctor's office." Stella's income was reduced, but her husband made a good living and provided everything the family needed. Even though George had a life insurance policy and some savings, neither was adequate to see their children into adulthood. "It was a profoundly important moment for me, seeing how I had taken so much for granted," she says.

With the help of her family she not only got back on her feet, but she also discovered a new passion. "Working with patients is incredibly rewarding. I enrolled in school to become an obstetrics nurse. In addition, I have become serious about saving and retirement planning, as well as mapping out an investment plan for my children's college educations."

While the loss of her spouse was devastating for Stella and her children, the tragedy forced her to reclaim her power. "For so many years, it was me, me, me. And that self-centeredness actually stripped me of my power because I assumed my husband would take care of everything. Now I am competent, strong, and completely self-reliant. It's a great feeling."

IN HER OWN WORDS

Sonia Gardner

PRESIDENT AND MANAGING PARTNER OF AVENUE CAPITAL GROUP

Sonia Gardner is the cofounder, president, and managing partner of Avenue Capital Group, a global investment management firm focused on the distressed markets. Since she cofounded the firm with her brother in 1995, Avenue Capital Group has grown to thirteen offices worldwide and currently manages more than $17 billion in assets. Sonia, who has more than twenty years of experience in the financial world, is the recipient of the 100 Women in Hedge Funds' 2008 Industry Leadership Award. This honor recognizes individuals whose professional dedication, innovation, passion, and ethics set a standard of excellence for the industry.

How do women become as successful (and honored) in their careers as you have become?

First, you have to be passionate about what you do and truly love it. I didn't face the same career challenges that many women in our industry face in working their way up the corporate ladder. It was just my brother and me when we started, so there was basically nobody else on the ladder. But I faced different challenges—at the top of the list was the challenge of building a firm that not only was financially successful but also had a reputation for maintaining its integrity at all times. I have always believed that the most valuable asset you have as a leader is your integrity—and the only way to become successful and maintain long-term success is to ensure that your integrity is never compromised.

(continued)

Tell us more about how you found yourself working in hedge funds.

Getting into this business for me was an accident, which is often the best way for careers to start. My brother had left RD Smith to start his own business, and he needed a lawyer he trusted to work with him. I had just graduated from law school and didn't have a job at the time, so I said I would help him until I found another job. The rest is history—I loved the distressed investment business and the challenge of building our own firm. In 1990 we started our own brokerage firm, Amroc Investments, specializing in distressed debt. It was a big risk at the time because we had no capital and it was just the two of us. We built the company slowly, and over the next ten years Amroc became the largest privately held boutique brokerage firm in the distressed market. In 1995 we started our second business—Avenue Capital Group—with just $7 million under management. We decided that it was a good idea to start a money management firm and effectively create a hedge against our distressed brokerage business. In 2001, we closed Amroc to focus exclusively on Avenue, which in hindsight turned out to be the right decision.

The moral of the story is to have an open mind and be willing to take risks. My brother and I built the business gradually, and made changes when necessary. We always gave it 100 percent and we were never worried about accomplishing goals on a rigid timetable.

How do you define "success"?

Success is not only defined by the amount of money you make! Success is about building an organization that you are proud of and passionate about, being respected in your industry, and earning the confidence and loyalty of your clients and employees.

Holding on to your values defines *success*—that is a very important piece of the puzzle. I believe you should never compromise your values for some kind of "perceived" success. You will never achieve success if you allow yourself to justify unethical decisions or make decisions that clash with your core values. Success is about "doing the right thing" and being committed to maintaining high standards

(continued)

of ethical behavior throughout the organization. I strongly believe that establishing an ethical tone at the top is what ultimately sustains an organization over the long term. A commitment to maintaining the highest ethical standards of the firm must be ingrained in the culture. That's true whether you have one employee, hundreds, or even thousands.

If you want to become successful, you also have to surround yourself with people who not only act with integrity but also are the best at what they do. Having people more knowledgeable than you in a particular area should never be viewed as a threat. We have always strived to hire people who are experts in their area because they help to improve and grow the organization.

How do you deal with volatility in the market, job landscape, and economy?

You have to learn to adapt to the ups and downs of the market and be willing to shift your business in response to changes in the economy. In a business like ours, which is literally defined by volatility and risk, I've found it to be essential, regardless of what is going on around me, to keep things in perspective and to remain calm and focused. This philosophy is definitely being put to the test in these unprecedented times.

How do other women make the leap into an area they are passionate about?

I was willing to take risks and explore opportunities I had not thought about before. I encourage women to do the same, especially when you're young and have time, flexibility, and resilience. The only way to really know if you like something is to try it. Internships, even when they are unpaid, are a great way to learn and build experience. Women should reach out to other women in the industry who have established successful careers, and join professional networks. Most important, every woman needs to believe in herself and should not allow anyone to tell her that she can't accomplish her goals.

SPEAK UP . . . THEN SHUT UP

Doing business, getting ahead, negotiating, and asking for (and getting) what you want, are incredibly scary propositions for many of us. There are two things we have to learn how to do in order to conquer what's keeping us from getting ahead: shutting up and *not* shutting up. The tricky part is in understanding when to do one and not the other.

Speak Up

There are many times at work or at home when we have to do some talking—not complaining, not explaining, but straightforward, upfront talking. Asking for what we deserve—a raise, help, information—is difficult for many of us. Recently I needed to get some information about one of my investments. I called the investment manager many times, but he would not return my phone calls. It was hard for me to understand his unresponsiveness because I was a good client who had entrusted a sum of money to him to invest. Besides, I have been in his position myself; returning client phone calls and providing information was always a priority for me and should be for anyone working in a customer-service-oriented business.

What made the situation even more infuriating was the rudeness of the manager's assistant. She tried to minimize my concerns, hushed me up, refused to answer questions specifically, and generally tried to make me feel as if it were not my place to be calling about my account. Although my anger was justified, I always maintained my composure when calling and e-mailing the office. As hard as it was for me, I also sent continuous good thoughts the manager's way, and wished him well (it does no good to wish ill of anyone). Finally, after weeks of calling, I received the answers I was looking for.

Requesting appropriate compensation is also a challenge. If we are sure we are entitled to more money or a better position, then why are we hesitant to ask for it? An old and dear friend, Donna, is a freelance physical therapist. For many years she struggled with how to set her hourly and day rates. "Since I am in a helping profession, I felt I shouldn't be charging a standard rate once a patient's insurance ran out and she was paying me directly," she says. Donna felt especially guilt-ridden about setting market-rate fees when working with elderly people living on fixed incomes.

About a year ago, Donna was talking to one of her colleagues about what she charged patients. "I was coaching her on negotiating fees. About a week later she told me how successful my guidance had been." Donna had to laugh, otherwise she would have cried. "I had to work up the courage to start taking my own advice." When she did, Donna was amazed that no one even blinked at her new, more standard rates, including clients who paid her the old rate. She realized there had been no reason to feel guilty about asking for a standard rate, instead of one that was much less than the majority of PTs charged. "Some of them even told me they thought I had been *undercharging*."

Making a case for advancement is another tough one for many of us. Some women sit back and wait (hope?) for a promotion to come along, but reward and accomplishment don't often happen that way. Jenny, a twenty-four-year-old media-marketing manager, took a more active route. She started her career right out of college at a magazine publisher as an assistant to an editor. After a year on the job, she told her boss that she wanted to sell advertising. "She told me I was too young to sell. Well, I thanked her for considering my request, and also told her honestly that I would be looking for a job in sales." Jenny knew she would be good in sales. "I explained to my boss that I wanted to be the person presenting, selling, and talking to people, taking clients out. I did not want to be the person sitting in the office." Jenny's boss didn't want to lose her to another company, so she referred her to another company publication. At the time, magazines were establishing Internet arms, and they were looking for people who had media experience.

That publication was impressed with Jenny's enthusiasm and started her out as a sales associate. "It meant making cold calls to small accounts and closing tiny deals for five thousand dollars. Now, just a few years later, I am making five-hundred-thousand-dollar deals," says Jenny. After two years she was promoted to account executive. Yet she had her sights set on becoming a regional sales manager. Again, her supervisor told her she was too young to do the job. "I didn't stay silent. I told them I was already doing the job I was asking to be recognized for." The company offered a small increase that was within their standard guidelines.

SUCCESS SECRET

The Velvet Threat

When Jenny wanted a raise she used a technique that I call the Velvet Threat: giving a polite, honest response when a valid request is denied. This technique can be effective only if you (1) are delivering the goods, (2) know that you can easily get another job if need be or are willing to lose the one you have, *and* (3) use the technique sparingly. Like ultra-hot chili sauce, a small dose of the Velvet Threat is enough—you do not need much to make an impact. And don't be the girl who cried wolf. If you threaten your boss all the time, no matter how soft and lovely your delivery, eventually she will tire of your constant demands and send you packing. Timing is important too. Should you threaten to quit during a recession or at a downtime in your industry when competitors may have imposed hiring freezes? Maybe not.

Once again, Jenny said thank you, but she would have to go. "The director of HR asked what she could do to keep me on board. I reiterated what I had said before, that I wanted to be a regional sales manager at a particular salary." While the company thought about Jenny's request she wasted no time and talked to other companies. "I interviewed at other firms, and received two job offers with the titles and pay I wanted. I brought the offers back to my company and said, 'This is what I could get elsewhere.' Once a company knows other people want you, you have power." Her old company could not even come close to what the other jobs were offering, so Jenny took one of the jobs, and left on good terms. She might be back someday, after all.

It's been only five years since Jenny started working, and she is working on top accounts and has two people reporting to her. "I am probably one of the youngest regional sales managers in this company, but it took a lot of hard work, risk, and speaking up. If I had not talked about what I wanted I could still be sitting at my old company letting other people make decisions for me." Many women are afraid to do what Jenny did. Even *she* admits that she was worried that her boss might just fire her. And certainly that can happen, but not as often as people fear.

Shut Up

You may not get what you want right off the bat, like Jenny did, but you increase your negotiating success if, after you speak up, you *shut up*. Many women have a tendency to overexplain, apologize unnecessarily, and try to justify their very existence when they ask for more of anything. Silence is golden when we are asking for a raise or a promotion, or even a favor. Ask, and then stop talking, or do what I call, simply, the Shut Up Success Secret (see box). For example, one of my bosses had promised to give me a bonus if I met certain sales goals. I met the established goals, which he acknowledged. I waited a few weeks, and then asked him about the extra bonus he promised. I sat in his office and did not say a word until *he* broke the silence.

I cannot tell you how difficult this was for me. The five minutes we sat there not saying anything seemed like five hours. Finally, he broke the silence and agreed to honor his word. Later on he told me I "won" because I confidently asked for what I wanted, and did not give a laundry list of reasons why I deserved the money. I *shut up* and waited for his answer. Because he agreed to the bonus earlier I don't think I won anything; he simply gave me what I was promised. Had I argued or complained, I would have been "showing my hand" and he may well have found a way to get out of his promise. The more information you give, the more they have to use to deny your request

---

SUCCESS SECRET

Shut Up

Use this technique to ask for what you want:

1. Ask for what you want.
2. Stop talking, and let the other person respond.
3. Never break the silence ("fill the void") by offering a laundry list of reasons why you need a raise or a promotion or whatever it is you are requesting.

(continued)

So many of us, when asking for a raise, have to mention that it will help pay the rent, get us out of credit card debt, or cover our bills. As hard as it is to believe, most bosses usually do not care. Once you start explaining, you have lost before you have even begun.

One minute can seem like an eternity when you are waiting for the other person to speak. To make the void less tempting to fill with your words, try the following three techniques:

+ *Sit on your hands.* I am not sure why this works, but it does. Maybe it reminds you to sit on your tongue!
+ *Think about what you will do for dinner tonight.* Make a recipe in your head, or imagine yourself sitting down in a restaurant and ordering a four-course dinner.
+ *Count to one hundred.* Concentrating on sequential numbers makes time go faster, but be sure not to lose your train of thought when the other person starts talking.

IN HER OWN WORDS

Nina DiSesa

CHAIRMAN OF MCCANN ERICKSON NEW YORK AND AUTHOR

Nina has worked in the quintessential boys' clubs of advertising for almost thirty years. In 1994, she became the first woman executive creative director for McCann Erickson New York, the flagship office of the largest advertising agency in the world. In 1998, she was made chairman as well as chief creative officer of McCann New York. In 1999, Nina was chosen by *Fortune* magazine as one of the "50 Most Powerful Women in American Business." In 2005, she received the Matrix Award, given each year to a select group of women in communication. In 2007, she was inducted into the Hall of Fame for CEBA (Creative Excellence in Business Advertising). She is the author of the book *Seducing the Boys Club.*

(continued)

Can women make a lot of money working for a big company?

I always felt if you were happy and good at what you did, money would come as a byproduct. As I moved along in my career I became conscious of the sucker factor—was I making less money than my counterpart because I was a woman and the other guy was a man? Probably. Even though I loved what I was doing, it didn't take me long to realize that women don't stand up for their rights in terms of income. But yes, I think we can do very well. With salary and bonuses I was able to make a very good living, as are other women I know at high levels of business.

So how do you get there?

It's hard in the beginning to judge what your compensation should be. You are not supposed to know how much other people in your office are making. You have to trust that the person you work for values your work and pays accordingly. I'll let you in on something. When I was in charge of compensation, I had three categories of people. Everyone who manages people has these categories: the stars, the almost stars, and the worker bees. They all fulfilled a function, some more valuable than others, or should I say some less replaceable than others. I would try to take care of the stars first so they would not get away. You have to stay ahead of the curve in terms of your most valuable people. Then I would go to the second tier, the people who were talented enough that I also did not want to lose them to a competitor. Finally, we get to the worker bees, people who were good but who I could live without if I had to.

Hmmm . . . so how can we use this information?

Find out which of those categories you are in. If your boss considers you a worker bee, you want to get into the second tier. If you are in the second tier, you want to find out how you can become a star. When you are a star you *know* your contribution is recognized. If you're in tier two or three ask your boss, "What can I do to be seen as a player?" and then do whatever that is. This is a more sophisticated way to get a raise and promotion than listing your accomplishments for the past year.

(continued)

Why?

This tactic—of listing accomplishments—is often seen as defensive. You are assuming that your boss does not know what you have done, and this makes you seem pathetic. The star never does this, and the second tier people rarely do it. The third tier people *always* do it. They constantly feel they must reaffirm their value. And that, in turn, affirms to the manager that they belong in the third group. You have to see yourself as important and deliver on the goods.

What's the antidote?

I was on a panel last year with a high-ranking woman at an investment house. She said something powerful. I'm paraphrasing, but basically, she said, "When someone comes to me and says, 'I understand you are getting ready to do xyz project. I will do anything to be on your team and I want to be part of your success on this project,' I am impressed. It's not "What can you do for me?" but 'What I can do for you and how can I be essential?' and that was refreshing to me." I love that—what a great attitude. She put that person on the team. That thinking makes you different. It's not "What's in if for me?" You have to answer that question for your boss. What's in it for *her* if she gives you a raise or a project or a new challenge? Women do this naturally—offer themselves—but they do not know how to merchandise it into success. They come off as being servants rather than players or people who solve problems.

So how do we change that?

It's a matter of approach. A man will come to the table as a problem solver but a woman will say, "Oh, I'll do anything; I'll scrub the floors." In the process she diminishes her value and her skills. It's a different point of view. Yes, you should be willing to do what it takes, but come with ideas, solutions. Don't come with the attitude that you're the nice girl who will do the dishes and empty the wastebasket.

Any other advice?

I've always had conversations about moving ahead rapidly when I felt like I was in a good place, and made a point of not doing it when I did not feel valued. Your own mood comes across, so take it into account beforehand. But in the beginning, I just worked my tail off and didn't think about anything else.

WORRY NO MORE

Okay, this all sounds great: you are going to claim your power, get that raise, look for a better joy, charm your competitors, but . . . what if this whole thing doesn't work out? What if you try to make it on your own and fail? What if everyone wakes up tomorrow and decides they don't like you? What if no one loves you and you never find a boyfriend? What if you ask for a raise and get laughed out of the room or out of a job? What if nothing works out and you are left weaker than when you started? Gosh, that sounds awful!

Worry (a close cousin of fear) is an enemy of personal power. It stops us from taking action, using our skills, speaking up, shutting up, and asking for more. Worry kills the fun. But we all do it anyway. I know men who never worry, but I've yet to meet a woman who doesn't. Many of you are probably impatiently tapping your feet right about now, thinking, "Excuse me, Marianna, but I have a lot to worry about!" Okay, but I bet you have more things to do than you have to worry about. Let's cut to the chase and get rid of worry. Then we can put the worry energy into something more useful, like practicing our power moves. Here are three effective strategies to help you stop worrying, once and for all.

Circle the Worry

Let's make a place to write down and acknowledge your worries as important so you can think about them later and not be distracted by them now. Worry can fill your mind and push out more important creative thoughts—but be assured you will have time for your worries later. A worry circle is a simple and effective way of getting rid of worry. Cut out an eighteen-inch-diameter circle from a piece of sturdy paper that you can fold and put in your purse. Even easier, download the worry circle from my Web site, liveitloveitearnit.com. Keep the folded worry circle nearby, and every time an anxiety crops up, write it down on the circle. While writing, acknowledge the worry, and recognize that your concerns *are* important.

However, instead of worrying right this minute, let's instead fret about your anxieties, troubles, and fears at a scheduled worry time. I suggest getting out your calendar and scheduling a specific time to worry one hour this week. How about Sunday from nine A.M. to ten A.M.? At that time, take out the worry circle, which will be filled with all the anxieties, troubles, and fears from the previous week, and worry about each one of them. For now, simply go about the business of life worry-free, knowing that you will worry about all of your worries on Sunday at nine o'clock.

When Sunday at nine A.M. arrives, I suggest sitting in a comfortable chair with the circle, and begin worrying very hard about all the things written on it. When the women in my workshops do this they always come back the following week and share one of three observations:

1. "It was a relief to write down my worries because I worried less. I knew I had a worry hour scheduled on Sunday."
2. "When Sunday finally arrived, I realized that a lot of my worries were gone and had been resolved. As for the rest of the worries, when I actually started in on worrying, I realized that it was a waste of time. I ended up tossing the circle, which felt very liberating."
3. "I did spend some time worrying, and it was a relief. I ended up resolving some issues, and I worried less the following week."

Exaggerate the Worry

Another good way to stop worrying is to laugh about it through exaggeration. Hyperbole helps reveal our worries for what they are: thoughts that either have no basis in reality, or real concerns that don't warrant the amount of time and effort we've been devoting to them. Even if your worry does have a basis in truth, it is more productive and feels better to think of a solution and act on it that it is to idly fret about the problem.

"What if I get fired?" That's a common worry. Go completely crazy with worry about it, really over-the-top. How outrageous can you make it? Feel free to embellish the worry any way you like. Let it go on and on until you start laughing because it becomes so "out there" that it's just never going to happen the way you're describing it.

What if I get fired?
Word will get out and no one will ever hire me again.
I'll have no money coming in and I'll end up penniless. That
means I'll have to move out of my beautiful apartment to a dan-

*gerous neighborhood. I won't be able to eat out again;
I'll have to go on food stamps. My expensive shoes will become
ruined, I'll have to sell all my clothes, and I'll end up in rags.
I won't be able to afford to take care of myself. My hair will fall
out, and my teeth will become cracked from eating shoe leather.
Eventually I'll be living under a bridge with a shopping cart
full of other people's garbage . . .*

■

Reverse the Worry

How about turning a worry on its head? Worry does not come from reality, but from your negative estimation of where reality might lead. Switching a negative worry into a positive one demonstrates that there are two sides to every story. If we're set on worrying, we might as well worry about all the wonderful things that might happen. You can reverse *any* worry. Try it, and be surprised at how quickly the worry fades away:

Worry: *"What if I go on all these interviews and I do not get a job?"*
Reverse worry: *"Wow, what if I go on all the interviews and get all the jobs and don't know which one to take?"*
Worry: *"What if I call my colleague to ask for advice and he says no?"*
Reverse worry: *"What if I call my colleague to ask for advice and he gives me so much information I need a tape recorder? I'd better get a tape recorder."*

Reverse and exaggerate worry techniques can be combined to create a worry that is sure to lighten things up:

Worry: *"What if I ask my boss for a raise and he fires me?"*
Reverse and exaggerate worry: *"What if I ask my boss for a raise and he says yes? What if he gives me a double promotion? What if he triples my salary, moves me into a corner office with a view, and tells me to hire two assistants. What if he sends me on a three-week vacation to the Caribbean so that I can refresh myself before I start my new job? I better get my bathing suit out of storage."*

Worry: *"What if I go out on all these dates and no one wants to marry me?"*

Reverse and exaggerate worry: *"What if I go out on all these dates and every guy wants to marry me and gives me an engagement ring? Then I will have six engagement rings. Can I possibly wear all six rings?"*

If there is one message I hope this chapter has conveyed, it's that true personal power comes from taking control of your life and making it work for you, not against you. True power is self-mastery. It's important, especially during the tough times that we all inevitably face throughout life, not to be so tempted to give your power over to someone or something else. When you can hold your own, you can do anything.

Claim Your Power Summary:
- Choice is power, and power is your choice.
- Identify your power drains.
- Use the power of your femininity.
- Don't relinquish your power, or the promise of security, to a man.
- There is a time to speak up and a time to shut up.
- Release the power worry may hold.

7.

Act As If

"If you want a quality, act as if you already had it."
—WILLIAM JAMES, AMERICAN PSYCHOLOGIST

ONE OF THE many great aspects of living in a democracy is our right to free will, to self-determination. We can make our own decisions, seek our own fortune, and access information without interference from anyone else. Moreover, to-morrow we can become whomever we want to be regardless of who we are today. Some of our most successful female entrepreneurs have transformed themselves from being unknown and financially bound to becoming widely respected and financially free. Oprah was a local reporter before her modest daytime talk show became a substantial and vibrant media brand. Madonna first tried her luck at dancing, and eventually, after singing in out-of-the-way downtown clubs, became a pop phenomenon. Martha Stewart was a young broker on Wall Street and became an internationally recognized lifestyle guru after buying a rundown house in Connecticut and renovating it.

If you feel permanently stuck in a certain situation and believe that change is out of your hands, think again. If you do not like where you are now, you have the power to transform it anytime. Some may be tempted to argue, "Well, society has classified me in a certain way (e.g., woman, minority, "poor," "not smart enough," etc.), and I can't break out of it." That's a misconception, an error in thinking. Society, family, friends, and colleagues do not define who you are. You do.

The secret is deceptively simple: Act As If. That means to behave, dress, and speak like the person you want to be. Acting As If is not about being phony or fake. Acting As If is another way of educating and improving yourself. The beauty of it is that it's free and it's fun. It's truly on-the-job training for a new life. What Acting As If does not mean is that you become less "you." Rather, it is you new and improved. I used and continue to use Act As If in so many ways without compromising my authenticity, or betraying or denying anything real about myself. I developed the qualities that I admire in others without abandoning the traits that make me uniquely Marianna.

For instance, before I started working in the corporate world, I never gave the rituals of fine dining much thought and, frankly, rarely ate at top restaurants. Certainly, I could tell the difference between a water goblet and a wineglass. But I was thrown into situations where I had to learn the rules of formal dining very quickly. How do I eat asparagus? Or shrimp? Which spoon do I use for soup? Or dessert? Whenever I took clients out to dinner or attended corporate events, I would wait to see what fork the person across from me picked up to eat their fish or salad with, and then followed suit.

In a larger sense, Acting As If could cause major shifts in attitude. Happiness, for example, can be achieved by one's own energies and attitudes. One of my favorite expressions, and one I live by, comes from Abraham Lincoln: "People are as happy as they make up their minds to be." Happy people seem to attract great things. They are more fun to be around. When you Act As If you're happy, you will actually *be* happy despite the ups and downs and ebbs and flows of life. It works. I have always Acted As If I am happy, and have, by and large, stayed that way. I am not pretending; it's not a gimmick: I *am* happy.

As I entered the business world, I watched how people introduced themselves to strangers at industry conferences and social gatherings and I did the same. I emulated my boss's behavior when he was in a business meeting: he was confident, sure of his decisions, but not arrogant or a bully. He had a bit of humor and a lot of compassion when relating to other people, and that was a style I could convey with authenticity. I looked to successful women in my field, and made note of how they interacted and dressed, their manner, and how they carried themselves, adapting their styles to my personality.

SUCCESS SECRET

"As If" Tips for Getting Ahead on the Job

If you work in an office and want to get noticed so you'll get that promotion, raise, or plum project, you can Act As If you are the most valuable employee ever, and become one in the process.

+ *Act As If You're Irreplaceable.* Do what needs to be done to finish any task. Go above and beyond the call of duty. Your boss will soon be wondering how he could ever live without you.
+ *Act As If You Meet Every Responsibility.* Be clear about what responsibilities your job requires, and meet all of them.
+ *Act As If You Can Do More.* Ask your supervisor for additional responsibilities that you are confident you can handle—and meet those as well.
+ *Act As If You're Capable.* Make sure both your supervisor and your colleagues know what you are capable of accomplishing through words and deeds.
+ *Act As If You're a Student.* Continue to learn about your field and refine and build your skills. Keep on the look out for new and more challenging opportunities.
+ *Act As If You're Calm and Confident.* Anxious, stressed-out, paranoid employees are never looked at favorably.

A woman I know successfully used Act As If tactics when she made a drastic change in her career. Brooke was an executive vice president and partner in a large international law firm. She traveled the world to work with clients, open local branches of the office, and consult on cases. Brooke is a very straightforward person and a marvel when it comes to organization, making a clear and concise argument, and motivating employees—all the qualities it takes to be good at her job. Moreover, Brooke was instrumental in designing the corporate handbook, ensuring that the firm's formal atmosphere was maintained. Brooke was very conservative in dress and manner at work (she wouldn't even wear a pants suit).

The time had come for a change. "I had put in thirty years, starting as an assistant right out of college—so retirement was an option I could take when I turned fifty. I jumped at the chance because there was another dream I wanted to fulfill." Brooke and her husband sold their East Coast city apartment and moved to a small, charming town in the South. "I wanted to open a yoga studio and become a teacher," she says. Brooke was already certified as both a hatha and Bikram yoga teacher, and had many years of practice and part-time instructing under her belt.

Brooke was savvy, and found a great location for her studio, a place convenient to the many young families, college students, professional people, and active retirees who lived nearby. She negotiated and signed a lease that had terms that were very favorable to her. Her mission—to empower all people through yoga—was clear and strong. She used all of her organizational, business, and management skills to put a strong foundation in place.

After a week of teaching classes, Brooke noticed something disconcerting. Some of the students, enough so that it was noticeable, did not return for a second class. She was dismayed. "I thought, uh-oh, we have a problem here. What's going on?" The studio was beautiful, the location perfect, and her prices were reasonable. "I asked one of my teachers to observe my classes. Maybe she could see something that I was missing."

After participating in a day of classes, Brooke's teacher said, "I know what the problem is—you teach like a corporate vice president, not like a yogi." This was an aha moment for Brooke. "I knew exactly what she was talking about. As a woman I felt I had to try extra hard to be matter-of-fact, businesslike. My personality fits very nicely with that, but—people can translate this as being a bit cold."

Brooke took her teacher's advice and started Acting As If she were her. "My yoga teacher is very loose, engaging, humorous, and gentle, so I emulated those qualities. My teacher gave me a videotape of one of her classes, and I practiced running my classes the way she ran hers." After a few weeks, Brooke's new approach to teaching became second nature, students responded favorably, more students started signing up, and Brooke is in the process of adding more classes to the schedule. Her commitment to Acting As If helped her succeed at making what would be a difficult cultural and professional transition easier and more enjoyable.

Super Modeling

Here's an effective and fun way to implement Act As If. It's similar to playing adult dress-up. Who do you want to be? Research the best people in your field and how they behave (their manner, dress, habits, etc.), and then do the same. I always say if you want to be a good swimmer, swim with the best swimmer you know. You may not become an Olympian, but you'll be the best possible swimmer *you* can possibly be. For instance, if the best swimmer gets up at five A.M. for a two-hour practice, start getting up at five A.M. and swim for two hours. If the best swimmer has an egg white omelet, orange juice, and green tea for breakfast, have the same. If the best swimmer works out with weights three times a week for forty-five minutes, do that as well. After Super Modeling for a while, I guarantee you'll see positive results beyond your wildest dreams.

FIND A MENTOR

As you Super Model people, or behave like the people who most closely resemble the type of person you want to become (see the exercise above), keep an eye out for one or more who could also be mentors. A mentor could be someone in a business similar to yours or in a business you hope to break into. Mentors are invaluable in showing us the ropes in a new role or industry, making introductions, helping find solutions to challenges, and advising us on career next steps.

These teachers and advisers are especially helpful for women, because we don't always have access to "boys' clubs" that help men naturally climb the ladder in a male-dominated company or industry. The best mentor is usually at a time in her life when she wants to start giving back and has the time to do so. Look for a person, as I did, who has done very well in his field, has at least five years' experience (ideally ten or more), and has already achieved great success and respect.

A mentor can work at your company (although she should not be a boss or supervisor—awkward!). Alma maters, professional organizations, industry groups, and even nonprofits may offer mentoring programs, so check with them as well as with your employer if you have not had luck finding a mentor on your own. These organized arrangements often require filling out a questionnaire for assessment purposes, and so that the right match can be made. That's a good idea, and I want you to fill out a *Live it, Love it, Earn It* questionnaire too (see the exercise on page 173).

Using a formal mentoring program can be a good way to begin to work with a mentor, especially when just starting out or changing careers. Sometimes prearranged or structured mentoring relationships can have a stiff or artificial feeling, however. You may not feel a connection with the person. Like any good relationship, "chemistry" makes the magic happen. That's why I believe finding a mentor on your own is really the best way to go. I have found that these pairings usually provide a more lasting relationship than one that has been provided by an employer or organization.

If you want to find a successful solution to your problem or an answer to your question, find someone who has gone though what you are going through successfully and ask her how she did it.

■

After identifying a few potential people who you think might be willing to be your mentor, introduce yourself and tell them who you are in a positive, upbeat way. A mentoring relationship should develop naturally, and, like any relationship, it might start immediately and it might not. Don't be disappointed if it does not fly right away. Ideally, I would suggest not to "formally" ask the person to be your mentor unless the situation presents itself. I never said a word about it to my mentor; our friendship just developed naturally into a mentoring relationship that has lasted more than ten years. Do ask the person to share their experiences; people love to talk about themselves and offer advice.

Before I even met my mentor, I knew about his fine reputation and heard colleagues talk about him in complimentary ways. Naturally, I was interested in meeting him. As miracles often happen, I was walking to a conference in Geneva and bumped into a friend of mine who was walking with this man. After we were introduced, I said, "I've heard so much about you and would like to talk to you for a few minutes when you have time." Once we were both back in New York, I sent him a note that read, "John, you are the best in the business. I would be honored if I could spend a few minutes talking to you about how you have become so successful. Maybe we can have a coffee sometime." He was so flattered he gave me more than a few minutes, and a relationship developed from there, slowly and over time.

When a mentor's advice works, tell her immediately, and thank her: "What you told me is really working. Thank you. Can you give me some guidance on this . . ." and so forth. I can't put too much emphasis on showing your appreciating and thanks—mentoring or guiding another person takes time and commitment, thought and dedication. The mentor's reward is seeing you grow and prosper (people love to take credit for other people's success). So don't forget to acknowledge the gift you have received from your mentor by expressing your appreciation, often with a handwritten note, a token gift, or by picking up the tab at lunch.

My Mentor Is . . .

Before you search for your mentor, clarify what you want from the relationship and assess who might be good candidates for the role using the two steps below:

1. Write down both the qualities you want in a mentor and what you hope to accomplish.

   Industry: _____

   _____

   Gender (if that's important to you): _____

   Skills you would like to develop with your mentor's assistance: _____

   _____

   Advice you want: _____

   _____

   Specific industry questions you would like answered:

   _____

   _____

   People you would like to be introduced to:

   _____

2. Next, write down all the people you can think of, whether you know them or not, who have the qualities you are looking for. When you are done, review the list and circle the names of three people you feel comfortable approaching right away. Ask them for just a few minutes of their time, tell them you always wanted to meet them, offer to take them for coffee, and tell them something specific you would like to talk about ("I'd like to hear about your success on Project X," or, "I'm eager to learn about how you started out in the business"). If all three people work out, lucky you—three mentors are better than one.

Greta had two mentors at different stages of her career; each changed her life and career in significant ways. "I met my first mentor was when I was working at a publishing company. Evelyn was an older editor, very stylish and smart. We took a liking to each other and we would have many discussions about books and our jobs over lunches." At the time when Greta was developing her friendship with Evelyn she didn't think of her as a mentor in a formal way. "I just thought Evelyn was a great woman to know—she had so many years in the business and had so many insights and great information. I treasured her friendship."

One day Evelyn asked Greta into her office and closed the door. "That was odd, so obviously my curiosity was piqued. It turned out that Evelyn was planning to retire in a year, and she wanted to groom me for her management-level job. It would be a big step for me. It had not occurred to me that the job would be available—let alone that the very person doing it had pinpointed me as her successor!"

Greta and Evelyn started spending more time together, and Greta became her right hand—learning the way she did her job, helping her select books, and mastering the management and finance parts of the position. When Evelyn retired, Greta was promoted and flourished in her new job. "I had stumbled, by accident, onto the value of a mentor."

A mentor can protect you, speak on your behalf and in support of you, help you find another job if necessary, and clue you in on things that may affect you that are happening behind the scenes in your office. "When a news service hired me to write for them as a freelancer, the man who ran the company became my mentor. Since I was not a full-time, salaried employee, the mentor relationship was appropriate," says Greta.

This man saw talent in Greta and showed her the ropes of reporting, writing a news story, and tracking down leads and sources. "At the end of five blissful years writing for his company, I had become a very good reporter. That would never have happened if I had not taken the chance on something new, or if I had not had this man by my side, helping me— showing me how reporters think, act, and organize their thoughts." This experience took Greta in a whole new direction, and today she has fulfilled her longtime dream of becoming a successful journalist.

IN HER OWN WORDS

Elizabeth Hilpman

PARTNER AND CHIEF INVESTMENT OFFICER
AT BARLOW PARTNERS

Elizabeth Hilpman is a partner and chief investment officer at Barlow Partners, an investment management firm that focuses on investing in hedge funds. Liz has also been an investment manager at Global Asset Management and an investment officer at Dartmouth College. For nine years she was at Commonfund, serving as vice president during her final years there. Liz has been a positive force for women in the financial industry for many years—and is one of its most respected and notable members.

Why or how did you choose the financial industry as a profession?

You have to be passionate about investments if you want to be successful in it, and I happen to love the idea of how people make money. When I began my career, I did not set out saying I wanted to be in the hedge fund business. It was still a cottage industry and most people did not really know what it was about. But I liked what I did—meeting smart people, deciding whether they would be good money mangers, and then making the decision of whether to allocate capital to them.

(continued)

Was it tough being a woman when you started?

Men have historically dominated the industry but I think I tried to make the most of it. I see myself fortunate to have encountered this since it compelled me to work harder, which created a foundation that helped me to get to where I am. Perseverance, following my gut, and making thoughtful decisions about what I would do next all contributed to my accomplishments. When I entered the hedge fund business, it was nonmainstream and more open to women, since it did not appear to be a route to power and money for men. Money was not always the motivation—I just wanted to do something that I looked forward to doing each day, and am lucky I found it early on. I wanted to be self-sufficient, I didn't want to define myself by the accomplishments of a husband, I wanted to achieve my own success. Nevertheless, I enjoyed working with smart men.

How has your career evolved?

Early in my career I left a nonprofit that was well respected and decided to go with a Wall Street style. It was hard for me to make that transition, and I ended up quitting without having something in place to step into. It did not take me long to find another job. I was hired by Dartmouth College to help manage its endowment. The job allowed me to engage with a savvy community where I was able to network extensively. It was also about helping others with regard to investment insights as well as with their careers. I stayed just short of three years, and went back to a much more financially competitive landscape at a London-based investment firm. Then about eight years later the principal of Barlow Partners invited me to join as his partner. The mind-set when you are an owner or partner in a business is very different. It changes the way you manage your time. It forces you to identify what is important for your clients and ultimately their investment returns. You have real obligations to your clients because they have tangible needs. The questions in the forefront of my mind are: How can I be most efficient? How can I get the best results for my clients?

(continued)

What's the most important thing you've learned over the years?

After I left my first for-profit job, and before I went to Dartmouth, I realized that so much of life has to do with your relationships, your network, and giving back to people. I realized that despite the great exposure I had in the Wall Street jobs to talented and bright people, I made the mistake of not cultivating them as part of my network. The more generous you are in life and the more helpful and supportive of others, the more you benefit, and the benefits come back to you in many ways. My focus was to be recognized as an investment expert, but you need a network of people in order for that to happen.

Also, as I matured and really started to watch how men networked—they play golf together, for instance—I saw that there was more camaraderie and helping each other and sharing information and also getting feedback from one another. As soon as I started to become more conscious and aware of that, I became much more proactive. I started asking myself, how can I be helpful to this person? Life, work, relationships—none are one-way streets. Helping others is essential for your own success.

ACT AS IF YOU ALREADY HAVE IT

Acting As If can be applied to every aspect of life. My position is that if women can talk themselves into believing they are too clumsy, too fat, not pretty enough, not rich enough, we can talk ourselves into believing the opposite things too.

I met a woman in the doctor's office the other day. She was looking at the "reasonable weight chart" on the wall of the waiting room. I caught her eye as she turned to sit down, and she smiled, saying, "I thought I'd be free of checking weight charts when I got out of high school, and here I am doing the same thing at forty." I laughed and agreed it's a tough habit to break. She went on to say, "If women used all the energy they use thinking about their weight to thinking about cancer, we would have a cure by now." So true! As she turned to leave, she offered one more sassy thought, which has stuck with me ever since: "Let's enjoy our behinds today! They're beautiful." Ridiculous as it sounds, we can all Act As If we have great rear ends, and the world will no doubt agree.

A friend of mine told me an amusing story about how her elderly mother starts the day. Each day her eighty-something-year-old mom gets up, looks into her dresser mirror, and exclaims with great cheer (anyone in the house can hear her down the hallway), "God, you're gorgeous!" She tells me her mom is and always has been a very attractive woman, but, as my friend tells it, "Everyone always thought of my mother as very beautiful, even though she wasn't into fashion, endless primping, and grooming. I don't think she went to a beauty salon more than a few times when we were growing up. She did her hair herself. One year she even won a local beauty contest—she had sent in a snapshot on a whim!"

Do try this at home. Why not get up tomorrow, look in the mirror, and say, "I am beautiful"? Then Act As If you are beautiful all day. Perhaps you'll stand a little taller, suck in your tummy, and thrust back your shoulders. You'll take extra care dressing and grooming. You'll feel good about yourself. Don't be surprised if heads turn—when you Act As If you are pretty, you *are* pretty.

I believe, as do many other people, that if you Act As If you already have abundance, happiness, balance, and grace, those things come to you. This can be the most difficult aspect of Acting As If for people to understand. On one level, it is an inexplicable phenomenon—luckily we do not have to understand how it works for it to work. Which is kind of like not needing to know how electricity works to turn a light on.

Spiritual adviser Jonathan Sonnenberg recommends that before starting your day, carve out a few minutes to contemplate what it is you would like to present to the world that day. "Close your eyes, breathe deeply, and fill yourself with clear thoughts of beauty, grace, calmness, whatever it is you would like to project." I do this, so I can tell you it works. How will you feel? Relaxed and confident, with a spring in your step: for some unexplained, miraculous reason this practice actually opens us to receiving the abundance we want and it comes to us more easily. When you feel calm and balanced, you'll be at ease in the world. You'll be filled with confidence and comfort as you glide through the day. If you do it continuously on a daily basis, people will begin to see you in a different way, and may begin to feel that you deserve abundance and help you achieve it.

The beauty of Acting As If we have great abundance is that it does actually attract abundance. If we behave as if we have great wealth, we will have great wealth. We make good money decisions and treat our money well. We have a positive view of money, and money is attracted to that. It's motivating and invigorating to start behaving abundant right now, and quite enjoyable.

Acting As If is a way of actively participating in our effort to change our own lives, mind, and situation. Change is difficult; Acting As If makes it easier and faster.

Act As If Summary:
- Act As If you are the person you want to be.
- Super Model.
- Find a mentor.
- Act As If you already have *it*, whatever *it* is.

8.

Take Action!

"You cannot change anything in your life with intention alone. . . .
Intention without action is useless."

—CAROLINE MYSS, AMERICAN MEDICAL INTUITIVE, MYSTIC, AND AUTHOR

YOU MAY HAVE heard or read about the Law of Attraction, which essentially means that thoughts produce events. I agree that thoughts *are* powerful. Action, however, is what turns thoughts into reality. We will never earn a million dollars watching TV all day; meet a terrific guy while hiding in our apartments, never going out or answering the phone; or find a new job without networking or interviewing. We must *take the next right action* in order to achieve any goal, and the same is true if that goal is to achieve a rich and happy life. In fact, I don't believe there is any such thing as taking too many actions.

Unfortunately, inertia, or the fear of failure, often prevents us from taking the first step. How do we get unstuck? How do we go from inertia to movement? From inaction to action? All of us face tasks we dread doing. When we are job hunting, how do we make ourselves pick up the phone and call the person we want to work for? What do we say after "Hello"? How do we overcome the apprehension running through our minds? Recently I was stuck about making the first call to someone whom I wanted to do business with.

No one wants to talk about what happens when we are stuck, but it's very real. Each time I picked up the phone my heart started beating so hard I could feel it, and I was physically shaking. So I would hang up. My stomach hurt, and I couldn't eat. A couple of times I woke up in the middle of the night filled with overwhelming anxiety. I wanted to do business with this company and knew I had to make this phone call, but the more I put it off, the more I spiraled into a deeper rut. I felt like a deer caught in the headlights.

Days passed, and I started to feel depressed, lethargic, and cranky. I became angry and down on myself as I procrastinated more, not being able to take such a seemingly simple action, but for some reason I was stuck and didn't understand the reason behind it. Why couldn't I make this phone call? This piqued my interest and I wanted to learn why we become stuck over some things and not stuck over others and how to overcome it.

As I started researching and talking to a psychologist friend who specializes in mental and emotional blocks to learn about stuckness and how to get over a block, I discovered the simple secret of getting unstuck, and it's really quite easy. After working with many patients trying to get over their blocks, the psychologist's findings were that every one of us has unique blocks. He found that people could spend days, months, and even years struggling to uncover the origin of a block and trying to unravel it through analysis. After talking with him at length, he told me there was an easier, simpler way of getting over a particular inertia. The secret of getting unstuck that works best for me is to stop thinking about it. Just dive in and do it! Overthinking and overanalyzing were my problems. Imagining all the "what ifs" paralyzed me. Dwelling on potential negative results from "messing up" the call created inertia. As soon as I stopped thinking about the call and all the possible outcomes and made a decision to just do it, it was uncannily easy to pick up the phone, press the numbers, and start talking. My philosophy is "Do it and let go of the results." It works.

Once we learn how to take action, we get hooked. Action becomes addictively fun. We never know when or where results will come. My suggestion is to take every possible action and not to dwell on what the results might be. Just continue with taking the next right action. You don't know which specific action will create what result, so you have to continue moving forward, leave no stone unturned, until the desired results show themselves. Here are three ways to put this simple strategy to work and get through the procrastination and inertia that may be holding you back:

1. The past is perfect
2. The future will be there when you arrive
3. The present is a gift

Bookending

Bookending is a system of support that helps you on both ends of a task. Before I start any task that I dread, I make a call or send a text to a trusted friend or abundance buddy and tell that person what action I am about to take. My buddy has preagreed to be my book-end partner. She does not give feedback, but is there to support my action (unless I am about to do something dangerous or completely misguided). She offers encouraging words such as "You can do it" or "I know you'll succeed." If I can't get through to her, I leave a mes-sage on her answering machine or send a text to her phone saying I will take such-and-such action. Then I take the action—make the call, attend the meeting, whatever it happens to be. Afterward, I call or text my friend and tell her that I took the action. Speaking to my friend first and then knowing that I can talk to her when my task is done fills me with courage and makes me feel like we are doing this together. Bookending reminds you that you're not alone. Bookending also helps to hold you accountable: you feel that you have to take the action because you told someone else you were going to do it. It's much easier that way.

Tear It Up, Sit, and Talk Through Your Fears

Let's release our fears once and for all. This is a good exer-cise to do with your abundance group or a buddy. Each simple exercise to get over your fears can be done at any time, in any order, or only do the ones you want to do. When I have a fear I go through all of the exercises and by the end my fear has lifted and I am ready to take action. Use this exercise anytime you feel fear around taking a particular action.

1. Tear It Up: Each of you writes out all your fears about going for your goal. Read each fear aloud and after each one say, "My fears are not facts." Tear the paper into small pieces, and as you toss them into the waste-basket say, "I toss all my fears away."
2. Sit on Your Hands: While sitting in a chair, place your hands underneath you and sit on them. Close your eyes and feel the fear as you send it through your body; feel it as it passes through and out.
3. Talk It Through: Set a timer for ten minutes. Tell a trusted friend or abundance buddy what you are afraid of without interruption. Ask her to listen without offering judgment or feedback. Get all your fears out. Then do the same for her. This is a safe, unstructured block of time to purge all your fears. Remember, *no feedback, please.*

THE PAST IS PERFECT

Regret over yesterday's so-called mistakes keeps us from reaching fresh goals. All the "I should have's," "I could have's," and "why didn't I's," keep us stuck in the past. We've all been there.

IRENA'S DILEMMA

A Wall Street colleague of mine, Irena, was bemoaning that she should have never left the company she worked for fifteen years ago. Mind you, today Irena has her own very successful and profitable advertising firm. The reason for her regret? "Marianna, did you see the *Times* the other day?" she asked with a crack in her voice. I had, but I didn't know what she was talking about. "There was an article about how [Company X] had been sold for a large sum of money."

"And?" I replied, wondering what she was thinking. "Don't you see, Marianna," she said, "I should have stayed there. I would have been a top executive by now, have earned shares in the company, and be making three times what I make running my company today. I would have probably received a large sum of money if I would have still worked there and cashed in my shares. They would be writing about *me* in the *Times*! I just can't stop thinking about how stupid I was to quit and go off on my own." She had to be kidding, right? No, Irena was very serious, and seriously upset.

The next time I saw Irena in person, I walked her through the Past Is Perfect exercise. First, we talked about the fact that there was no way she could predict the outcome she imagined. Many things can happen in fifteen years. There is no way she could say with certainty that if she had stayed at Company X, her net worth would have grown by leaps and bounds, or that she would have been happy at the company for all those years. Then we looked at what would have likely happened, based on evidence, if she had stayed at the old company. She would have had to work eighteen hours a day every day, nights and weekends, with limited time off and under a very difficult and demanding boss. At least that's what the newspaper article had said about the people who worked for Company X. She would have had to travel extensively, not to glamorous hotspots but to remote places where the company had advertising clients.

Irena would never have met her husband if she had been working all those hours and traveling that much. She would never have created a new business that makes money, employs people, and allows her creativity and the freedom to devise and implement original business strategies. And even more important, she would have given up her dream of starting a business and creating a beautiful family, not fully exercised her talents, and not have had the beautiful and fulfilling life she enjoys today. Yes, she did make a good choice to leave Company X when she did. Her past is perfect just the way it is. Irena was finally able to let go of her feelings of regret.

Let's get unstuck from our past so we can free up our thinking and be open to bigger and better things. Experiences are instructive, not destructive. We have to learn to glance back at our history instead of staring at it endlessly for hours every day, until those hours turn to months and years. If we relentlessly focus our attention on what we could have, would have, and should have done, the past becomes a ball and chain. It's so freeing and exhilarating to get unstuck from the past and spend more time living in the present.

BETTY'S EPIPHANY

A former colleague of mine, Betty, had a destructive block that prevented her from moving forward in her career. She had made a substantial amount of money when she started an e-commerce business in the 1990s. It was the peak of the dot-com boom and Betty was flying high—investors and customers flocked to her business. The news media covered her success. Betty was only about twenty-eight at the time. She had many social activities tied to her fame around town, and enjoyed the attentions of a boyfriend who was impressed with her fame and success.

One night Betty took twenty people, including me, out for dinner to a fabulous new restaurant, and had even hired belly dancers as entertainment. The champagne was flowing, paparazzi captured our images as we partied, and the photos made the society pages the next day. What a night, with Betty in the starring role! A few months later the dot-com boom went bust. Betty had been worth millions on paper and then the bubble burst and poof: no more money. Her boyfriend, no longer enamored with Betty, walked out on her, along with some of her newly found friends.

Ten years later, Betty was still stuck in the past, wondering what could have happened if she had sold her company before the industry took a nosedive (could have, should have, would have . . .). She wouldn't even try to find another job because she was afraid of being laughed at by prospective employers. Betty feared they would scoff at her past failure and reject her. She constantly reminisced about "the good old days." She could not bring herself to start a new business either; she couldn't bear to fail again.

Whenever I would run into Betty, she ruminated about her failed enterprise as if it were the defining moment in her life. She had actually created quite an extraordinary business at a very young age. It would have been difficult for her to predict the extent of the technology industry's collapse. Yet she continues to beat herself up about what she sees as her failure to foresee what would happen to the market.

The last time I saw Betty and she started in on her "poor me" story, I smiled and said, "Wow, Betty, your past is perfect!" She looked stunned for a moment, then curious. "What are you talking about?" she asked. I suggested we get a cup of tea. When we had settled into a nearby café, I asked Betty if she would consider looking at her experience a bit differently, even if it took some time and work on her part. She agreed to do it.

Betty was willing to try the Past Is Perfect exercise. It helped her release the past and all her regrets. The exercise ended her tendency to analyze and reanalyze what happened so many years ago. Immediately after trying the exercise she started feeling lighter, as if she had let go of a heavy burden. Betty has started to move beyond the past, and she has started living in the here and now. A year later, Betty now has a new look about her. She has started a new business in Internet ad sales. It's going so well, she has hired three people and is already on her way to another success.

The Past Is Perfect

When you are feeling bound by your past, this exercise should help release the hold it has over you. Carve out a half hour if you can, and do the steps in order with your abundance buddy. Or devote an abundance group session to this exercise.

1. Write down all your regrets—your "should have's," "could have's," "why didn't I's," and resentments regarding the past. This may take a while, but it is time well spent.
2. Once the list is complete, look at the first item. Say it out loud: "I regret not taking the job in the city"; or "Maybe I should have married that guy"; or "I wish I had taken that summer off to travel."
3. Your abundance buddy replies: "The past is perfect the way it is."
4. Next, agree and tell her why. For example: "Yes, it's true that my past is perfect the way it is. If I had taken the job, I would have never started my own business." Reverse roles and do the same for your buddy.
5. Tear up your lists and say, "I release the past. The past is perfect the way it is."

THE FUTURE WILL BE THERE
WHEN YOU ARRIVE

Worrying about the future can burden your ability to take actions right now. How often do you find yourself daydreaming or worrying about future outcomes in ways that prevent you from moving forward? "What if this happens?" "What if that happens?" It's true that investment decisions, business planning, and saving should be based on future needs. However, we can still live very much in the present while visualizing results and goals and also planning for the future. Engage in activities that favorably impact your finances, health, and well-being going forward without getting caught up in trying to predict the future. Avoid basing your actions (or inaction, as the case may be) on this What If Syndrome.

It's simply not productive to overanalyze potential future stumbling blocks or problems. Anticipate, but participate. Here's what I mean. Say you have an idea that you'd like to present to your boss. You agonize for weeks about whether she will like the idea (what if she laughs, rejects it, thinks it's stupid), and about what will happen if the idea does not work out (total humiliation, loss of reputation, mocking by colleagues). These future predictions become so dire that your idea never makes it out of your head and onto a page, let alone lands on the boss's desk. Rest assured that the future is going to happen, and that you will be there for yours. That's very good news. No amount of thinking changes that fact.

When you become aware that you are slipping into the What If Syndrome, give yourself a little pinch to shock you back to the present. If pinching doesn't feel right, get up and do a few jumping jacks. I like to tie a red ribbon around my wrist and every time I look at it say to myself, "I'm in the here and now." The point is to do something brief and physical that brings us back into the moment.

SUCCESS SECRET

End the What If Syndrome

Copy these three cards, or print them from liveitloveitearnit.com. They are easy to slip into your purse or a wallet. When you start making unrealistic predictions based on little or no actual evidence or knowledge of the future, take the cards out and read them to yourself. Doing so will immediately remind you that possible outcomes go both ways and that focusing on the positive possibilities is healthier and inspiring.

What if . . .
all my dreams come true?
■

What if . . .
everything is wonderful?
■

What if . . .
everything turns out better than
expected?
■

THE PRESENT IS A GIFT

We are living in the present moment, so why not take advantage of it? Right here, right now, is our moment. It's the best time, whatever time it happens to be. *Now* is the only time you can take action. *Now* is where you are standing this minute; take advantage of it.

Some of you might be wondering how I can say "Live in the now" and also tell you to make a vision board, or visualize the future in a positive way, as if these ideas were at odds. They are not at odds. Making a vision board, for example, is doing something in the present that impacts how we behave today, and that leads to a better tomorrow. Visualizing is a way of putting ourselves in the situation we want to be in *today*, in our minds. Again, that stimulates us to take actions in the here and now that are beneficial.

Here are my top five tips for living in the present:

1. *Focus* on and respond to what is happening today.
2. *Do* things today that will have a positive impact on tomorrow.
3. *Concentrate* on completing tasks at hand without thinking about the outcome until the task is completed.
4. *Go* about the day's business with a feeling of purpose. In other words, approach everything with full engagement and attention.
5. *Move* from one task to another with ease, conscious energy, and recognition. For example, silently say, "I can do that; that's easy," and do it.

Pernille Spiers-Lopez

CEO OF IKEA NORTH AMERICA

Danish-born Pernille Spiers-Lopez moved to the United States twenty-three years ago. She joined furniture powerhouse IKEA North America in 1990, and has served as president of IKEA North America since 2001. It may be Pernille's humanistic leadership philosophy that gives her an edge over the competition. When she took the reins at IKEA NA, staff turnover was at a high 75 percent. By the next year she had reduced that number to 56 percent. IKEA is now consistently named a "Best Company to Work For" by both *Fortune* and *Working Mother* magazines. She talked to me about thriving in retail and being a leader.

Is being a woman an advantage in your business?

This business is about being relevant to women. In home furnishings you want to make the woman happy because they make 90 percent of buying decisions. So being female gives me an advantage in that context. I can connect with the important things in women's lives because I am living a similar life; I'm married and have two teenage sons.

What about succeeding in general in your industry?

If you want to be a retailer you also have to know and understand all aspects of what you are selling. I started selling furniture in a small store in Florida, and would work in as many different areas of the store as I could so I understood the business inside out. If a woman wants to be in retail, she has to get to know the product so she can feel authentically passionate about it. There is no one single way to get to the top of your profession—I started as a journalist in Denmark. It's a career that prepared me for life, for dealing with different situations and a variety of people. It was a good start for me.

And what about success?

Ultimately if you want to be a leader, it begins with self-examination. And *you must like what you do and do it well.* Along the way we all make choices and decisions; don't beat yourself up about them. Meanwhile, keep an eye on the future.

BABY STEPS GO LONG DISTANCES

When a baby starts to walk he does not start running right away or taking long, confident strides. First he crawls. Then he pulls himself up by grabbing on to the leg of a table. He slowly begins to put one foot forward. He's pretty wobbly at first, and sometimes he falls. But he gets right back up, and takes more baby steps, and gets more confident. Pretty soon he's running so fast you can't catch him. That's the way it's going to be for you when you begin to take actions that lead to your goal.

Baby steps are an excellent way to start. They are a way of breaking down a big objective into small ones that can be tackled individually. After completing an action, let go of it and move on to the next one. That means not pinning all your hopes on one or even a dozen actions. Do what needs to done, forget it, and move on to the next right thing. Results come very organically if you keep moving and allow your actions to flow one into the other.

SUCCESS SECRET

Action List

At the end of each day I make an action list, not a to-do list. The word *action* is forward thinking and positive; *to-do* seems like drudgery. Then I review the list and put a circle around the most important actions. I find that when I write down all the actions I want to take the next day, I don't have to worry about them for the rest of the evening. I even sleep better.

Meanwhile, always keep daily, monthly, and even yearly goals fixed by putting them in writing and placing them someplace where you can see them. They will motivate you to keep taking baby steps. The first thing I did on the day my hedge fund marketing business opened was to write out my goals. I stuck the list on my computer screen so that I could see and read it day after day after day. I just came across that original paper recently, and my heart leaped at the realization that I had indeed accomplished my biggest goals by taking a lot of baby steps!

While I was building my business, I took *at least* one baby step each day. The first time I had a three-day business trip to London to sell the financial products I was representing, for instance, I could have easily been beset with anxiety at all that I needed to do beforehand, once I landed, and when I was back at home. Instead, I broke down the trip and made it into a written list of baby steps. I took the steps one by one until everything necessary was complete, from soup to nuts. I wrote down each of the baby steps ahead of time and then took action. Here's how it worked:

First baby step: I prepared, printed, and assembled the presentation booklets.

Second baby step: I booked the flights and hotel rooms and put together the itinerary.

Third baby step: I mailed information to the clients before the meetings to prep them for my presentation, and confirmed each meeting the day before it was to take place. I remember getting to the office at five A.M. to call potential investors for meetings in London. It was the time to catch them—before the rest of New York started calling them. I always got through at this hour.

Fourth baby step: After I called all the investors I knew, I asked other people in London for referrals, and made these calls next, knowing a referral had more potential than a cold call.

Fifth baby step: Once in London, I made sure to be on time for each appointment, had a productive business meeting, and respected the time I was given.

Sixth baby step: I followed up with e-mails and phone calls once I was back in New York.

Many of these tasks might seem trivial, or even boring and administrative. But they were necessary for my trip, and no one was going to do them for me. Breaking my trip into manageable baby steps made it seem doable and I wasn't overwhelmed by all of it at once. My organization and preparation were very calming (surrounding yourself in chaos, on the other hand, is extremely dramatic and upsetting). The trip went smoothly and was successful.

One of my favorite baby step stories involves Emily, a friend of mine who found a way to mesh her passion for design with an exciting new career at age forty. And it all started with one bold "cold call." Emily had been married for several years, devoting herself to her husband's hotel and hospitality business. Because she got married right out of college, the only business experience she had was working in hotels, first managing the staff, and then renovating some of the hotels they owned. "I am not diminishing what I accomplished, but my work was in partnership with my husband, so I didn't really have conventional office experience," Emily says.

About six years ago Emily and her husband split up. "I just had drifted away from my husband, I think because I had gotten married so young," she says. Her husband was angry and hurt. Even though she had spent nearly twenty years helping him grow his business, and had never received anything for it, she did not pursue alimony. There were no children involved, so Emily simply moved on. "I went from Texas to New York with one suitcase of clothes and thirty thousand dollars in the bank. I have always liked home fashions and accessories, and I was good at sales, so I thought I could get a job as a salesperson in a design store. What actually happened was very unexpected."

SUCCESS SECRET

Put It in Your Shoe Box

When a specific problem threatens to take over your life, put it in a shoe box (I use a shiny red box that came with a pair of shoes I bought years ago). Write your problem down, take one step toward resolving it, and then place the problem (on paper) in the shoe box. The next day, take the shoe box down from its shelf, do what you need to do to solve the problem, and put the shoe box back on the shelf and continue with your life. Do this every day until your problem is solved.

Life took an interesting turn for Emily. "I started selling beautiful home accessories on my own. A friend of mine made these absolutely gorgeous napkin rings with chandelier crystals, natural shells, beads from all over the world, and other found objects. No two were exactly alike, which intrigued me. Napkin rings change your table and give it a different look even if you use the same china and flatware. I told her she should be selling them at Bergdorf Goodman or Barneys."

Emily's friend challenged her to try to sell them for her. If she met with success, she would split the profit with her. "So I cold-called Bergdorf's, Barney's, and Saks Fifth Avenue, and asked to speak to the tabletop buyer at each store. I made an appointment, and each of the buyers really liked the rings, and they all placed orders. I really enjoyed selling and I thought, 'Hmmm, I am going to keep selling these napkin rings.' I ended up writing orders for *twelve thousand* napkin rings. That one call launched me into what I am doing now, which is representing and selling home fashion products that I believe in."

When other home design companies heard about Emily's success, they wanted representation as well. "I developed good relationships with store buyers and they came to trust my taste and ability to find unique items. They were always curious to see what I had come up with," she says. Soon, Emily started to realize that she had created a viable business. "I started to take what I was doing very seriously. I attended trade shows at New York's Javits Center and in Atlanta and High Point. You meet so many buyers face-to-face at these shows. I also continued cold-calling and building my network."

By the end of just a few years, Emily had built up a client list of more than one hundred manufacturers she represented exclusively to New York City's best department stores and boutiques. "I carry such a diversified line, including throw pillows, coffee table books, soy scented candles, beautiful stemware from Europe, finely made toys and games, and French stationery. All the things I would love to have in my own home."

Baby Steps

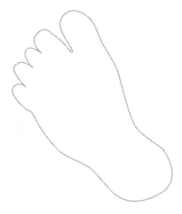

Here is a baby step. Isn't it adorable? Copy this step, or download a free version from my Web site, liveitloveitearnit.com. Make eight to ten copies, and write on each foot one small action step needed to fulfill your chosen goal. Pin the steps to a corkboard reserved for this goal. Each time you accomplish a baby step, draw a smiley face, a checkmark, or the word *DONE* across it so you can see what you have accomplished. Begin working on the next step. By the time all the steps are removed, you will have met your goal. Congratulations!

Ambassador Brenda La Grange Johnson

FORMER U.S. AMBASSADOR TO JAMAICA

"The most philanthropic and generous people in the world are the Americans," says Brenda La Grange Johnson, former U.S. ambassador to Jamaica (2005-2009). As ambassador, she chaired the Caricom HIV/Aids Conference in 2007. Before that Ambassador Johnson was a partner, since 1977, with BrenMer Industries, importing and marketing consumer products. Ambassador Johnson has been involved in many groups and associations as a leader and organizer, including The Nasher Art Museum, the Women's Board of the Madison Square Boys and Girls Club, the President's Advisory Council to the Arts (PACA), the American Cancer Society, and the National Institutes of Health National Cancer Advisory Board. Ambassador Johnson has also worked with HRH Prince Charles and the Prince's Foundation for the Built Environment to restore Rose Town in Kingston, Jamaica. Ambassador Johnson is also a busy wife, mother, and grandmother: She and her husband have four children and six grandchildren.

How did your career lead to becoming the ambassador to Jamaica?

First off, being an ambassador is the best job in the world. I feel very lucky to have been appointed to the job. There are various ways to become an ambassador—going into diplomatic service, for example. The majority of people starting to work for the State Department are smart young women. Once a person works for two to three years in the home office, they often move to a new job in a foreign country. This is a wonderful chance to travel, learn a language, work with people from another culture, make new contacts, and so on. One can also be appointed to a post by the President; that's the way I became ambassador.

Becoming appointed by the President must mean becoming top in your field, well known in certain circles, and well respected. Could you share your networking secrets?

(continued)

There are several secrets to meeting people who can advise and help you, or those who could be influencers and mentors. First, work for the party of your choice. I did more than twenty years of political fund-raising, and I was more often than not one of the few women involved. Most involved in this work are men and so you will meet very influential people. Another secret that is often overlooked is going to places of worship. No matter what your religion is, go to a place of worship; you meet many people there from your community. Finally, be prepared for a lot of hard work. It was very hard raising money for both Bush administrations (it's a "hard ask" since contributions are not tax-deductible).

What has being an ambassador taught you about success? Are there any ambassador's secrets that would help women in business and life?

Well, there's an open secret, and that is ask for the job you want. When George W. Bush was elected I was appointed to the President's Advisory Council of the Kennedy Center, and later to the Kennedy Center Board of Trustees. Many people I met would say, "You would be the perfect ambassador. You should ask for it." People might not know your interest in a job so let it be known. There is nothing wrong with being your own best advocate, and in order to be one you also need to be qualified for the job. Continue to advance yourself, keep learning. While I was building my career, I was teaching and working, and, at the same time, going to school at night.

Second, seize the moment. When you are in a situation where you will be in front of the right person, take advantage of it. I was at a White House pregala event for the Kennedy Center Honors program, and was in the receiving line for a photo opportunity with the President. I knew then that I would have twenty seconds alone with him, and I decided I was going to ask to be considered for an appointment. I started to say that I would be honored . . . and before I had a chance to get the rest of the words out, President Bush asked, "Are you interested in an appointment?" I nodded and said, "I would like to serve." He looked at me and said, "Consider yourself under consideration." Three weeks later, I went to the White House for an interview and the President asked me, if I were offered the job, would I take it? Of course I said yes.

(continued)

How did you balance family life and the obligations of your job?

It's almost impossible; you have to do the best you can. I have a wonderful husband; he's very involved with our family. I make sure all grandparents' days at my six grandchildren's schools are marked on my calendar. I put my job as ambassador first, but I also make time for these special events and would fly from Jamaica to New York, even if it was only for twenty-four hours, to see my grandchildren. Some women do not have the kind of support system a married woman has, so it's even more difficult for them, but not impossible. A single mother has to create an alternative backup plan and support system.

TAKE CREATIVE ACTION: START A BUSINESS

Starting a business is an aspiration for so many women. Every day I meet at least one woman in a workshop, at a coaching session, or socially who tells me about her idea or dream to work for herself. I often meet the same women months, or even years, later and ask them how their new business is going, and they reply, "I don't know where to start"; "It's so hard to make the time"; or "I really want to do it, but have too much going on." While it is challenging to strike out on your own, and it certainly was for me, it's worth the risk and hard work is required if you believe strongly in your idea. The most important aspect of starting a business is preparation, and this includes putting your business idea down on paper, researching the field and your competition, writing a business plan, calculating financial needs, and seeking investors if necessary. Let's take a look at these crucial steps to making it on your own and hear from some women who have done exactly that.

FROM FUZZY TO FIRM

Some women I know have about five businesses floating around in their heads and they never write any of them down. As a result, none of these ideas ever materializes. The first action needed to start any business is to formulate the idea on paper. When the idea is staring at us in black and white it can be read and reread, revised and changed. Otherwise it is just a bunch of fuzz in our heads.

Dream Business

Use this space to write down some business ideas, or download more sheets from liveitloveitearnit.com. Once they're on paper, pick the idea that excites you the most, and work on that one.

My dream business is . . .

SEIZE THE MOMENT

Oftentimes we have a perfect business opportunity staring us in the face but we choose to ignore it. Either we are not tuned in to ourselves enough to recognize a prospect with potential or we brush it aside, choosing not to get out of our comfort zone. If you are in sync with what's important to you, when opportunity does come knocking, you'll be able to act quickly, without missing a beat.

That's what happened to Katherine Cohen, Ph.D., when she started a new business after working for years in education. When Katherine was still in high school she began working for The Princeton Review after taking a class from the test-prep and publishing company. "I took one of the first classes offered when there were only two people running the company, one on the West Coast, where I am from, and one on the East Coast. The head of the L.A. division thought I was smart, so after the course was over, he offered me a job when I was a senior in high school. I did assistant work, and became a teacher for Saturday courses."

Katherine continued building her experience during summers off from Brown University, where she went to college. "I would come home and teach at The Princeton Review. When I graduated, I returned home and tutored in Beverly Hills and found it to be a lucrative business. Plus, I loved working with teens and students. I hired five people to help me who specialized in different subjects. My day started at two P.M. and went to ten P.M. I loved it."

One day, a mentor from Brown called Katherine and suggested that she apply to a Ph.D. program in Latin American literature at Yale. Katherine thought about it, said why not, and applied. "I didn't think much about it. I used a pencil to fill out the application the night before FedExing it in time for the application deadline!" What do you know? Katherine was accepted with a full scholarship and a stipend. "I taught undergraduate courses while I was working toward my doctorate. I loved student life and ended up getting a position as a first reader for Yale undergraduate admissions. That's when the proverbial lightbulb went off that I could help other students get into the college of their choice."

Fill a need and fill your pockets.

■

Katherine finished Yale early that year, and went to UCLA extension to obtain her college-counseling certificate. After completing a required internship at a high school, she went back to the West Coast and talked to one of the only independent college counselors in the Los Angeles area about working with her. "She shot me down, saying that I did not have any experience and she had no room for me." Undeterred, Katherine thought, "Okay, I'll start my own business. It will be better if I move to New York because it will provide a more active client base."

Shortly after she had made the decision to move cross-country with her fledgling business, she got a call from *Vogue* magazine. The editors had heard about Katherine and her knowledge of school admissions from the academic grapevine. "The editors were putting together a college issue and the woman I spoke with said she needed information about colleges and related trends." The editor was impressed with Katherine's breadth of knowledge and kept calling her with questions, and Katherine was happy to accommodate her. "When the *Vogue* editor called the final time, I was in the thick of setting up my business in New York. She told me she wanted to put my name and number in the issue as a resource, and she wanted to know what my 800 number was!"

Pursue every lead and you will get there.

■

Quick-thinking Katherine, who did not have a number, told the woman she would call her right back. "I quickly called an 800 number service and once I signed up I called the editor back with a newly minted 800 number, 1-800-IVY-WISE. It literally took a couple of minutes." The *Vogue* issue came out in August 1998, and Katherine's name and the name of her company, Ivywise, was printed in the resources section. "Since mine was the only college-counseling service listed, I think I got about five hundred phone calls from all over the world that month."

As she struggled to answer every last call, Katherine knew that she had a very viable business on her hands, and that she was filling a need that had been underserved—helping high school students with the college application and admissions process—for a long time. "I immediately had to hire an assistant. Within the first year I rented office space on Fifty-seventh Street in New York. Today I have ten counselors and a team of tutors who work all over the globe. We are a high-end boutique service, starting with admissions help for preschool and kindergarten, but college is our core business."

If Katherine had not been thinking on her feet and seizing every moment, answering every knock on her door, she would not have started teaching when she was still in high school, started a successful tutoring business, been paid to go to Yale, started her own business, or gotten herself mentioned in *Vogue* and established a thriving business.

DUE DILIGENCE

Once deciding to make a business happen, some digging around is required. Researching a proposed business is helpful in learning how to best approach the business from your individual perspective and writing a business plan. New York City matchmaker Janis Spindel started her business seventeen years ago after having an epiphany. "When the fourteenth couple I had introduced called and said they were getting married, I looked at my husband and said, 'I think I have a business here.'" That got the ball rolling, but before Janis hung up her shingle, she did a substantial amount of research.

"I call it due diligence. I picked the brain of other matchmaking businesses and they shared tips and pitfalls with me," she says. It is a smart idea to talk to other people in the business you want to be in. They are usually flattered and generous with information. In fact, most every industry has networking organizations specifically for the purpose of exchanging experiences and information with other people in similar industries. Janis also went out of her way to contact legal and financial advice before opening up shop. "I found the best lawyer to draw up contracts and other legal paperwork. I found an accountant who could set up an accounts payable system before I accepted a dime from anyone. I had the entire structure of my business in place before I had one client, so I was ready for him." Again, Janis's strategy paid off. She is still successful, even though other matchmakers have come and gone in the nearly twenty years she has been in business.

Hire the best accountants and lawyers you can afford.

■

"My business is recession-proof; even during tough times people need love, maybe even more so," she says. "What I do, connecting like-minded men and women, is priceless. And there are always single people; they never go away. This year alone, even in a huge economic downturn, my business is up twenty-three percent. I continue to expand my presence and react to new trends in technology that make connecting with customers easy," explains Janis. She attributes her consistent success to the groundwork she laid in the beginning. "It has provided me with a solid and lasting foundation. I do not have to worry about the basics because they are in place. I can focus on growing my business."

A WOMAN WITH A PLAN

The best business plans are clear, concise, and convincing. I started with a 10-page business plan. Some people might ask, "A ten-page business plan; that's it?" I know people who have written 110-page plans, but mine was a very tight plan covering all the points I needed to make: a description of the business, why it would be successful, how the business would operate, a look at who was already in business, and financial information. Financial data includes a one-year detailed description of projected income and expenses, and a five-year projection of overall income and expenses. Even if a business does not need investors, it's a good idea to write a plan because it formalizes how the business will run and outlines estimated finances. This is useful information for both a sole proprietor and a large company. It can also be used as a measure against which to check monthly and yearly progress.

The 5-Step B-Plan

Creating a business plan is easier and less time-consuming than you probably think. While some business plans are as thick as phone books, there is no length requirement. As long as your business, strategy, numbers, and projections are clear and realistic, you can be succinct. Business plans are important for two reasons: one, so *you* can be clear about your business, its mission and your financials; and two, so you can present your business in a clear and concise way to outside investors if you are looking for cash.

1. Executive summary: This is a very tight and to-the-point one- to two-page overview of your business idea and its general strategy. My business idea was to sell financial products to investors. But whatever your summary, make sure it gives the reader a clear snapshot of your intentions, whether it is a jewelry business, physical therapy practice, e-commerce Web site, etc.
2. Marketing: This section describes how a business will find and keep customers—after all, without customers there is no business. It should include more information about the products and/ or services you offer, your unique selling plan, pricing strategies, sales or distribution plans, and advertising and publicity strategy.
3. Finances: This can be one or two pages explaining how much money is needed to start your business (based on administrative and material needs, including everything from rent to office supplies), how much money you will need over a three- or five-year period, including unforeseen expenses and downtimes in your business, and when you expect to break even and make a profit.
4. Management: This is a listing of employees, contracted workers, and other professionals that you need to run your business and a brief description of their job responsibilities. Maybe you do not need anyone but yourself. In my case, I did the management and even clerical work myself for the first year, and needed only part-time assistance after that. I hired outside professionals on an as-needed basis for accounting, legal work, and other

financial operations personnel. If you plan on manufacturing something, you may need to work with a factory or craftspeople, or source materials. Supporting data such as the résumés of your principles (as well as your own résumé), licenses, and other legal documents such as operating agreements are included in this section.

5. Competition: This is a summary of the other players in your field as well as an analysis of why your business is different or better than existing businesses. How does your business fill an existing but unaddressed need?

Financial Data

Your financial projections can be in the form of a spreadsheet, and some people include a graph. Projections need not be complicated, but they should be realistic. Create a spreadsheet detailing all of your first year monthly fixed and variable expenses, including equipment and supplies. I suggest creating a five-year projection for total expenses and income, showing your estimated break-even point (when your expenses are equal to your income) and time frame for projected profits (when your income is more than your expenses).

Ask for Money

Not every business needs to be funded by outside money. Many small, home-based businesses will have little overhead, so start-up money needs may be modest. However, there are many enterprises, such as manufacturing businesses or businesses that require a certain location to be effective or have sizable start-up costs, that may need funding above and beyond what you can afford. In that case, you need to find investors who are willing to take a risk. This is actually the primary reason why a business plan is necessary. Investors want and need something on paper that explains your idea and gives financial background to support your business. They will use this information to evaluate whether or not they want to place their money in your hands.

Believe it or not, I was turned down for both personal, small business, and women-oriented bank loans. I first went to the bank where I had a relationship and asked about women's loans. The banker said that it was a long application process, and that at the end of it I probably would not qualify for many different reasons. One reason was that the consumer or retail bank did not fully understand the business I was proposing because hedge funds at that time were not well known or very regulated; furthermore, I did not have many personal assets that could be used as collateral against the loan, and did not find a cosigner. Of course, in a tough economy, conventional bank loans may be even harder to come by. Banks have now gone back to being risk-averse and are disinclined to write many small business loans.

Private investors, personal savings, and even family loans are often the best ways to raise capital for your business. I chose to ask private individuals who I knew had the cash to invest, a belief in my abilities and idea, and an interest in my industry. Without these three things, an investor will usually not plunk the money down.

Whether you know the person you are seeking funds from or not, it takes guts to ask someone to write a check and trust that you know what to do with it. People invest in other people's businesses for many reasons: they like your business model; they see themselves in you; they want to diversify into different areas; they are interested in the industry you are in; or they have other personal or business reasons. But most often they want to *make* money, not lose it, and investing in someone else's time and toil *can* be a good way to do it.

There were two people whom I considered to be potential investors in my business because we were like-minded in our view of the industry. At the time not many people were doing what I wanted to do: market hedge funds. I knew that there were plenty of opportunities for me in this underserved area of the financial sector. These two investors saw that in the 1990s hedge funds were a growth industry. They also saw that I was young and motivated, had experience in the business, and was hungry to make money. They were already invested in financial products that I worked with, so they already had a business relationship with me, knew what I was doing, and saw how good I was at it.

As I got to know these men, I would tell them about my aspirations to start my own marketing company. I asked them if that was something they would be interested in learning more about. Each of them asked me for a business plan. I estimated that $150,000 would be necessary for my start-up expenses, and demonstrated confidence in my ability to bring in business. I was always humble and grateful.

One of the investors agreed to my terms, became my business partner, and provided me with $120,000 in drawdown money. Drawdown money is similar to a line of credit, meaning the money is there if and when you need it, but you are not obligated to use it. You need to pay back only the money you actually borrow (plus interest and fees and any other monies stipulated in the agreement).

My partner was a silent partner, meaning he was not working with me day-to-day. Therefore, each month I kept my partner aware of what was going on in the business, including supplying him with a list of expenses, money coming in, and other detailed information. I was fortunate to have a good working relationship with my partner. Without him I would never have been able to start my business. Some investors want to be active partners and get involved in daily business. It's up to both of you what kind of partnership terms you agree to establish.

Find the Right People

Whether you plan on hiring a staff or not, you still need good people to help you with administrative, legal, and financial paperwork involved in starting and running a business. Professional conferences and references from friends and colleagues in your business are the most tried-and-true ways to meet people. I met a really good lawyer at a hedge fund conference who had experience in the business that I was starting. He drew up the partnership and operating agreements when I first started and client contracts periodically. Likewise, people who want to start an entertainment business need an entertainment lawyer; a woman who wants to go into the purse and handbag business needs a lawyer from the garment or manufacturing industry, and so on.

I also needed a good accountant. While I could do basic bookkeeping myself for the first year, professional help in filing my taxes and setting up the right business accounts was crucial. The second year of business, my accountant took over all my record keeping and books. I found him through a referral from a business colleague, and I have worked with him for more than ten years. I trust him with everything. If you do not have *the* best accountant and *the* best lawyer you can find, you are not going to have a good business. Do not skimp on legal and accounting advice. This is not the place to cut corners. Credible, up-to-date advice saves money and time in the long run and prevents problems from happening.

If you do plan on hiring staff, whether it's one person or twenty-five, finding the right fit is a priority. Tisha Collette, owner of Collette designer consignment boutique says, "Hiring the appropriate people is the key to a successful company. I am an owner, but also a worker among workers. Everyone in my company has something to contribute. I consult each worker for their thoughts and feedback, and usually blend everyone's ideas. We're all in this together." Hire people that are more knowledgeable in specific areas of your business where you lack wisdom and experience. This gives you and your company an advantage. "My employees look to me for guidance, but at the same time, I look to them for guidance. My employee's also have a feeling of ownership and it works—it makes the business more successful."

Manage the Cash Crunch

Many businesses, more than you might think, face a cash crunch within the first few years of business. All of a sudden expenses become so great that income is not enough to cover them (usually a result of unexpected external events), and there is no money in emergency reserves. The jewelry maker faces a spike in gold prices. The public relations person discovers a need to upgrade computer systems sooner than anticipated. Or the market for a particular business bottoms out and goes through a long rough patch. The economy turns sour and all businesses are affected. Industry regulations change the way a business must be run, but in a negative way. Suddenly, we are faced with a business that is operating at a loss.

The easiest way to survive tough times and unexpected low points in your business is by building an emergency cushion or cash buffer into your expense budget and keeping a lid on unnecessary expenses. A business cushion fund (similar to your emergency fund in your FSP) should be equal to 20 percent of your total expenses. If nothing is coming in from a business, then as little as possible should be going out of it. I can't stress this point enough: it is not only how much income we make, it is also *how little of it we spend*. Even my mentor, who is very wealthy, watches expenses. It does not matter if he has millions in the bank from one business; when he starts a new venture he keeps an eye on every dime to ensure that he keeps his costs to a minimum. He spends only what is necessary.

Unfortunately, some women believe everything can be expensed—travel, dinners and lunches, cab rides, even clothing—and that these things are then "free." NO! Every expense you incur comes out of your bottom line: income minus your expenses equals profit. Anytime an expense can be reduced, it should be. For example, is there a cheaper office, can you share it with another small business, or is an office outside the home even necessary?

I needed my office to be located in an established and recognizable area of town, a place where well-known and reputable hedge funds were located, so I chose Rockefeller Center. A large number of my clients were international and recognized the area as being the home to highly regarded hedge funds that they would also be meeting with. Having an office there gave me credibility with people who were not familiar with me (remember, I was just starting out).

Had my office been located in the more artsy and casual Lower East Side of New York, I might not have been seen as professional and serious in the financial business. I might have worn the same suit almost every day, but having a tiny office at a respectable address was important for my business image and to help grow my clientele. The office was a necessary expense. But an assistant to fetch me latte in the morning or a full-time accountant? I don't think so.

Day-to-day expenses can be curbed. Is it necessary to have an expensive business lunch every day? Could you instead have coffee meetings or visit a client in her office in the morning or afternoon, or have telephone discussions? Do you have to take a cab or car to work or appointments? Or can you instead take public transportation? Even if I was going halfway around the world to make a presentation, I never said to the client, "I need a first-class ticket." I was grateful to be working for him, and booked a seat in coach.

Expenses Aren't Free

Some companies reimburse employees for expenses 100 percent. This is not the case for the self-employed. "What is sitting in your wallet is the most important thing, and not what's leaving it," says Howard Samuels, CPA. I could not agree more. When you keep expenses down you raise your income. Why? Because the tax write-off you think you might be getting from all those business dinners and business-class plane tickets are costing you much more than you think. Meals and entertainment, for example, are not deductible at a favorable rate.

This simple example makes the point crystal clear: Say you spend $100 on a meal. Half of it (50 percent) is generally 50 percent deductible, which means that you can deduct $25 off your taxes. Assuming that you are at a 25 percent tax rate, you will actually save just $12.50. The $100 "write-off" you thought you were getting actually cost you $87.50 out-of-pocket. Think about this next time you have a choice to take someone out for dinner or meet for coffee. I'm reminded of two entrepreneurs I know who illustrate why expenses shouldn't be taken advantage of.

Doreen has a clothing business selling exquisite one-of-a-kind dresses that are manufactured by hand in India. Her designs are sold in small boutiques in Los Angeles and Miami. After three years in business, she is now looking for an investor. Doreen tore through all her original capital on inventory and extravagant expenses, such as first-class trips to the factory in India, taking buyers out to expensive dinners at trendy restaurants, and buying beaded trim for her clothing at retail, instead of shopping wholesale.

Doreen met an investor who put $100,000 into her business specifically to produce more clothes. Without clothes there would be no business. Instead, Doreen used a chunk of the money to buy a first-class ticket from Los Angeles to Hong Kong (that's $16,000, in case you're wondering) and took friends out to lavish dinners on her expense account. She does not seem to understand that the money she is spending is coming directly out of her business. Her investor isn't happy and is not giving her another dime.

Sandy has a leather goods business and found herself in a similar situation. Luckily she decided to do something about it before it was too late. After Sandy had one good year in business, she was feeling pretty confident. Orders were up, and her beautiful purses and gloves were featured in a couple of fashion magazines. She had even secured a high-end department store as a regular customer. Within weeks, she rented a high-priced office, hired a staff of five, installed a phone system with six lines, and contracted with a car service to drive her around town. She even expensed a spa day and haircuts for everyone "on the company." Yikes!

By the end of the year Sandy was in a cash crunch. She was spending more on cars and drivers than she was making from leather sales. After taking a good look at her expenses, the numbers she was spending on phone lines that never rang, a staff that duplicated itself, and cars that would drive her a few blocks in the rain were astronomical. Sandy decided it was time to get real. "My car service bill was in the five figures!" she told me, astonished.

She moved her office back into her home; cut her phones lines down to one; walked, took the bus, and occasionally hailed a cab in bad weather; and fired everyone except one part-time assistant who helped her pack and ship orders and keep track of manufacturing and inventory. Everything else she did herself, except for tax work (she kept her accountant, whom she used a couple of times a year). By the end of the third year, Sandy was slowly starting to make a profit.

DIRECT TO SUCCESS

For many women, the idea of starting a business from scratch is appealing but daunting—because of the financial investment required and the mandatory 24/7 long hours. One way you can fulfill a desire to earn money on your own, with a flexible schedule, is through direct selling. Haven't you heard of women who have made millions selling make-up, kitchen products and other items? If you have the right personality and like to sell, it is a way to start a business and learn a great deal about organization, management, bookkeeping, sales, and marketing—all the skills you need to be a success in any career.

Debbie Rotkvich is one of the top multimillionaire sellers at direct marketing jewelry company lia sophia. She says she got her start with a $149 investment, which included a starter kit of about $1,100 worth of jewelry. She was trained by a friend who brought her into the business (a common practice among direct sales companies) and she was off and running.

In the beginning, Debbie says the work gave her tremendous flexibility— she worked when she wanted to and was able to learn the ins and outs of the business over time. She started doing small home shows, inviting ten or twelve ladies to come to see her stylish jewelry, learn about its lifetime replacement guarantee, and so on. She also helped other women get started too. Debbie was really good at both selling jewelry and bringing in other women to start their lia sophia businesses too. When she realized she could create a great business and great wealth she became very serious. So serious that, "I grew my business into an eight-thousand-person team. Now, nineteen years later, my team is like a large corporation."

Even though Debbie receives support and infrastructure from the home office of lia sophia, like most direct selling opportunities, it's up to her to make the business a success. "I feel this is definitely my own business, I am an independent contractor, so how and where I can take my business is up to me. My amazing team of women does an average of $10 million a month in jewelry sales, so I am truly blessed." But with that enthusiastic group of salespeople comes a lot of responsibility and management responsibilities, which Debbie embraces.

"I have a strong work ethic. You must be very disciplined," says Debbie. "It's easy to say 'I have my own business, I can work from home, I can be flexible,' however, you must put the time in to get results. I am up early answering e-mails, making phone calls, and working on big projects. Having your own business means you have to be a self-starter; no one will do it for you. Procrastination does not work. I work my business from home as if I were going to an office. A lot of elbow grease is involved."

As Debbie became more successful and realized she could grow her business, she created a strategy. "I realized that if I made a plan, and stuck to it, I could be more successful. I focus on doing two home jewelry shows a week, and bringing on one to two teammates each month. My goal was to be making six figures in two to three years, and I have far exceeded that. So my advice, if you want to start a direct selling business, or any business, is to always have a plan of action for any endeavor, be consistent, and be very disciplined."

FAILURE IS A GREEN LIGHT ON THE ROAD TO SUCCESS

Remember Betty, who could not bring herself to take another career chance after her Internet business failed? One failure and she felt as if she could never try again. Nonsense. Successful men and women have failed numerous times but just pick themselves up and try again. That means they have taken more actions, and are willing to try again after a disappointment, until they reach their goal. Successful people have an open mind; they are flexible and willing to modify or adjust plans to suit market conditions or to correct errors they noticed the first time around. They never get locked into one way of doing something. So as we embark on action taking, remember that not every action results in an as-hoped-for outcome. It does not matter. Keep going.

Take Action Summary:
- The past is perfect.
- The future will be there when you arrive.
- The present is a gift, so live in it.
- Baby steps go long distances.
- Take creative action and start a business.
- Failure is the green light on the road to success.

9.

Live with Gratitude

"Gratitude is riches. Complaint is poverty."

— DORIS DAY, AMERICAN SINGER AND ACTRESS

GRATITUDE AND THANKS remind us that we are never alone—there is always someone near us who can offer support. Certain family, friends, and even colleagues can pull us ashore when we are drifting, extend a helping hand because they believe in our abilities, and give us a place where we can laugh or cry (open twenty-four hours). The recognitions that our efforts are part of something bigger than ourselves equip us to handle the challenges that are always found on the road to success and happiness.

That's why it is so important to say "thank you" for a favor, a gift, assistance, kind words, or good wishes as recognition of another person's thoughtfulness. Yet living in gratitude means so much more than writing a simple thank-you note and expressing kind words. Gratitude is a shift in thinking, a change in attitude. A famous theologian observed that in ordinary life we tend to forget that we receive much more than we give. By recognizing this truth through gratitude our lives become richer. Inner peace and contentment result naturally. We are able to put day-to-day stresses in proper prospective and proceed with life in a calm, happy frame of mind.

Gratitude also allows us to understand other people and be sympathetic and empathize with their situations. None of us lives in a bubble.

Gratitude shakes us out of self-absorption—we're not the center of the universe. Think back to Gabrielle, who piled up disastrous debt and nearly lost her will to live, saying, "I was so miserable that everything looked bleak and hopeless."

When she woke up from the nightmare she realized how much she had, literally (she shopped in her own closet for new clothes she had forgotten she bought) and spiritually. "When I looked around for the first time in a long time, I saw that, first and foremost, I was alive. Thank you! I had wonderful people in my life, a fulfilling job teaching children, a beautiful daughter, and much more." This shift pulled Gabrielle out of herself and gratitude filled her up. For so long she had been unable to give of herself, and once she embraced gratitude, she found that she had generosity to spare. She saw life as sweet, not sour.

Once you start to practice thankfulness, even for the smallest things, the more you have to be grateful for. Think about how it feels to receive good news or an unexpected gift: happy, lucky, relieved, satisfied, at peace. Doesn't it seem as if other areas of our life magically improve and appear better than you previously imagined also? It's not magic; it's gratitude. The great feeling you have when you are truly appreciative is infectious. When you are grateful for one thing, all the other stuff around you starts to look pretty good too. The idea is to make the feeling last, and not fade when the excitement of the moment passes.

I remember first understanding the power of gratitude during a college spring break. Four friends and I had taken an inexpensive package vacation to Cancun, Mexico. When we arrived, we found the hotel to be rundown. Our room was small, especially with five girls crammed into it. But the drab quarters didn't affect my mood. I was taking a real vacation, on my own, for the first time, as opposed to working myself to the bone. For the few hundred dollars the trip cost, I'm not sure we should have expected much more than that.

During a bus tour around town, one of my friends turned to me and said, "Marianna, this is so lame, I can't believe you are sitting there smiling and humming." I was happy and grateful. To me the trip was fantastic. I had been outside of the country only once before. Mexico was yet another exotic, foreign country I was exploring. The weather was sunny and hot, the beaches were beautiful, and the ocean was warm. Moreover, I was *traveling*, seeing a new place. Everything seemed pretty good to me.

The lesson here is that gratitude makes wherever you are and whatever you are doing look better, and from this it naturally becomes better.

SEE THE GOOD AROUND YOU

Showing gratitude every day keeps us grounded. For instance, this morning, as I do most mornings, I took a moment to reflect on what's good in my life: "I am so grateful that I can work from my home; I am so glad that today is sunny and bright; I am grateful it's the holiday season because it's so festive; and I am looking forward to having lunch with an old friend today." This small ritual shifts me away from any possible negativism and puts my day on solid footings. At the end of the day, as I lie in bed, I do the very same thing, and say thank you for at least three things that happened over the last twelve hours. I often name very specific events, whatever comes into my mind.

Sweeten your day with the kindness of saying thank you—
to the butcher, the baker, the dry cleaner, the doorman—
to anyone who makes your life a little more pleasant
in small and large ways.

■

When you thank your lucky stars every day, magic happens. The world actually becomes a rosier place and your own beauty and loveliness increase. There is so much good around you: spying a beautiful flower on your way to work; catching a cab in the rain; finding the perfect sweater to complete an outfit—on sale; receiving an unexpected check in the mail. Every joyful happenstance and small pleasure counts, and recognizing them is guaranteed to make the day go better.

 ## Gratitude Alphabet

The blues can come along at the least expected times and for any reason—in the office, at dinner with friends. It's human nature to have an occasional sense of melancholy; the trick is

not indulging it. When I feel world-weary I say my gratitude alphabet, and it unfailingly increases my spirits.

Start with *A* and go through to *Z*, thinking of one thing you are thankful for that begins with each letter of the alphabet. It can be simple. As in *A*, I am grateful for aerobics because they are a fun way to keep in shape; *B*, I am grateful for my baby, who is so cute and in love with life; *C*, I am grateful for the cash in my purse; *D*, I am grateful for my dad, who taught me the value of a dollar; *E*, I am grateful for the beauty and twinkle of the evening stars in the clear sky; and so on. Try this the next time you are feeling blue. I guarantee that by the time you reach the end of the alphabet you'll be feeling happy and blessed.

TO COMPARE IS TO DESPAIR

Someone once said that to compare is to despair, and I could not agree more. You always feel ungrateful when you are measuring your life, level of success, or situation against others who you feel have more or better. My attitude has always been not to expect anything, but just to be grateful for what happens. Everything that came to me as a result of my efforts was icing on the cake. I studied hard and was grateful that I got an A on a test. I worked hard and saved and was silently thankful that I could buy myself something that I wanted with the extra money.

Instead of distracting yourself by constantly comparing yourself to others, put self-judgment aside and work toward what you want. Constant comparison creates an overall attitude of "The grass is always greener on the other side." It isn't. The problem with comparing is that you start to believe that everyone has it better than you. That belief, in turn, leads to despair, discouragement, and defeat. Gratitude for what you do have allows you to feel more fulfilled and be more productive.

A friend of mine told me about a very successful man he knew, a great art collector who had amassed a marvelous array of paintings and sculptures. His home was filled with museum-quality work, some of which had become so valuable as to be priceless. Best of all, he really appreciated and enjoyed his art. The man was proud to welcome friends to his home and tell them about each piece.

His enthusiasm rubbed off on his guests and they always left his house feeling lighter on their feet and happier than when they had arrived. In fact, he inspired many people to become interested in art. His attitude changed, however, when visiting a grand museum. He would walk into the Metropolitan Museum of Art in New York City, the Louvre in Paris, or the Hermitage in St. Petersburg and be filled with anguish and misery. Why? The man would compare his great collection to those at these large museums and feel very poor and inadequate.

Now, it may seem outrageous that anyone would compare his art collection to the greatest museums in the world, but this man took pride in his art and the disappointment he felt was very real. Though it may be on a smaller scale, we do the same thing in our own lives. Learning to accept and be grateful for what we have is something everyone has to learn, no matter the circumstances. The benefits of doing so are immense: gratitude is good for your health, emotional well-being, and frame of mind. When you are in a grateful state of mind, your mood is enhanced. You realize that life is really sweet. Gratitude boosts your energy, makes you more attractive, and increases your excitement about life. Gratitude allows you to digest all the good things you have so that you can have more. Living in a thank-you state of mind keeps you grounded, humble, and connected to your community and the world.

Thank You! More, Please!

Before you can have more of what you really want you have to digest what you already have, and then ask for more. Sometime during the day, jot down at least three "gratitudes" in a small notebook. Once a week take inventory of your list and say to your higher power, God, or the universe, "Thank you. More, please." Each time something wonderful happens during the day, always take a moment to say, "Thank you. More, please." By acknowledging thanks you are digesting what you have received and making room to receive more.

There's an old fable that explains beautifully how destructive envy and ingratitude can be. A young woman, Cassandra, lived in a small village. She was descended from royalty and considered an important member of the community. Cassandra was known as a dreamer, and imagined that someday she would be very wealthy and have everything she wanted. Unfortunately, there was a problem or flaw with every job she took (the hours were too long; coworkers were not friendly enough; the work was beneath her), making it impossible for her to remain in any one position for more than a few weeks.

Cassandra went to the village elders and complained that she was not well trained enough for a good job, so they agreed to provide her with special education. Cassandra attended the training academy, but didn't take it very seriously. She thought the teachers were silly, and the other students stupid and boring. Still, she was anxious to get the piece of paper that proclaimed her ready for a high-level management position at the local factory. After graduating, she was installed in a management position and took advantage of the perks that went with it. She felt trapped by the job, and realized it was actually a lot harder than she imagined.

One day Cassandra noticed that the girl next door, Thea, had started to wear very nice clothes. She observed workmen coming and going from Thea's house during the day. Her curiosity was overwhelming, so she asked her neighbor what was going on. "We're having some of the rooms redone," replied Thea. "I can afford it now that I've been promoted at the factory." What kind of job could she possibly have that allows her to have such fine things, Cassandra wondered. She works at the very bottom rung of the factory.

Cassandra became very jealous of Thea, and spread rumors about her, telling neighbors that Thea was probably stealing from the poor to make herself rich. Soon, she went to the village elders and asked them to intervene and stop Thea from making money. Because she had the support of her angry neighbors, who had come to believe that Thea must be involved in wrongdoing, the elders complied. They confiscated Thea's home, and drove her from the village.

Before Thea left she stopped to wish Cassandra farewell. "I am so grateful for all the things that came to me, and for this experience," she told her neighbor. Cassandra burned with rage. How could this woman be happy when Cassandra was so miserable? "What could you possibly be thankful for?" she asked. Thea had lost her home, her job, and her money. "I know what I can accomplish, and I am thankful for my health and freedom," Thea replied. "I can start over and create a better life somewhere else." With that, Thea left the village, never to return.

Fables exaggerate important lessons so that we don't miss them. Here, the story reminds us what can happen when we forget that we are in charge of our own happiness, when we neglect to count our blessings and appreciate our potential. Ruining someone else's life gives no comfort, and it never results in abundance for yourself. Ingratitude turned to jealousy fueled Cassandra's destructive actions. Predictably, she reaped what she sowed. Cassandra also never realized that gratitude makes you beautiful. It affects the way you look in a positive, radiant way—from the inside out.

EMBRACE THE PERFECTION

Ingratitude rears its ugly head every time we think something has not gone our way. It happens to me, and when it does, I have to snap myself out of it fast. It's helpful to decide that whatever is happening is the perfect thing, and to be thankful for it. Before you can realize the abundance that is waiting for you in the future, you must accept and be grateful for the perfection of what's going on today.

For example, many years ago I was between jobs and out of work for nine very long months. In classic form, I felt like a failure. There was a dark cloud over my head. I was worried and upset, angry that nothing was coming my way, and resentful that I couldn't find something that I wanted to do. I finally realized that my attitude was not helping me find a job. What would happen if I embraced my unemployment? What if I saw unemployment as a special time? It gave me the freedom to explore opportunities, and more time to devote to reading, exercise, and other pastimes that working prevented me from doing frequently.

Besides, I reminded myself, my emergency fund could see me through this lean time. I had a roof over my head, good friends and a supportive family, and great professional experience. It dawned on me that my value as a person was not defined by whether I was working. Unemployment was just a fact. It wasn't until I accepted that I had left my job voluntarily, and that "right now" I was not working, that I was in a position to move forward and find another job. Once I assumed an attitude of gratitude, I felt happier and lighter. It was not long after that that a job came my way.

My attitude of gratitude was lost in the fray again a couple of years ago. In my late thirties I was single and wanted to get married and start a family. A few months earlier my long-term boyfriend and I broke up. I was meeting men, but frustrated that I was not meeting the right one, someone I wanted to marry and make a new life with. I'd say to myself things I'd heard from other women in my situation: "There are no great guys out there"; "I'll never find the right one"; "What if I never get married?"; "What if I never have a baby?" Woe was me. I simply did not want to accept these outcomes and fought against them at every turn.

After a few months of spending too much time feeling lousy, I made a decision and said to myself, "You know what? I am going to be happy and accept where I am today. So I don't have a boyfriend. I love my career. I have great friends and family. I travel and have fun with my life today." Everyone gets depressed and discouraged—even me—when results don't match expectations. After all, we're human. That's okay—but nip it in the bud by being aware of your feelings, making time to feel your feelings, and then consciously shifting them. So instead of being aggravated over not having a fiancé, I began to accept and become grateful about my circumstance. I was happy and satisfied with just about everything in my life. Soon after accepting the situation and regaining my attitude of gratitude I met the man who eventually became my husband. I truly believe this happened because I had shifted my outlook on life from being negative to being positive, radiant, and happy.

Emma discovered the magnetic properties of acceptance and being grateful when she started a family. "I didn't think my two-bedroom apartment would be big enough for all of us. A third bedroom would have really helped us out," she told me. Emma didn't want to leave the apartment building she was in, and was pining away for a three-bedroom unit on one of its upper floors. Meanwhile, her very happy, beautiful home for the last several years was starting to grate on her nerves. "I have to admit, I started resenting my two-bedroom apartment," she said.

One morning a couple of weeks later Emma woke up and looked out her bedroom window. The sun shone into the room at a nice angle and made everything sparkle. "I shook myself and said, 'Emma, you have to stop all this complaining about a three-bedroom apartment. This is a beautiful home, and there's room enough for everyone.' I decided then and there to be very grateful for my home," she said. And with good reason; Emma owns it free and clear. It's not the biggest apartment in the world, but it's bigger than a lot of homes people live in who have bigger families.

"I really started to fall in love with my place all over again," she said. Not surprisingly, the superintendent of the building called a couple of weeks later and told her a three-bedroom was available. "I was happy and expressed an interest in looking at it. But you know what—I am not desperate to move. If it happens, fine. If not, that's okay too. I'm at peace with where I live. It's the perfect home for us right now," Emma told me later.

Whenever we feel the pull of ingratitude, let's push it away. Stop. Take a deep breath. Accept the situation and say, "Thank you. This is perfect right now," and proceed as if that were the case (it is). There will be a positive difference in our actions and the reactions we receive.

SAY THANK YOU EVEN WHEN IT HURTS

The most challenging form of gratitude is also the one that has the biggest payoff. Thank everyone who has helped you, even those who don't seem helpful on the surface, and even if you don't think they deserve your gratitude. A friend of mine, Janet, a salesperson for a large Internet provider, was taken under her boss's wing when she was just twenty-four years old. He saw raw talent in her, so he trained her and taught her the business. Soon she had her own roster of clients and was making her own sales—a striking achievement when compared to most of her colleagues, who were at least thirty. Janet became a very good salesperson at a very young age.

A year or two later, palpable tension had developed between Janet and her boss, who felt that Janet was not giving him the credit he deserved for helping her along the way and for all her successes. Janet did not know what to do. Her work environment was becoming very uncomfortable. I advised Janet to use the Buttering Up Success Secret (page 223) by acknowledging his help and saying, "Mr. Jones, thank you for all the help you have given me and everything you have done for my career. Without you I would not have been able to make any of these sales and become so successful so quickly."

"No way!" replied Janet. "Why should I give him credit for sales I am making on my own?"

"Because he really did help you, Janet, and what's the big deal about thanking him and telling him how great he is? Doing so does not make you less successful. Tell him he is the best thing that ever happened to your career. He'll help you even more if you do, and there will be no more discomfort," I explained.

Well, Janet kept resisting, and a few weeks later, when Janet was still complaining, I said, "Janet, cough it up and tell him thank you. Acknowledge him and tell him he's great." Finally, she did it. The tension broke, and Janet's boss was so flattered that he continued to help her and supply her even more sales leads. It worked!

Another friend of mine, Angela, was having a major difficulty with the company she worked for. She had parted ways with them, and was negotiating the exit terms of her employment contract. Angela and the partners in the firm were on opposite ends of the spectrum when it came to how much money each party thought she deserved. Obviously, Angela thought she deserved a lot more than the firm wanted to give her. Angela called me and complained bitterly about the people in her company. She thought they were "out to get her" and confided in me that she was tempted to call the company's clients and tell them not to do business with her old firm. She wished the worst for all of them. Meanwhile, negotiations had come to a complete halt, with neither side budging.

"Angela, you've got to put the brakes on your emotions," I said. "You can't wish these people ill. You certainly cannot talk about the company in unflattering ways because that will put you in both legal trouble and a karmic mess." Angela conceded that calling clients was just a fantasy, which was a relief. But she continued to say nasty things about her bosses. Finally, I suggested that Angela try an experiment. Instead of thinking and saying nasty things about her bosses, why not try thanking them and saying great things about them?

"Are you kidding?" Angela sputtered.

"No, I am serious," I said. "Give it a try. In fact, I want you to imagine your bosses being super successful. Picture them with lots of new business and money coming their way. Pretend you like them. Every morning get up and say, 'Thank you, John and Charlie, for everything you've done for me.'"

Angela said she would think about it. A few days later she called and said that because nothing was happening with her negotiations she would give my suggestion a try. She started to think kindly of her bosses. At social gatherings she would heap nothing but praise and compliments on her old firm whenever someone asked about it. She visualized lots of money coming toward her bosses whenever they entered her mind.

Several weeks after that Angela called and told me a remarkable story. Her bosses had called her and told her they were going to give her what she wanted. They met all the terms she had asked for and they parted ways amicably. "Marianna, after I started thinking and speaking highly of the company, I started to feel so much better," she told me. "I totally forgot how angry I was, and actually stopped being consumed with worry and anxiety. Then, very unexpectedly, I got a call from them and everything was settled very quickly and favorably for me."

SUCCESS SECRET

Buttering Up

When someone sincerely flatters us it makes us feels good. Try to identify one quality you admire in a person and comment on it sincerely. This is a special way of thanking someone just for being her, and recognizing that her uniqueness is appreciated. This strategy works wonders when you are networking, building business and personal relationships, looking for a mentor, asking for advice, or seeking insight into the qualities you admire in another person. Likewise, be sure to accept a compliment when someone butters *you* up. Do you sometimes reject a compliment by downplaying it? When you are being buttered up, look the other person in the eye, smile, and say thank you. Accepting a compliment graciously allows another person to give something to us.

GIVE BACK

When you are grateful you know you have abundance, and you are more willing to give of yourself. Practicing gratitude shows you that you always have riches on hand. When you come from scarcity you do not see that you have anything to give. One of the most significant and powerful ways to give thanks is to give back. There is an exquisite and enchanted flow to giving and receiving. They work in unison to produce a never-ending supply of abundance. For example, giving back a portion of my time and money to charity, my church, and organizations I am passionate about has made me wealthier both in spirit and in dollars.

The more I give away the more I seem to attract, and the more I have to give in the future. It's a wonderfully circuitous situation, and proves that abundance never runs out. This can be a tough concept for some people to grasp—how can giving away money, time, or knowledge result in more? It's called the Law of Circulation: all things in the universe are constantly flowing back and forth at an ever-expanding rate. What you give to one person you will receive from a different source in a different form.

It's absolutely essential that you give without expectation of getting something back. That's why we should always feel good about giving; it has to be done of our own free will and can't feel forced or done out of a feeling of obligation. One way to begin giving is to offer that which we want for ourselves. Sounds odd, I know, but when we do this, we get back what we've provided tenfold.

For example, if you want love (say, a relationship), give your love away. If you want to make more money, donate money to a needy person or a cause. If you want to learn about something, mentor someone or share what you know with someone who can use the information. Giving and receiving are equal opposites on the spectrum of abundance. People who have the most love, wealth, knowledge, and happiness are the ones who give and receive the most of those things.

SUCCESS SECRET

Give from a Happy Heart

Giving must come from a happy heart, especially when you give your time—make sure you volunteer for those activities that you feel most strongly about. And don't spread yourself too thin, or you will

(continued)

become resentful and be of no use to anyone. There are just so many charity tickets you can sell or cookies you can bake before exhaustion sets in. Temper enthusiasm with common sense.

Giving has to be genuine, so you should not do it until you are ready; otherwise you may feel simultaneously guilty and resentful. Once you have decided that you want to give, base your donation decision on whether the cause is one you truly believe in. An organization that is closest to your heart will benefit the most from your dollars—whether it's cancer research, helping the homeless, or an animal shelter. When something is given with genuine love, it has unique power.

The question is, how much should you give? Some people feel they should give away 10 percent of their income (this is often called tithing, and it is tied to some religious beliefs). To me, it's the principle of giving. I believe that everyone should give what they are comfortable giving and give back in their own way. Charity has to come from a place of *wanting* to give. Moreover, giving should be fun. You want to feel good and happy about what you give, not pressured or obligated. When you feel obligated it takes away the importance and magic of giving. Giving should come from the heart and give you great energy. I also believe that giving is not only about money. We can give in many different ways: with our time (by volunteering), our expertise (by offering advice or through mentoring), our possessions (old clothes, furniture), our service (helping others), and through our thoughts and prayers. There is always some way that you can start the cycle of giving.

Many young women call me with questions about getting into the financial industry, and I enjoy sharing what I know, giving them contacts, and offering guidance. They ask me many questions about contracts, non-paying clients, legal advice, negotiating, and hedge fund marketing, as well as about daily problems that come up in general work situations. I am always honored to impart what I know. Sharing my knowledge makes me stronger, not weaker.

Hospitals, elder-care facilities, pediatric wards, animal shelters, soup kitchens, and schools will embrace your desire to lend a helping hand.

Donate a percentage of your belongings (or an amount that you are comfortable with) to a woman's shelter. Whatever you offer will be appreciated and come back to you in boundless and unpredictably delicious ways. Give as much as you feel comfortable giving. I believe that putting giving in motion, even slowly, brings incredible results.

We can give back in small ways every day; some people call this engaging in "random acts of kindness." To me, it's gratitude in action. Help someone cross the street; offer a shoulder to cry on to a friend; give advice to an intern in your office; buy a stranger his coffee one morning; take your fiancé's mother out to lunch; call your grandmother or aunt to say hello; send a funny postcard to an old friend; or simply offer a thought or prayer to someone in need.

 Show Your Gratitude

> Take a few minutes and think of three small things you can do for someone else tomorrow, and don't tell anyone that you're doing them. Can you pick up some groceries for an elderly neighbor or sweep her front steps? How about taking a friend's dog for a walk so she can relax after work? What about bringing a helpful coworker a flower or a cup of tea? Small gestures change the world.

ACCEPT THANKS WHEN IT IS OFFERED

Women tend to have a hard time with this one. Giving is grand, but receiving is also essential. Never refuse anything that is offered in kindness. If something is offered for the wrong reasons—a gift is given to entice us to do something that is not in our best interests; or there are ethical, moral, or legal consequences to accepting something—then by all means decline it politely.

If someone offers a gift out of kindness or affection, take the gift and respond with a genuine "Thank you," even if the gift itself is not exactly what was hoped for. It really *is* the thought that counts, and that is what we can be grateful for. If someone wants to pick up the tab at dinner, don't argue; accept graciously with thanks. When someone pays us a compliment, as in, "You look gorgeous," or, "You are so talented," don't demure, don't protest—*don't negate the gift that has been offered by disagreeing with it.* Say thank you. And mean it.

Some of us have strongly held beliefs about receiving gifts. We could feel that accepting something from someone else makes us susceptible to her, or puts us in a position of obligatory reciprocation or of one-upmanship (now we have to give that person something even better than what they gave us, to prove we're worthy). Discard those beliefs.

Accept all offers made with love or friendship with poise and dignity. If you receive an item that you don't like or need, pass it along to someone who can use or enjoy it. Everyone wins. When we refuse gifts, compliments, and kind deeds, we are blocking the flow of abundance in our own life *and* in the giver's life. When we accept a gift we are completing a cycle of giving and receiving, and abundance flows freely.

IN HER OWN WORDS

Congresswoman Marsha Blackburn

MEMBER OF THE U.S. HOUSE OF REPRESENTATIVES
FOR TENNESSEE AND AUTHOR

Wife, mother, small business owner—Marsha Blackburn also happens to be the first woman ever to be elected Tennessee state senator for the 23rd District. The congresswoman has long been a champion of women, and has mentored and encouraged many women to assume leadership positions and become politically active. Marsha is also the author of *Life Equity: Realize Your True Value and Pursue Your Passions at Any Stage in Life* (Thomas Nelson, 2009).

Why is gratitude so important for a successful and happy life?

Gratitude and graciousness have to be part of our thought pattern. Expressing gratitude and graciousness daily grounds us, focuses us,

(continued)

and serves as the underpinning for our efforts: "This is why I am doing what I'm doing; these are the people and events who have enabled me to pursue my goal or passion." We are not islands; we depend on those around us to help pull us forward. My mother taught me this lesson, and it's one that I have passed on to my children.

What would you tell women who may not be feeling very grateful because of a slight or disappointment? There can be so many on the road to success.

Instead of becoming frustrated or angry, develop an attitude of graciousness and reframe the situation to see how it fits into your mission. I remember working diligently to raise funds for a nonprofit organization, and it was a *very* successful effort. The chairman of the board of the organization took all the credit, but he hadn't had much to do with fund-raising. Instead of getting mad and giving up, I stuck with the job. I exerted my graciousness and gratitude because I felt the project was important. Eventually I became chairman of the organization, and was in a position to empower and encourage the staff. I could treat others in the way that I had wanted to be treated. Had I let my disappointment at not being recognized override my mission and passion, had I given in to ingratitude, it would have been a missed opportunity.

Politics can be an especially rough-and-tumble world. What have you learned that could help other women stay strong even when the daggers are flying?

There are numerous times when we work our hearts out on an issue that's important to us, and naturally we think, "My goodness, everyone should be supporting my efforts." That's a myth. There will always be those who don't support our goals. When an individual is standing in your way, you have to keep focused on what you want to achieve. You can't worry about the things you can't control. Worry gives you wrinkles. And of course, you have to learn to bite your tongue, even when someone has been hurtful and inappropriate.

That said, there are ways to deal with the vitriol of politics or any

(continued)

situation where emotions and passions can outpace courtesy. I pace my bedroom practicing a speech I would love to give [to the person who has said something hurtful]. That's a constructive form of venting. Ask a friend to let you practice your speech in front of her. Get those feelings of hurt off your chest because they can eat away at you. And realize too that the person who has hurt you has made a conscious choice to do so. What does that say? I think of the Ten Commandments: Thou shall not kill. We think of this in the physical sense, but there are people who do this emotionally every day. Your strength, gratitude, and graciousness allow you to rise above the hurt.

How do you incorporate gratitude into everyday life?

Through celebration. It's so important to celebrate successes—our own and others'. What a lovely way to express gratitude, by recognizing achievements. It gives us a chance to pause and thank those who have helped us reach the benchmark we're celebrating. Never pass up the opportunity to express pleasure and excitement when you've reached a goal; that's gratitude in action.

My husband, Chuck, and I have an antique dining table that has been in our house for nearly as long as we've been married, thirty-four years. Old tables never come with chairs, so thirty years ago I thought, why don't I buy six or eight different chairs? I found a large bishop's chair for one end of the table, and a smaller chair for the other end. We call them the king and the queen chairs. When our children were small, if one received an A on a test or finished a mile run, he or she sat in the king chair to celebrate. We still do that today! Every Sunday we have lunch as an extended family. Even after all these years, when my grown children come to the door they always ask, "Who will be sitting in the king's chair?"

And of course, when we say grace before a meal, we never forget to say thank you.

Acceptance, generosity, and gratitude are all part of the same cycle of abundance and prosperity. One can't really work without the other two. As we end this journey, I want you to remember to keep an open heart and an open mind so that you can receive everything you want and stay the course even when it seems uneven or unfair. Whatever you release comes back to you in a more divine form. Release anger and it turns to love. Let go of old, confining beliefs, and new, more energizing ones take their place. Exercise and eat right, and health will come your way. Donate your time and money, and both will find their way back to you, in multiples. Think in loving terms, and love will always be yours.

Finally, at this very moment, I want to tell you something that you have perhaps started to conclude yourself: right now, this minute, you *are living, loving, and earning it*! So continue on your journey; don't stop now. The fun has just begun.

The Five-Years-from-Now Letter

Carve out at least thirty minutes for this exercise. Take out a piece of stationery and a pen, or sit at your laptop, and write a letter to me, Marianna. Post a date five years from today at the top of the letter. Picture yourself where you would like to be five years now. For example, you might be sitting in your beautiful new house curled up on your bed sipping a cup of tea and looking out the window at the beautiful trees in your backyard while your two children are playing in the other room.

Write the letter in the present tense, as if what you are saying is happening right now. Describe what your life is like, with as many Live it, Love it, Earn it details—and dreams realized—as possible. When you are done, put the letter away in an envelope (print it out if you wrote it on a computer) and place the letter in a drawer—somewhere safe but also a place where you won't completely forget about it. I want you to open that letter five years from the day you wrote it and read it. How many of the things you talked about have been realized? If you have maintained a Live it, Love it, Earn it attitude, they all will be yours and more.

Live with Gratitude Summary:

- Gratitude is more than an attitude; it's a way of life.
- See the good all around you.
- To compare is to despair; recognize the value in what you have.
- Embrace the perfection of your life at any given moment.
- Say thank you, even if it hurts.
- Give back.
- Accept thanks when it is offered.

Conclusion:
Live It, Love It, Earn It . . . Forever!

EVEN THOUGH WE have come to the end of the book, I hope that your journey to financial freedom continues and gets better and better. The nine tools you've learned are not to be used within a finite period of time, only to be abandoned after immediate goals have been met. Live it, Love it, Earn it tools work at every stage of life. I have fulfilled many of my own dreams—created my own business, became financially free, surrounded myself with a great family and friends, and created a balance and peace in my life. Yet I have other dreams, desires, and goals to reach. I continue to use the tools and success secrets in this book to pursue new interests and ideas, start new businesses, help others with their dreams and goals, and take part in exciting adventures and travels. You will see that once you start using these strategies, the possibilities and opportunities in front of you will multiply and you will start to live a life beyond your wildest imagination.

Just as mine have, I know your dreams will come true, and I invite all of you to tell me about your successes using my nine tools. I can't wait to hear from you! Share your stories with me at liveitloveitearnit.com.

Acknowledgments

THERE ARE SO many people I want to thank for their tremendous support and encouragement with this book. I realize how fortunate I am to be surrounded by incredible family and friends who have always been there and always will be there for me. I couldn't have done it without you.

First and foremost, I would like to thank my husband for his support and encouragement and for always being there for me through the ups and downs of book writing. A special thank you to my parents, Albert and Sandra Olszewski, and my siblings, Michele, Rose, Theresa, and Al, for helping me with the details, being there every minute of the way and for their tremendous encouragement and support. I am so lucky to have such a great family.

A very important thank you to Deborah Briggs for suggesting the inspired title *Live It, Love It, Earn It*. I appreciate your being very much a part of the process, and will be forever grateful to you for your constant guidance and support.

Thank you to my agents John Steele, who started the ball rolling and stood behind me from the start, and Farley Chase, who took the ball, ran with it, and continued to guide me every step of the way. To my publisher, Adrian Zackheim—thank you for believing in me, for your wisdom and experience, and for making it possible for me to share my message with a wide audience of women. And to Adrienne Schultz, my editor, thank you for your insightful editing and making the book the best it could be. It was so much fun working with you. I also want to offer thanks to the Portfolio team—Will Weisser, Maureen Cole, Brooke Carey, and all the other talented and hard-working people who were involved in getting the book from manuscript to bookstore.

A special thank you to Debra Schuster Tanger for empowering me to tell my story; Thomas Farley, Daniel Cappello, and James Pine for offering expertise I could not have done without; and Annabelle Bond for putting me in touch with my agent in the very beginning, when my book was just a dream.

Incredible thanks and gratitude to all the successful and courageous ladies (and a few men!) who shared their insights, wisdom, experience, joys and challenges: Senator Marsha Blackburn, Elaine Crocker, Nina DiSesa, Jessica Einhorn, Sonia Gardner, Elizabeth Hilpman, Ambassador Brenda La Grange Johnson, Tamara Mellon, Muriel Siebert, Pernille Spiers-Lopez, Barbara Stanny, Diane Von Furstenberg, together with Corinne Amato, MaryAnn Brumbaugh, Katherine Cohen, Bobette Cohn, Tisha Collette, Teresa Colley, Nancy Curtin, Marichris Dela Cruz, Colette Draut, Mary Beth Evans, Steven Fales, Susan Wood Frehse, Fruzsina Keehn, Aida Khoursheed, Lisa Heiden Koffler, Kristin Mayer, John McGillian, Malcolm Milton, Martha O'Brien, Anna Olsson, Cecelia Ongteco-Smith, Emily Owen, Kerri Pacello, Debbie Rotkvich, Howard Samuels, Lisa Selby, Janis Spindel, Tom Sherwood, Jonathan Sonnenberg, Tracy Stogel, Lisa Talamini, Elizabeth Webb, Joan Willette, Daniela Zahradnikova, Barry Zischang.

Finally, I would like to thank my writer, Karen Kelly, for her dedication, energy, and brilliant writing skills. Thank you for going above and beyond to make this book a success. I appreciate all of your work and cannot thank you enough!

Further Reading

Chatzky, Jean. *Make Money, Not Excuses: Wake Up, Take Charge, and Overcome Your Financial Fears Forever.* New York: Three Rivers Press, 2008.

DiSesa, Nina. *Seducing the Boys Club: Uncensored Tactics From A Woman at the Top.* New York: Ballantine Books, 2008.

Frankel Ph.D., Lois. *Nice Girls Don't Get the Corner Office: Unconscious Mistakes Women Make that Sabotage Their Careers.* New York: Business Plus, 2004.

Johnson, Spencer, and Kenneth Blanchard. *Who Moved My Cheese? An Amazing Way to Deal with Change in Your Work and in Your Life.* New York: G. P. Putnam's Sons, 1998.

Johnson, Spencer. *The Present: The Secret to Enjoying Your Work and Life, Now!* New York: Bantam Books, 2003.

Moran, Victoria. *Living a Charmed Life: Your Guide to Finding Magic in Every Moment of Every Day.* California: HarperOne, 2009.

Ponder, Catherine. *Dynamic Laws of Prosperity.* California: DeVorss and Co., 2007.

Scovel Shinn, Florence. *The Game of Life and How to Play It.* Wilder Publications, 2009 (reprint).

Stanny, Barbara. *Secrets of Six Figure Women: Surprising Strategies to Up Your Earnings and Change Your Life.* New York: Harper Paperbacks, 2004.

Waitley, Denis. *The Psychology of Winning: Ten Qualities of a Total Winner.* New York: Berkley, 1986.

Resources

HOW TO REACH MARIANNA OLSZEWSKI:

300 South Pointe Drive, #3506

Miami, FL 33139

LiveitLoveitEarnit.com

Marianna@liveitloveitearnit.com

FINANCIAL ADVICE

Nancy Curtin, CLTC

Certified Long-Term Care Specialist

SmartFuture, LLC

331 West 57th Street, Suite 434

New York, NY 10019

Phone: 212-767-1500

njcurtin@gmail.com

http://ltclife.biz/

Tom Sherwood, CPA

Lilling & Company LLP

10 Cutter Mill Road

Great Neck, NY 11021

Phone: 516-829-1099

tsherwood@lillingcpa.com

Howard Samuels CPA, MST S&C LLP
Certified Public Accountants
30 Two Bridges Road, Suite 205
Fairfield, NJ 07004
Phone: 973-439-5600
Fax: 973-439-6900
hsamuels@s-cllp.com

Barbara Stanny
Barbara Stanny, Inc.
2023 E. Sims Way,
Suite 328
Port Townsend, WA 98368
Phone: 360-385-0600
Barbara@barbarastanny.com
barbarastanny.com

Barry Zischang ChFC CFP CIMA
Wealth Strategies Consultant
RBC Wealth Management
Four Landmark Square
Stamford, CT 06901
Phone: 203-351-9314
Fax: 866-947-3313
Barry.Zischang@rbc.com
rbcwealthmanagement.com

ENTREPRENEURS

Katherine Cohen
Ivy Wise
140 West 57th Street, Suites 3C and 3D
New York, NY 10019
Phone: 212-262-3500
Fax: 212-262-4100
inquiries@ivywise.com
ivywise.com

Bobette Cohn
Bobette Cohn LLC
333 East 53rd Street, 4M
New York, NY 10022
Phone: 212-644-9187
bobettecohn@hotmail.com
Styling: thomastreuhaft.com and thomastreuhaft.com/Bobette_Cohn/
    bc_women.html
Collection: gift-library.com

Tisha Collette
Collette Designer Consignment
10 Main Street
Southampton, NY 11968
Phone: 631 725 9300
Colletteconsignment.com

Colette Draut, makeup artist and eyelash specialist
Pierre Michel Salon
131 East 57th Street
New York, NY 10022
Phone: 212-755-9500
beautybuyme@hotmail.com
pierremichelbeauty.com

Fruzsina Keehn
Fruzsina Keehn Jewelry
Phone: 646-684-4891
fruzsina@keehn.cc
FruzsinaKeehn.com

Aida Khoursheed
Estarise
36 East 20th Street, 3rd floor
New York, NY 10003
Info@estarise.com

lia sophia jewelry
www.liasophia.com

RELATIONSHIP ADVICE

Janis Spindel
Phone: 212-987-1582
JanisOnline@janisspindelmatchmaker.com
janisspindelmatchmaker.com

Elizabeth Webb
Phone: 646-649-4036
info@lavidafemme.com
lavidafemme.com

MIND AND BODY SUPPORT

Malcolm Milton, certified master physical instructor, NASM, CES
Dodge YMCA
225 Atlantic Avenue
Brooklyn, NY 11201
Phone: 917-533-7962
Malcolmaziz1@optonline.net

Jonathan Sonnenberg, spiritual healer
The School of Vibrational Healing
1133 Pleasantville Road
Briarcliff Manor, NY 10510
orkie.com

Lisa Talamini, vice president, Research and Program Innovation
Jenny Craig, Inc.
5770 Fleet Street
Carlsbad, CA 92008
Phone: 760-696-4000
jennycraig.com

Index